Around the World On a Bicycle

ROUTE OF THE AUTHOR AND BUCEPHALUS
COUNTRY OVER WHICH NO OTHER BICYCLE
HAS EVER TRAVELED
EXPLORATION OF REGIONS NEVER BEFORE
PENETRATED BY A FOREIGNER WHO LIVED TO
TELL THE TALE

ROOF OF THE WORLD

Foo Loo LAUNDRY

N
W — E
S

Indian Ocean

C. F.

Around the World On a Bicycle

By Fred A. Birchmore

with black and white
snapshots by the author

Around the World on a Bicycle

Peddle the planet and relive history with Fred Birchmore, the first person to circle the globe on a bicycle.

Copyright © 1996 by Cucumber Island Storytellers

Library of Congress Cataloging-in-Publication Data
Birchmore, Fred A. (Fred Agnew), 1911-
Around the World on a Bicycle / by Fred A. Birchmore;
edited by Willa Deane Stuckey Birchmore;
with Foreword by Melinda B. Musick.
p. cm.
Originally published: Athens: University of Georgia Press, 1939.
ISBN 1-887813-12-8

1. Birchmore, Fred A. (Fred Agnew), 1911- – Journeys.
2. Voyages around the world. 3. Cycling.
I. Birchmore, Willa Deane Stuckey. II. Title.
G440.B6B57 1996
910.4'1 -- dc20
95-53821
CIP

Layout and Design by Becca Hutchinson

David C. Lock, Publisher

Published in the United States by Cucumber Island Storytellers
P.O. Box 920
Montchanin, DE 19710

Please visit our site on the World Wide Web.
http://www.cucumberisland.com

Montchanin, Delaware

Dedicated to
Father, Mother, Aunt Janie,
And to
My Niece Sarah Jane
Who Came
As I Went –,
Born the Moment
I Started
Around The World

ACKNOWLEDGMENTS

To WILLA DEANE STUCKEY BIRCHMORE, my dear wife of 56 years, for her encouragement and her unwavering love and support, for her help with text revisions and additions, and for typing these 400 pages of text. Without her, most of my later adventures would never have been possible.

FOREWORD

When my father bicycled from Norway to Saigon in 1935 and 1936 he found a world quite different from today's cosmopolis. The far corners of the Earth not merely seemed but truly were remote. Many regions were isolated by poor roads, by illiteracy, and by limited communications systems. By this isolation disparate cultures retained their ancient customs and manners. Changes evolved at an erratic and slow pace. Cars were a rarity abroad, and correspondence was primarily by post or by spoken word, for radio was yet in its infancy.

It was a hazardous time to be abroad in a world stirred by political unrest. Travel was limited to the privileged. Those who ventured into newly accesible but still uncharted lands were the brave, the reckless, and the truly adventurous.

These travels and adventures on a bicycle were undertaken in the spirit of Lindbergh, of Admiral Byrd, and of Amelia Earhart, in a time when the great heroes were adventurers. The literary style of the book is consistent with the inherent romanticism of that era.

Some of these adventures are so fabulous as to seem fantasy, and there are some who have doubted the veracity of our father's adventures. But we who have accompanied him on many of his later travels can attest to them, and to his remarkable strength and endurance, his uncanny ability to find adventure, and his wonderful way of making friends with all along his way.

Melinda Birchmore Musick, M.D., Ph.D.
January 12, 1996

[iii]

PREFACE

I've biked through cold,
I've biked through heat,
I've baked my brain,
And I've frozen my feet.

I've bucked through wind,
I've bucked through rain,
I'll never buck a bike
'Round this tough old world again!

That I should take it into my head to cycle around the world, was not at all surprising to parents and friends acquainted with my past life. Though an almost helpless invalid and "sissy" for the first ten years of life, and afraid to let Mother get out of my sight, nature seemed to have endowed me with more than the usual amount of wander-lust inherent in every normal person.

At the age of two, I started out on foot around the world. Just around the corner, I turned for a last look at the old homeplace, when to my horror, I discovered that it was already out of sight. In terror, I retraced my steps and ran screaming into Mother's sheltering arms.

At the age of ten, my first real adventure away from home was almost as disappointing as that eight years earlier. My Dad took me on an overnight camping trip nearby; I shivered through a fearful, sleepless night, listening to the screeching of owls, the chirping of crickets, the creaking of katydids, the singsong sawing together of cicada legs, and sounds of other direful denizens of the dreadful meadow wherein we had pitched our tent. Little did I dream that fourteen years later I could snore peacefully in my bamboo bed in the depths of the jungles of Indo-China, with giant snakes and man-eating tigers as my only companions.

Thereafter, until college days, I satisfied the craving for adventure by reading everything within reach from Treasure Island, Pilgrim's Progress, and Junior Classics, to Stoddard's Lectures, National Geographic and other travel magazines and novels.

Early in my reading I ran across a poem which struck my fancy:

"No matter what I wish to know
Of Heaven above, or earth below,
Some modern sage or saint of old
Will tell me all that can be told.
Prose writers, playwrights, poets, wits,
Strive in the way which best befits
The mood I happen to be in,
My praise, my tears, or smiles to win.
Good books to read, a mind at ease.
A place to dream in when I please.
Can I not claim by right Divine, my crown,
And say: 'The world is mine'?"

However, I soon learned that second-hand experiences are not fully satisfactory. During the next three summers, my love of nature carried me to the top of nearly every mountain of any consequence in the Appalachian Range.

The last week-end before my final examinations in the University of Georgia was spent in solitude on top of Blood Mountain in the Blue Ridge range. Invitations to commencement exercises had already been mailed, and as I was openly and notoriously advertised by the Old Home Town as the recipient of M.A. and LL.B. degrees simultaneously, the slightest slip-up in my examinations would spell tragedy. However, my mountain retreat proved to be ideal for the concentrated study which enabled me to pass the exams.

College days were marked by other experiences of a mountain-top nature, figuratively speaking.My Robinson Crusoe life in a cave on the Isle of Capri was not the first experience of this nature. For six weeks, I lived alone on a little island in Lake Junaluska. Here I had my first experience cooking potatoes in a tin-can oven in the middle of a blazing camp fire.

The following winter, the call of the open road lured me on a hitch-hiking (for the first and last time in my life) trip to Miami, Florida. Though the entire trip cost only 15 cents (the price of a package of dried figs and a cup of hot ovaltine), it nearly ended disastrously among the Seminole Indians in the Everglades along the Tamiami Trail. Such experiences seemed to intensify, rather than to satisfy, the wanderlust.

Four years as a member of the college boxing and other athletic teams had equipped me physically for any adventure; after a semester of study as American Exchange Scholar at the University of Cologne, Germany, I was ready to set out on the long, long 25,000-mile trail on a bicycle (also 15,000 miles on the seven seas) through 40 countries around the world.

With my bed in the great Out-of-Doors, and motive power the visceral dynamics in my legs, the only expenses of the trip were for food, film for my camera, passport visas, and other incidentals.

Bucephalus, the faithful old bicycle which carried me around the world, is now resting summa cum laude in honorable retirement in the United States National Museum, in the Hall of Mechanical Heroes, alongside Colonel Lindbergh's Spirit of St. Louis, and Admiral Byrd's conqueror of the South Pole, the Floyd Bennett..

It may sound silly and sentimental to some, but when one's only companion during eighteen months of awful, beautiful, and horrible experiences is a bicycle, it becomes more than a mere inanimate piece of metal—it is a real friend. When I think of the thousands of miles of jungle mud, desert sands, and rocky mountain sides my old "iron horse" had to plow over; the scores of snow-blocked passes making its life miserable in my mad mid-winter dash through the Dolomites, Bavarian, and Tyrolean Alps, and how, like old Job in the Bible, Bucephalus came through with colors flying—well, I just can't keep from loving that old bicycle as a true friend much more trustworthy and "human" than many human beings.

After perusing this book, the reader perhaps will be generous enough to agree that something more was required of me than a maximum amount of physical endurance and a minimum exertion of common sense. The greatest single factor in the success of the trip was my faith in humanity. I went alone through the wildest regions in the world on the theory that there are more good people in the world than there are bad.

If the present volume does nothing more than substantiate this theory—to shed a little more light upon the "touch of nature which makes the whole world kin"—these pages will not have been written in vain.

*　　*　　*　　*　　*　　*　　*

And now, after writing this book of my globular wanderings, I try to bury my treasured travels in the most hidden sarcophagus of my mind. But at most unexpected times— while writing legal papers in my law office, looking over old court records, eating dinner, in the middle of a conversation with a friend about commonplace things—like a bolt from the blue, these ghosts of the past break through the lid of ordinary living with which I try in vain to hold them down, and I see a lightning flash of pictures: a camel caravan I met in an emerald vale of Central Afghanistan, a band of wolves encircling me one still starlit evening far out in Sinai Wilderness, a stormy night at the pilot wheel of my homeward bound freighter with 60-foot waves threatening to tear me off the bridge, a twilight from the apex of Cheops Pyramid on the edge of the Garden of Allah, a 3 a.m. 10-mile ride in a ricksha after seeing a Chinese show in Saigon, a certain little Norwegian mountain girl with a smile on her face and a song on her lips. So strong is the call of these haunting memories that I must clench my fists, grit my teeth, and fight them back into their coffins lest I arise and follow them once again beyond the blue horizon.

With a tinge of wistful nostalgia, I close the lid upon them and again resume my task of trying to live like a normal person just as though I had never really seen Moonlight on the Matterhorn, sunrise on Sinai, Arabian nights, and Northern Lights—only dreamed of them!

August 1, 1938   F.A.B.

"Who has known heights and depths, shall not again
Know peace—not as the calm heart knows
Low ivied walls, a garden close,
The old enchantment of a rose.
And tho' he tread the humble ways of men
He shall not speak the common tongue again.

Who has known heights, shall bear forever more
An incommunicable thing
That hurts his heart as if a wing
Beat at the portal challenging
And yet—lured by the gleam his vision wore
Who once has trodden stars seeks peace no more."

Mary Brent Whiteside

CONTENTS

PART ONE: European Prologue

PART TWO: Bucephalus Becomes a
            'Round the World Reality

PART THREE: Exodus from Egypt

[xii]

"They have cradled you in custom, they have primed
        you with their preaching,
They have soaked you in convention thru and thru;
They have put you in a showcase; you're a credit to
        their teaching;—
But can't you hear the Wild?—it's calling you.

"Let us probe the silent places, let us seek what luck
        betide us;
Let us journey to a lonely land I know.
There's a whisper on the night-wind, there's a star
        agleam to guide us,
And the Wild is calling, calling—let us go."

                                    Robert W. Service

PART ONE

EUROPEAN PROLOGUE

CHAPTER I

I Discover Bucephalus

Early one June morning I arrived in New York, and after gaping up and down at this monstrous metropolis, with the awe of a little boy watching a hippopotamus yawn, I embarked on the good ship Black Osprey, a freighter bound for Rotterdam. As the ship rolled into the waves, sending a spray of salt water over my position in the prow, I opened my mouth regularly and methodically, thereby allowing the spray to alleviate my blistered tonsils—a result of the mid-day visit to Manhattan.

Being a very typical landlubber, I served on the ship in the capacity of painter, dishwasher, winch-wiper, boxing coach to the more martial gobs, and nursemaid to four of the five other workaways, who had difficulty in getting their sea-legs. For amusement, the captain suggested that I play shuffleboard with a twenty-pound rust scraper.

After twelve days alone on the Atlantic, the Black Osprey nosed into the crowded English channel from which poured an endless row of ships. It was like emerging from a desert into a crowded city thoroughfare.

The ship crawled up the channel and the river to Rotterdam where, after docking, I was honorably discharged; I received the regular salary of a workaway: one cent per month! I wrote a receipt for my salary and gave it to the captain.

After two days of sight-seeing in Rotterdam and The Hague, I left for a short visit with friends in Gotha, Germany. There I purchased an excellent Original

[1]

Reinhardt bicycle. It was a case of love at first sight. The moment I first laid eyes on the beautiful blue steel frame of this sturdy steed, I knew that Bucephalus was meant for me. It was merely a matter of seconds before I had dashed into the bicycle shop, flung sixty-seven Reichmarks on the counter, and breezed out the door with my new found friend.

In company with an eighteen-year-old German boy, Werner Faber, I left Gotha on July 9 for the North Sea and Norway. At once there were interesting customs and beautiful scenes for our enjoyment: picturesque landscapes; beautiful country lassies; a town crier with his "Hear ye, hear ye, people of this village!"; famous Wartburg castle at Eisenach; dialect of people unintelligible even to Werner! Finally, to bed on fresh hay in a delightful barn in Wahlburg. (One gets permission from the Burgomeister before one is allowed to remain in a village over night.) We traveled light, planning to cook most of our meals and spend the night wherever the end of the day found us.

In a day's journey we wound through scores of Westphalian villages with their needle-spired churches and ancient inns with inner courts. Between the villages we traveled through impenetrable forests, dotted with feudal castles.

Occasionally we passed funeral processions. The horses were draped in black sheets, with black hats. The pallbearers walked behind the black stage coach wearing swallowtail coats and high silk hats. Then followed all the relatives of the deceased wearing long black robes and riding bicycles, some of them five-passenger models, with two babies in a basket in front of mama's (or papa's) handlebars, and two more children in a basket behind the seat.

On July 14, after bicycling 640 kilometers through northern Germany in five days, we crossed the border into Denmark, singing lustily the marching song of the "Canadian Infantry."

[2]

In Denmark, as in Germany, there were special roads for bicycles only, and even though the wind was against us, we pedaled through the entire country—from south to north—in three days. On the fourth day, we looked out of our barn window to see the sun rise over the sea.

All in all, Denmark is a wholesome and hospitable country, filled with friendly and solid people. This is a land of beautiful horses, fine cattle, oceans of grain, potatoes, turnips, strawberries—a land carefully tilled and scientifically managed—a land of comfortable homes—a land where life is worth living—a land where the simpler virtues and wholesome customs abound.

We left Frederickshaven docks bound for Göteborg, Sweden, on a little 18-foot sailing skiff laden with a cargo of fish, as the guests of the captain and first mate, who constituted the crew in toto. Even though this toy boat nearly turned a flip at each wave, my sea legs held firm and I still could look forward to my first experience of sea-sickness.

Our entree to Sweden in the afternoon was via a ten-mile trip up one of Sweden's famous fjords, for Göteborg, like Rotterdam, is not on the coast. All the way to the city cold, gray stone hills frowned down upon us. Even after we hoisted our "iron horses" ashore and got into the familiar saddles again, the outlook still loomed gloomily. We found it too dangerous to ride in Göteborg, with traffic laws the reverse of those to which we were accustomed.

Nosing our bicycles into a driving wind and rain, sweeping down from the north, we plowed up a muddy highway winding between giant grey cliffs, endless rock fences, and villages of big, top-heavy wooden houses.

Night-fall found us sitting in an old stage coach in a barn twelve kilometers from Monkeyville on the road to Kunslav, with a half gallon of fresh milk, a loaf of black bread, and a pound of cheese for supper.

In the twilight a large steamer was gliding up a little

[3]

stream of water between two fields of rye which were in turn between two stone cliffs. The boat seemed to pass through the fields, dodging the haystacks in a game of hide-and-seek, for the river could not be seen from the ground level.

One can go all over Scandinavia by boat, train, airplane, bus, or last and least used, bicycle. As our weary wobbly legs were stern reminders that we had not chosen the easiest means of transportation over this rugged region, we did not regret crossing on a ferry into the black forests and green vales of Norway, a pleasant change from the cold, grey, stony coast of Sweden.

In spite of days marked by constant head winds and rain, noonday swims in icy fjords, time out to eat wild berries, and for frequent visits to old Swedish castles, during ten days we pedaled our bicycles nearly 900 miles, over what were for the most part very bad roads.

CHAPTER II

My Bonnie Norwegian Lassie

Norway! Haywalls, most of them several hundred yards long and resembling giant caterpillars from a distance; beautiful fir-covered mountain peaks seeming to touch the azure sky; clouds like distorted wind-blown bubbles; myriads of hemlock "log run" rivers, silvery lakes and fjords winding beneath the high mountain cliffs; hundreds of giant waterfalls, which account for the fact that trains and everything in the country are run by electricity—even the poorest country home boasting an electric cooker.

We reached Oslo early one Saturday morning, and, after lunch, started on a wild ride to the northward, into the heart of the mountains and through the most beautiful scenery of northern Europe. We had planned to go west to Bergen, but found that it was necessary to detour several hundred miles northward in order to make the trip by bike.

We rode 134 kilometers the next day—very good considering that, except for 26 kilometers across a plateau 7000 feet high, we had been climbing all day. On reaching this plateau I saw what I thought to be a lake in the distance but it turned out to be a beautiful river flowing down from still higher snow-capped peaks. The next day we would cross those mountains!

Late in the afternoon we began stretching our necks—like turkeys preparing to fly to the roosting place—looking vainly for an abode for the night.

Once I smelled peculiar odors in the clear, clean atmosphere and we soon discovered the source. They emanated from a large fox farm where hundreds of these animals were raised for their fur. It is too bad that some one can't devise a scheme whereby the fox could be sheared instead of skinned. I tried to discuss with Werner this point of skinning a fox twice. He was puzzled when I told him that in Georgia—U.S.A.—I frequently "skint a cat" several times in rapid succession, in my younger days. He came to the conclusion that strange animals were raised in my country and inquired as to how many times an Indian could scalp a paleface.

We soon came to a little house perched up on a hill a few kilometers above the hamlet of Gjeilo. When we knocked, an old man and his granddaughter came to the door and, as both spoke German, we had little difficulty in conversing.

With permission to sleep in the hay loft in the barn, we were preparing literally to "hit the hay," when grandpa came over bringing feather mattresses and linen and invited us over to the house for a late supper. While we ate, granddaughter—beautiful and blonde—sang Norwegian folk songs in a clear soprano voice, to the accompaniment of her guitar. The supper was unusually good—nut-brown cheese made of goats milk, butter, fish

[5]

and bread. This bread, heavy as lead and with a crust about an inch thick, provided more "ballast" than a bait of sweet potatoes and buttermilk.

The next morning Cymbaline cooked breakfast for us and again sang while we ate. From the dining room window we could see the snow-capped peaks above us, and the more I looked at them the more I realized that, considering the energy to be expended in climbing, it would be essential to acquire that energy at this breakfast.

After about two hours of breakfast and songs, we overcame the inertia and prepared to be up and on the way. Cymbaline presented me with a large round loaf of bread about two feet in diameter. She explained that as she baked bread only about four times a year, this loaf was comparatively fresh, being only one month old. However, it was excellent even though the mastication thereof was an arduous form of exercise, quite reminiscent of my leather-chewing course of training for my college boxing team. Thus heavily laden, we sauntered down the lane, our hearts filled with lasting love and gratitude for Cymbaline. As we galloped over the hill, I looked back just in time to catch a last fleeting glimpse of this golden haired lassie waving a wistful goodbye, and then—gone!—gone from my sight (forever?), but never from my heart. There are girls, and girls, and girls; but never in all the wide, wide world will man meet maid more pure, or sweet, or fair, than my little Flower of the Norwegian Highlands.

After two hours of steady cycling, we stopped and took a swim in a river fresh off the ice and snow of the high mountain pass just above Gjeilo. We then pushed our bikes all day to the top of the pass. There a summer camper informed us that it was impossible to go farther except via railway, since there was no road of any kind— not even a trail—for the next 32 kilometers.

Werner and I decided to "do the impossible" and be the first ever to cross the pass on bicycles. It was 5:30 p.m.

[6]

when we started up the railroad tracks with our bicycles, through tunnels, over high bridges., but we had little fear of night overtaking us before reaching our goal. Even this far south it did not get really dark. The night before the sun had set shortly before twelve o'clock; there was a brief twilight period, and the sun rose again.

If Werner and I had "stuck to" our railway track we would have arrived at our destination in schedule time, but half-way across the pass he sighted what he thought to be a new road. He had grown weary of the dark tunnels protecting the tracks from snow avalanches.

Though somewhat dubious as to this trail, I had led Werner thus far, and turn about was fair play. Lead on, mon capitan, I follow. So my German friend and I lifted our bikes over three fences to the trail which turned out to be a new—very new—road across the pass. We, its first travelers, started merrily down its winding way. After we crossed twenty-two unbridged gullies, opened and shut about a dozen fence gates across our path, the "road" suddenly ended. We had made a record run of two and one-half hours on its one and one-half kilometers of length.

With only a turf swamp, a creek, and few more fences separating us from the railroad track, Werner and I put our bikes upon our shoulders and plunged forward. Each bike, with its two knapsacks, dangling pots and pans, and blankets, must have weighed one hundred and fifty pounds. It was nearly ten o'clock before we succeeded in reaching the railroad tracks—only two hours to travel the remaining twelve kilometers before the train would come thundering down the rails upon us, probably in the middle of a narrow tunnel or on a long bridge.

Again shouldering our vehicles, we ducked our heads against the wind, and clicked off the first few kilometers in grand style with scarcely a stop for breath. "Four kilometers to go and only eleven o'clock," I shouted back to Werner.

[7]

But Werner was too tired to answer at once. He had fallen across the rails and was breathing like an old war horse during a battle. "I-I c-c-can't go—on," he finally sputtered.

"But we've got to go on," I pleaded. "We're not only in the middle of a trestle, but over a river as well."

Dropping my load, I helped Werner to his feet and placed his bike on his shoulder. By the time I had again picked up my own heavily laden vehicle and was ready to resume the journey, I was as tired as he. But I knew that to stop and rest now would be fatal. We would perhaps drop off to sleep and "wake up dead" after the train had run over us or we had frozen stiff.

"We've got to rest occasionally, but let's be systematic about it," I muttered.

"Ya! Let us rest through fifteen deep breaths between every one hundred and fifty ties of ze remaining four kilometers," suggested Werner, when he had finally recovered his lost voice.

"Ausgezeichnet! Brilliant idea!" I rejoined. "By counting each cross tie, the time will not seem so long between rests, and by counting each long breath, rests will not seem so short between walks—is that what you mean?"

With a look of confusion and wonder plainly written across his face, Werner took the lead up the trail, mumbling half aloud and half to himself: "Perhaps you are crazy, perhaps I am crazy—perhaps both of us are crazy, but at least we are dead not yet!"

Ten minutes before midnight we pulled into the little station house just before a big engine was ready to start out across the pass. We had finished the first leg of our dash to Bergen without casualties. However, our ankles had swelled about twice their normal size and knife-like pains shot through our arms as if they were being cut in two at the shoulder. That night we were so tired that we slept in a bed.

[8]

The next day, en route to Eidford, we almost froze in a snow storm—snow in July! The road down the gorge was a magnificent piece of engineering, circling down like a gigantic corkscrew screwed perpendicularly into the side of the cliff.

We spent the night at Eidford on a bluff looking down the great fjord, where the wind howled and screamed all night. Many beautiful farms and orchards were nestled in the sheltered nooks of these fjords.

Three days later, after a wild ride over hills and dales— above the clouds and under—in rain, fog and snow, we pulled into Bergen. I felt fine except that my ankles were again so swollen from the strain of the past few days I could hardly walk.

We embarked on a Danish schooner for Stettin, Germany, and as we set sail at 7:00 p.m., the sun came out for the first time in three days. For the next fifteen hours the boat played hide-and-seek with the little mountain islands on our inland voyage down the Norwegian coast.

Upon arriving at Copenhagen, Denmark, we "took in" the city, while the boat was undergoing some minor repairs. I was especially interested in the collection of medieval armor and accoutrements in the museums; the knights in full armor on the horses recalled Ivanhoe— riders on their steeds wearing velvet gowns under their iron garments and plumes, "fore and aft." At Elsinore Palace, I looked for the ghost and recited Hamlet's solilo- quy while I paced up and down the cold stone corridors.

Then on to Stettin and Berlin, where Werner remained with friends while I proceeded alone to Gotha.

In spite of the circuitous route I reached Gotha in two and a half days, averaging more than 150 miles per day. I was constantly passing soldiers, tanks, giant air fleets and artillery. Nearly every community boasts of barracks and forts where the Government maintains its youth, training them for war.

Although I had been away from Gotha only a little more than three weeks, the green and red fields of grain and poppies had turned golden. I had ridden staunch old Bucephalus more than 2500 miles.

CHAPTER III

Mountain Climbing on a Bicycle

On a hot day in August, I cycled out of Gotha to the tune of many "Gute reise!"s and "Auf wiedersehen!"s. It was the same bicycle, the same rider, and even the same road that had started me on my Scandinavian trip a few weeks earlier—yet they were all entirely different. The first trip had served as a sort of trial run; the bicycle was broken in, and I was toughened up.

At Eisenach, I left my old trail and headed south through the heart of the Thüringen and Black Forests. Hops are seen everywhere in this part of Germany and their bright red blossoms contribute beauty to the landscape. An endless double row of trees lines both sides of the roads. These trees not only impart shade to the road, but bear nuts and fruits as well. I anticipated getting out of this district since the luscious apples and pears lying along the roadside retarded my speed. It was annoying to pass on without sampling them.

It was harvest time and each peasant family was busily applying hand sickles to the small patches of grain. Singing lustily with each sweeping stroke of the scythe, these sons of the soil seemed to radiate good cheer and wholesomeness, so simple yet so sincere are their lives in which industry, cleverness, thrift and love of nature are paramount.

Each day I discovered some new and charming characteristic of this people. While sitting on the Heidelberg roadside eating "mittag" of raw carrots, milk, and thick sandwiches of black bread filled with dried figs, butter and limburger cheese, ninety-three cyclists whizzed by. Of this number, sixty-one said to me "Guten appetit!"; nineteen said "Gute!"; eight queried "Schmacks gut?" and five, who apparently did not see me, said nothing. From this little observation I decided that though the coarse German bread and cheese might lack the "aesthetic fragility" of our American products, German manners were polite and polished to the point of perfection.

I felt as if I were at home with my mother when I stopped in several village curb markets along the route, bought gingerbread cookies, fruit, raw vegetables, and gossiped with a good natured old farmer or a proud grandmother in her green velvet dress with her grandchild in her arms. Like an old fashioned politician, I found that "bragging" about the children "gets the votes" in every country in which I traveled.

The Black Forest girls, dressed like pictures from an old family album, were so beautiful that I was tempted several times to betray my trust to Cymbaline—the Norwegian lassie.

All these healthy and intelligent girls wear the same kind of old fashioned black velvet jackets, but the skirts are of different colors, usually green with vari-colored stripes. This outfit blends perfectly with the picturesque landscape—the little road winding up through the purple twilight haze to a neat little thatch cottage at the end of each dale; it was all like a picture in an old fairy book. Though the Black Forest derives its name from the many black fir trees growing in it, the trees and everything, even the moss-covered tile or straw roofs of the houses are green.

At my first view of the Alps overlooking Lake Sursee, I could not refrain from uttering a reverent "My God!" Just across the border at Basel, Switzerland, a shower of rain washed and clothed the feet of the majestic Alps;

[11]

thunderheads swam around overhead like giant sea monsters in an ocean of clouds.

After a strenuous 24 kilometer climb, Bucephalus and I reached the top of Brünig Pass where we spent the night in a little alpine hut. As I sat down to write in my diary and looked about me, the view was quite the reverse of that at Basel. Instead of gazing upward, I peered down at the mountain peaks penetrating sporadically the ocean of clouds below, like little islands in a billowy sea. How I wished the rest of the world could be with me to enjoy this glorious panorama as the setting sun sent a rainbow of colors across the turbulent sea of clouds and snowy mountain peaks far below me.

Unfortunately, I was the sole heir to the great fortune of scenery which unfolded before my aerial hayloft. On my left, the sky was red from the sunset; on my right, the golden moon seemed to be playing hide-and-seek with the big thunderheads among the mountain peaks; several miles below—for one must speak in terms of miles and not feet, the lights of the village were just waking up and looking at themselves in the mirror-like lake. How I wished I had color film to retain the natural colors of the green and blue Swiss lakes.

Sitting in the twilight by a spring of pure water bubbling out of the mountain top immediately adjacent to my hut, I looked back in my mind's eye upon the beautiful scenery at Chillon and was convinced that the position of the poor prisoner in the dungeon was the perfection of pathos.

After several days literally pushing my bicycle over long passes, I stopped in Frütigen and bought hobnail shoes and wool socks. Without these necessary purchases I could never have pushed my bike the seventeen kilometers up the path of the 9000-foot perpendicular cliff from Kandersteg to my abode for the night—an old mountaineer's hut near the top of Gimme Pass.

The trip over this pass was a great experience, requiring

The Little Mermaid at Langelinie

A sailor's life is bold and free

Denmark is filled with friendly and solid people

Haystacks, Norwegian style (also roosts for wild turkeys and wandering bicyclists)

My bonnie Norwegian lassie

Pause before plunge into the mountains

maximum physical endurance and minimum exertion of common sense. Having heard that a man once made the trip across on horseback, I had decided to make the attempt with Bucephalus.

In spite of fine air and a comfortable bed of hay, I did not sleep well, as an old Swiss hen and rooster with their brood of fine robust "children" came clucking into my hayloft and continued to chatter all night.

At daybreak, I was on my way pushing Bucephalus up the narrow trail. After an hour or so, I removed my shirt and put on dark glasses. The exertion of pushing 150 pounds of steel up the cliff warmed me up in spite of the dazzling snow and icy winds. Every fifteen or twenty steps I would have to stop and "take a breather."

The path—which was only two or three feet wide—was very rocky and any false step might cause me to fall over the cliff. At times it would take several minutes to maneuver Bucephalus around a hair-pin curve. My back soon became sunburned and when I reached the top of the pass, I had acquired a first class sun-tan.

Before starting down, I stretched out on the snow and rested. In the nooks and cracks of the rocky earth many beautiful alpine roses grew. It was very interesting to study and examine plant life miles up in the air.

The ascent had been strenuous but it was not so dangerous as the descent. Had I let my bike slide faster than a snail's pace down the winding trail, for only a fraction of an uncontrolled second, it would have landed in the midst of the village thousands of feet directly below. It was necessary to lock the brakes on the bike, and wrap rope around the tires in order to keep it on the trail.

The trail was hewn out of the solid rock cliffs and was so steep that only my toes touched the ground on the ascent and only my heels on the descent. So high is the "obstacle" between the two villages of Kandersteg and Leukerbad that the trail is nearly twenty-seven kilometers in length, whereas the train, tunnelling straight through the mountain, travels only six kilometers. The trail goes over the very tip-top of one of the highest mountains of this region and yet it is a "pass." Misnomer, I call it.

I had named my bicycle Bucephalus, but I was tempted to change the name to Judas, for after carrying it up the mountain and sliding it down, it played traitor in my hour of need. Because it rolled over a large nail half way down to Leukerbad, I had to carry it across my shoulder—pack and all—the rest of the way down to the village; the last three or four kilometers were excellent for riding.

Not less than a score of cameras clicked pictures of me, trudging wearily into town late in the afternoon, bearing my burdens on my back. I met the town's brass band consisting of children, old men with long, white beards, and everyone else so fortunate as to possess a horn, even though, as the music intimated, he could not play it.

Of course, this music was not in my honor. It was a mere coincidence that I happened to drop in while the daily concert was in progress. However, the band did make it a special occasion, when it learned of my presence and of my trip over the pass with the bike, by playing the only American tune it knew, "My Old Kentucky Home." I believe I recognized the melody, but unfortunately the musicians who knew the piece least played the loudest.

Riding up the Rhone valley, I passed several monasteries with their many small individual "hermitages" or " studies," dotting the mountain sides. Many of the monks were spraying their meadows with water pumped from manure-filled wells—an effective method of fertilization which no doubt accounts in large measure for the excellent quality of the famous Swiss cheese.

Many dots of towns perked up here and there in the mountains, each town graced with a steepled church towering protectingly over the brown wooden huts huddled around its base.

[16]

Looking up the branch gorges of the Rhone, one sees hundreds of beautiful arched stone bridges for the roads and railways winding up the mountain-sides. The rivers and brooks are well controlled as every stream of water has artificial rock bed and sides.

In the evening I wound up the delightful little forty-one kilometer foot-path toward Zermatt and the setting sun to see moonlight on the Matterhorn. As I rode up the trail through picturesque little "villayets," and on up toward the soft twilight glow on the side of the snow-covered Matterhorn at the end of the trail, I thought this surely was God's greatest gift of beauty to the world.

I had just started to climb to my hayloft on the edge of Zermatt as the first shadows of night were creeping up the gorge, when a heavenly light swept suddenly across the side of the great Matterhorn. Looking to the left over the cold, blue-steel, starlit sky, I saw the full moon rising among the giant snow-caps of the highest range of the Alps.

Nights of the full moon do not occur every day, and clear starlit skies are about as often as full moons in Switzerland. Seldom does one find the two simultaneously, and hardly ever could one be so fortunate as to have both these phenomena of nature occur in the most beautiful spot in this country.

"What a view there must be tonight up there on top of the Matterhorn," I mused. "Why not climb the mountain! Yet how unromantic to have to make the ascent with the aid of a guide! But alpine guides are only human. If they can lead tourists to the top, why couldn't I carry myself up? Climb a snow-capped mountain alone? Absurd!" I laughed at myself for even thinking of such a thing. But the more foolish the venture seemed to be, the more fascinated I was at the possibility of the undertaking. As the words echoed and re-echoed through my brain "Climb the Matterhorn!" I pictured myself groping up the moonlit side of the rock-ribbed glacial monster.

My reverie was interrupted by a light touch on my shoulder. "Stranger, you are looking longingly at the Horn—like for me to carry you up tomorrow morning? Costs only one hundred and eleven francs—"

I looked around to find that the husky voice belonged to a sturdy Swiss mountaineer whose silver badge on the right lapel of his green coat plainly and conspicuously marked him as an alpine guide.

"One hundred and eleven francs is a rather high price, isn't it?" I queried.

"Well, considering that one hundred and eleven francs is the value put on our lives, I don't believe it's so much after all," he replied. "In fact, it's a pretty low price when you think of the high place it takes you to," he continued.

"Is it possible to climb the Matterhorn alone?" My question almost knocked him down.

"Mein Gott! How should I know?" He gaped in amazement. "No one has ever been known to do such a foolish thing, and I have not thought of the possibility."

"But is it possible?" I repeated.

His first reaction of startled concern and pity toward me gave way to a few moments of thoughtful meditation. Finally in a slow, thoughtful voice he said half to himself: "Donner und Blitzen! It might be possible after all! However, when several persons rope themselves together over the dangerous part of the climb it doesn't matter much whether one slips and falls or not, as the rest will hold and save him. But when a person is alone, he can't afford to fall because there's no one holding on at the other end of the rope. Yes, it's foolish to try to climb that Horn alone."

"If the guide is less sure-footed but weighs twice as much as his companion. wouldn't it be safer without a guide? The chances are that the heavy guide would be the one to fall and pull his companion to death with him," I

[18]

argued.

The guide at first looked at me as if he wondered what my question had to do with the price of eggs in China, then begrudgingly but sincerely remarked, "Perhaps you are half right. In more than one instance I have seen climbers make the whole trip without a single slip. Had they been alone they would have been successful in the climb. But, they were not alone, nor will any one ever climb the Matterhorn alone. It just isn't done!"

His closing speech sounded like an ominous prophecy, but my mind was already made up. "Why, for a little fellow like me, as sure-footed as the best of alpine guides, I had much rather risk my life in my own hands than with one of those big husky mountaineers."

I had just done the "impossible" by scaling Gimme Pass with a bicycle—why couldn't I climb that mountain without a guide?

CHAPTER IV

Climbing the Matterhorn Alone

With a pound of dried beef in my pocket, and wearing my hobnail shoes and snow mittens, I set forth from Zermatt in a broiling hot sun for Matterhorn's hoary head, without a guide, snow axe, goggles, or other usual equipment. After two hours of easy climbing I reached Schwarzee Hotel, and after two more hours of hard climbing, I stumbled into Belvedere Hut—altitude 10,000 feet, and such light atmosphere that it was easy to lose my breath.

At the Hut, the proprietor informed me that he had no room for me and that I would have to go next door to the Hotel, which was more expensive and which I had hoped to avoid.

Before I left the Hut, a donkey passed carrying down the

mountain the broken body of a young Italian who, though unconscious, had a vise-like grip on the donkey's neck as if desperately clinging to his last little thread of life. Three days before, a party of four had gone up the Matterhorn. One, this one who passed, had fallen into a crevice where he had remained crying for help for two nights and a day before he could finally be reached. Later I was to think back upon this scene.

I obtained a room at the Hotel, and went immediately to bed. Having heard that two Frenchmen were going up with a guide at two o'clock the next morning, I intended to follow along behind them. My host was to awaken me at 1:45 a.m.

As my "party" and their guide left their hut under the shadow of the mighty Horn, which seemed to be sitting on top of the world and penetrating into the sky, a fourth, uninvited and unknown, crept behind the light of their lantern only a few meters away.

The full moon was brilliant against a background of black, ominous thunderheads and a foreground of glacial mountains; for the first time I experienced that "moon-struck" feeling that I had heard people talk about. The moon was like a guardian angel over the sleeping white caps of the mountains, and the clouds were ugly demons trying to devour her. In Saint Paul's Cathedral in London, there are alternate statues of angels and ugly gorgon-head-ed demons for contrast, and so it was here.

But in less than an hour after my start up the almost per-pendicular cone of the Matterhorn, the moon vanished and I had to rely solely upon the lantern a hundred feet in front for light. In the darkness, with the light shining ahead, I thought of the old song "Lead Kindly Light—Lead Thou Me On." I crawled along following a light up the great mountain side, singing softly this old song. I remembered the days when I was a child attending camp-meeting, and listening to the old Methodist preachers under the stars

[20]

proclaiming "He who would attain the heights of salvation must approach with humility."

For the next five hours the clouds grew more angry and the wind more furious until finally, just before the party ahead reached the summit, the storm burst loose.

It was too near the goal to turn back, so I was glad to see the men climb on to the top. Here my "party" became aware of my presence for the first time as I came puffing up at their heels. We enjoyed the gorgeous view of gray-black nothingness for thirty seconds; then started back down.

The wind was deafening and the swirling snow blinding. Prompt descent was now a matter of life or death, so without taking time to ask why I was alone, the guide roped me in with his crew, and I became a full-fledged member of my "party." Since the steps cut in the ice up the steep slope were fast filling with ice and snow we had to race against time as well as unleashed and maddened nature.

Worst of all, I was very weary. It was not until I was standing on top of the Matterhorn with the flurries of snow too thick to see through, the clouds as dark as midnight, although it was eight o'clock in the morning, and the wind howling and blowing with the fury and roar of forty Niagaras, that I fully realized how utterly foolish I had been to attempt to climb the Matterhorn immediately after the two most strenuous days of my life, when all my supply of energy was exhausted. Too, I had just broken in my new climbing shoes and my feet had hurt all the way to Belvedere Hut on the first day up the mountain. When I had started out, I could hardly put one foot before the other, but strange as it may seem, walking was all right as soon as the steep climbing began.

For one fleeting second the long perpendicular trail I had just traversed flashed through my mind's eye. It had been hard enough to climb up the icy steps, as many of them were several feet apart, and my short legs could span the intervening space only with difficulty, but to go down when these steps were filled with ice and snow seemed impossible. Still, where it is a question of life or death, the seemingly impossible will always be attempted.

It is said that a drowning man has a vision of his whole past life in the last moments of consciousness, and that a freezing man dreams of green pastures, bright sunshine, home, and all that is good. As we clutched desperately for life in the snow and rocks, I thought of many things—of many pleasant scenes with the home folks down in sunny Georgia. I recited poems softly for pastime; it seemed that a century must pass before we would reach the bottom of that aweful arm of rock and snow which pointed so defiantly towards the heavens.

For some strange reason my head seemed clearer during the descent than usual—probably the high altitude had made me "light-headed" or delirious—and thousands of thoughts flashed through my mind simultaneously as I composed music to the poem, "The Cremation of Sam McGee."

On that memorable six-hour trip, or perhaps more accurately, slip, down the side of Matterhorn, only three of the four of us were on our feet at the same time, which means that even if we had been endowed with the nine legendary lives of the cat, all nine of our lives would have been extinguished had we been alone, for when one falls here, it is usually a funeral ride to one of the glaciers far below. Truly on our downward journey it was "all for one and one for all."

Several times I thought that in our hurry we would reach the bottom about a thousand times quicker than we wished. The other three men averaged at least one hundred and seventy pounds each; a few times one of them slipped over the side; the rest of us had to clutch the ice-covered rocks until our hands bled, till our companion regained his balance and released the pressure on the rope

[22]

which bound us all together in one common thread of life.

The mental strain must have been worse on my comrades as each had several successive falls, and had the rope snapped, it would have meant his death plunge; but the physical strain told worse on me as I had to help brace and back up two of my comrades when the third fell.

After six hours of eternity, we reached the bottom of the steep pyramid and what we thought was comparative safety, only a few miles above Zermatt. We were just congratulating ourselves on our victory when a deafening roar, as of mighty flood waters breaking through a great dam, froze us in our tracks with fright. The wind howling around one corner of the Matterhorn, the black clouds twisting and knotting like miniature tornadoes, the snow and sleet cutting our faces, made a perfect setting for the end of the world. Suddenly tons of snow and rock came thundering down the precipice across our path of a few moments back and plunged into the depths of the glacier below. If we had been a few seconds slower in our descent, we would have had first class tombs under tons of snow and ice, and perhaps a century or so hence our bodies might have made their youthful and preserved appearance to the people in the valley below! Or even if we had not been caught in this avalanche, we would have had a difficult time finding the way, in the dark clouds across the glacier ridge, after the path had been swept away. To say the least, this little anti-climax sent us trooping into Belvedere Hut as sober and pale as men can be.

As a cup of tea cost three francs and a square meal a small fortune here, the lonesome five-franc piece in my pocket told me that I had to go down to Zermatt where I had more money in my pack stored in the luggage room of the depot. My three newly-made friends were content to remain at the Hut for the rest of the week or until the storm was at an end. The Hotel proprietor informed me

[23]

that a guide had come up from Zermatt nearly an hour before, and that even then the trail was becoming impassable as far down as Hotel Schwarzee at the 2800 meter level, and that I had not a minute to lose if I made it.

It did not take long for me to decide what course to pursue. The memory of my first view from below this little hut precariously perched on a peninsula of rock cliff, surrounded by glaciers and with Matterhorn's arm pointing heavenward in the background; the memory of the donkey carrying the broken and bleeding Italian down past the hut to the hospital or morgue in Zermatt; these things made me long for good old terra firma.. On this high, wind-swept, snowy peak life hung too insecurely for me. Consequently I drank a supply of snow-water, buttoned my jacket, and plunged forth to end my trip as I had started it: alone.

Even though the snow was already seven inches deep and steadily falling faster, so that I had every reason to be anxious and worried, the mental strain and suspense of the last twelve hours climbing could be maintained no longer. My mind now forced itself to relax and grasp at every object for entertainment and diversion. I noticed that the snow was of different colors, predominantly purple in the trail before me and blue in the glaciers on either side.

Nearing Schwarzee I had to cross a glacier covered in several feet of crumbled rock. There is such intense heat and cold, frequently in the course of one day, that rocks are easily dislodged and crumbled. Twice on my downward journey, I had to climb over rock from fresh avalanches which partially obliterated the trail. At any moment a landslide might have buried me alive; but I was very well pleased that such did not happen.

On the Matterhorn trail, the rocks are of all shapes and colors. Often white crystal rocks were embedded in the center of a different type of rock. The changing weather conditions had caused the big rocks to crumble in half, leaving the smooth smaller rocks in place like a large diamond, or other precious stone in the setting of a ring.

I was so engrossed in my geological observation that, without realizing it, I walked down from the low ceiling of black clouds, snow, ice and danger, into a land of warm sunshine. At Hotel Schwarzee, which lay just out of reach of the furious snow clouds which bathe old Matterhorn's head in snow flurries almost every week, even during the summer, I stopped for more snow-water and was told that the day had been warm and clear in the valley below. All the time I had been clinging for dear life against all the forces of nature—gravitation, hunger, exhaustion and cold—I might have been basking in the sun only a few miles below!

From Schwarzee to Zermatt it was truly like drifting into the dream of a freezing man. I found myself stumbling down through a few warm fleecy clouds into a serene paradise. Never was the sun more beautiful or the day more peaceful!

As I walked down the main street with a poker face, a big fat tourist drinking tea on the veranda of the Monte Rosa Hotel inquired, "Back from the Matterhorn?" To my reply in the affirmative, he remarked, "My son climbed it last year. I understand it gives one an appetite." And not once during the twelve hours on the actual peak itself had I thought of food!

Looking back towards the setting sun, I saw only a few black clouds over the southwestern horizon. The Matterhorn could not be seen, but I knew she was there in the midst of those clouds; and I knew, too, that it was not nearly so peaceful up there as it might seem from Zermatt.

CHAPTER V

All Roads Lead to Rome

I said an easy good-bye to the Matterhorn and started out for Italy. I did not realize that Zermatt was so high until I had gone down the gorge for nearly fifteen kilometers before meeting some dark clouds coming up the gorge. For the next thirty-five or more kilometers down to Visp I was flying down through dense clouds and a down-pour of icy rain.

Suddenly, my journey almost ended on the rocks of the river far below. Recent rains had washed out a section of my little path, and I ran upon a chasm unawares. Quick maneuvering and the two wheel brakes stopped Bucephalus against the side of a boulder overhanging the gorge. The force of the impact wrecked the rear tire and I had a pleasant time repairing it in the rain.

Yet the most disheartening thing of all was to have to climb back over the same range of the Alps that I had been climbing down all morning—there was no alternative as the path ended at the chasm.

From Brig to Gonda I pushed and pulled Bucephalus 42 kilometers up Semplon Pass through the worst icy rain encountered since leaving Norway. The long trip up the pass was bad enough—perspiration and rain made me look and feel like a drowned rat—but the long downward journey over into the Italian border was like falling off an iceberg into the Arctic Ocean. I nearly froze. The scores of tunnels—some of them hundreds of feet long—with arched windows along the side for light; the road passing behind waterfalls; the alpine goats clustered under the rocky cliffs—registered as a flash of snap-shot pictures in a rather foggy background.

Just as I hit the Italian border at 4:00 p.m., the rain ceased, the clouds parted, and the sun came shining

[26]

through. Whether this was a good omen or not, at least it was a pleasant change to cycle down the broad warm Italian valleys winding between green sloped, less majestic but more gentle-looking Alps than those of Switzerland.

In one sense it grieved me to see so many fresh green fields and silver streams, for it meant that Italy had her rains as well as sunshine, and that sooner or later I should get my share. However, after enduring the icy rains of Norway and Switzerland, surely I could stand the warm showers of sunny Italy!

For two days, I cycled leisurely through the beautiful lake region of northern Italy, occasionally swimming in the clear waters of the lakes and picnicking between swims on fresh grape marmalade, ice-cold watermelon, and buttered rolls warmed by the sun.

When a fellow tires of riding, there's nothing like a puncture to make him wish he could ride. While cycling out to Venice from the mainland, sleepily watching the teams of horses pull boats up the canals, I was suddenly awakened from somnolence when "Judas" turned a flip following the explosion of the rear tire. After pulling the body together I surveyed the situation and found in the tire a hole large enough to surround a golf ball. With no spare tire anywhere nearby, I used my last patch to repair the tube and tore the tongue from my shoe to cover the tire from the inside. Alas! the hole was too large. Reluctantly, I completed the destruction of my shoe by fashioning a "boot" from the soft leather covering my toes. It worked!

Venice might as well have been a city in the trees as far as Bucephalus was concerned. As the road ended at the entrance to the city, I checked my steed and started out afoot. Even this method of transportation was not effective. Every time I started up a narrow sidewalk along one of the great labyrinthine canals lined with dirty yet picturesque houses—reminders of the New York East Side tenements—I found myself running into a blind alley that either bumped into a stone wall or dumped into a canal. After several hours getting nowhere fast, I abandoned my peripatetic method and went native. I really "went to town" when I "took to the water" in a rented gondola.

Landing at St. Mark's Square, I marveled at the four fiery bronze horses poised on their hind legs as if about to pounce off the parapet of St. Mark's Cathedral with the same eager readiness that my own iron horse responded to my call to action.

I roared delightedly at the bronze lion of Babylon; I sighed sadly at the Bridge of Sighs; I gaped awfully at the hideous ugliness and exquisite beauty of this coral reefed city. But the thing that impressed me most about this magic isle was its comparative peace and quiet. Imagine New York without its screaming subways, elevateds, tramways, auto roads and all its pulsating arteries of loco-motion; instead, only quiet waterways winding between the skyscraper walls, with the gentle lapping of tiny rip-ples against the buildings or the soothing swish of a gon-dolier's oar as the only sounds to break the silence.

In the American Express Office, I met an American lady from "Down East," who insisted that I talk to her—said she "adored my melodious Southern accent."

May I now take the liberty of ascending the pedagogical stool and proclaiming to the world and especially to the "damnyankees" that no genuine Southerner says "you-all" when speaking to only one person, and further, that the correct pronunciation in the deep South is "yawl."

Having seen Venice inside and out, via Grand Canal and petite canal, in moonlight and in sunlight, I joined Bucephalus and we headed south.

After a day of hot traveling, we stopped for the night at the first real Italian plantation I had seen. The big house of granite and marble nestled in the middle of a beautiful cypress grove. The scores of servants, the numerous small

[28]

houses on the place, the warm hospitality of my host, and the atmosphere in general recalled to mind plantation life in the Old South.

All the plantation peasants wore bright red bandana headgear, vari-colored blouses and aprons, all spotlessly clean, and each person—man, woman and child—seemed to have a donkey of his or her own to ride. Each donkey wore a bonnet to keep his head cool—whereas in northern Europe they wore blankets to keep warm. The courtyard of the great house was a bedlam of barnyard fowls, rabbits, goats, sheep, pigs, oxen, donkeys and more donkeys.

If carrying buckets, pitchers, vases, baskets and watermelons on top of their heads can give these peasants poise, they certainly should have it—anything that they can't put on the donkeys they put on their heads. A Georgia fieldhand, however, has the world beat, when it comes to carrying things on the head. Often, when visiting my grandfather at Twin Oaks, his plantation in Georgia, I would see one of his fieldhands climb a fence and come across a plowed field in a slow gallop with a round melon balanced aloft.

Though sworn to climb no more mountains, for the next two weeks I found myself pushing Bucephalus up one bigger hill after another—literally walking through most of Central Italy.

I challenge anyone to ride a bicycle from Padua to Rome via Florence, Bologna and Aquapendente during the month of August—the heat is awful. It took six hours with frequent rest periods to make the last forty kilometers into Florence. There for three days I rested from my travels, sitting in Uffizi Galleries and pondering over the wonderful gems of art dating back to the second century B.C. It seemed to me that the farther back a statue dated, the more intelligent were the features portrayed. Practically none of the statues of the Romans of the olden times resembles the modern Italian, but rather the modern

[29]

intelligent American business man.

In contrast to these "old timers," are some of the modern Italian soldiers strutting about like bantam roosters—the higher the rank, the more feathers he wears in his hat. It was amusing to see a group of these heroes bedecked with gaily-colored crosses, medallions and other "badges of honor" sold by merchants and pawnbrokers.

Easing out of Florence in "low gear," I soon got the last three days reserve energy into circulation and started the long climb to Rome. The road to Sienna lay like a great snake writhing through the hills and among the olive groves. "All roads lead to Rome!" but what terrible roads some of them are! Like weary legionnaires returning home immediately after a hard-fought battle, Bucephalus and I wobbled through the Arch de Triumph into the city of seven hills.

Reaching the Coliseum in the heat of the day and finding a slab of stone in one of its dungeons in the arena to be the coolest spot in Italy, I lay down for a nap. I must have dreamed that I was a gladiator waiting to tackle a roaring lion, for I heard the roar of the crowd above. Slowly I waked up and slowly I pulled myself together, yawning and stretching vigorously and emphatically all the time. As soon as I could open my eyes, I heard the crowd really roar. I braced myself for the attack, when I saw that I was surrounded by a group of laughing and squealing American co-eds on one of Cook's tours. They evidently mistook my seemingly lifeless, sun-blackened body for an old bronze statue until I bestirred myself. As soon as possible, I beat a hasty retreat into the arena.

-eyed
ies of the Black Forest

I obtain the latest gossip
and gingerbread from these
good-natured curb marketeers

ll social
ctivities
nd
stitutions
re
presented
the
avarian
illage
aypoles

Atop Gimme "Pass"

e trail was
wn out of
e solid rock
iffs and was
steep that
ly my toes
uched the
round on
e ascent
nd only
y heels on
e descent

Memory of my first view of this little hut perched precariously on a rock cliff, surrounded by glaciers, and with Matterhorn's arm pointing heavenward in the background – all these things made me long for good old "terra firma"

In a broiling hot sun I set forth for Matterhorn's hoary head

CHAPTER VI

Crusoe Comes to Capri

It was not until I reached the Isle of Capri several days later that I really caught up on my sleep. There, in a cave located at the end of a small peninsula overlooking the only land-locked inlet of the island, I spent six weeks resting and taking life easy for a change.

My Caprian cave bored through the cliffs, was only thirty feet above the water, and all I had to do for an early morning swim was to take four steps to the entrance of my quarters and jump.

At twilight the long rows of twinkling lights of Naples, with Vesuvius puffing out of its smokestack "astern," resembled a giant steamer in progress.

I spent most of my time dreaming in the cave, swimming in the bay, basking on the beach and exploring the island. There are many delightful trails winding like catacombs under the white-washed houses—through vine-yards, under masses of wisteria and bougainvillea, through olive groves. Capri has many natural bridges and arches and hundreds of solid rock-caves adorned with stalagmites and stalactites like the spires of the cathedral in Milan—grottoes in which the light is a ghostly blue-green twilight glow.

In the evenings, before retiring, I usually sat for a few minutes on the village Piazza and watched the motley procession of natives and visitors pass in review—hooded nuns from the island convent gliding through the city streets in groups of four and eight like penguins—visitors in bizarre costumes: togas, pajamas, bathing suits, Japanese gowns, ladies leading or carrying dogs—artists wearing trousers that were too short and tight and coats that were too long and baggy.

Often I left my cave and spent the evening at the villas

of wealthy Europeans who were spending the summer here. Capri is too lovely to stay indoors and the dinners were served out under grape arbors; a circle of electric lights, concealed behind the clusters of green and purple grapes, emitted a soft glowing light which blended perfectly with the twilight and seemed to make our rendezvous retain its soft twilight colors long after dark. After dinner, servants spread mattresses on the verandah so that we might observe the showers of comets without getting cricks in our necks.

One evening, my host, a young Oxford graduate who was resting here after passing his final examinations, assured me that every visitor aspired to three adventures while on the island: a boat trip around the island, a swim around the island, and a swim in the Blue Grotto.

My expedition to achieve the first was ill fated; after making the complete circuit of the island, my tiny canoe capsized just as I was stepping ashore inside the Green Grotto at the lower entrance to my cave-home, and I sprawled flat in the deep water along with my kodak and pocketbook. After recovering my camera before it sank very far in the deep water, I began diving for my pocketbook which was plainly visible at the bottom of the deep green bay. The pressure was too much, so I contributed about ten dollars to Davy Jones' bank account.

A German boy started out with me on the second expedition at 7:30 a.m., but had sense enough to quit at 11:00 when he started shivering from chills. He was considerate enough to find a boat to accompany me the rest of the trip, and before I had reached the original starting point a whole fleet of sail and row boats had joined the escort.

The bay is a regular maelstrom, for the wind whips around both corners of the island from the open sea and one must swim against the tide and choppy water in either direction. For only a few miles of the swim, when close to shore inside the small inlets, were the waters very calm.

Naturally, the first part of the swim was best; until the water seemed to freeze on me, I used an easy breast stroke, but changed into the crawl for the last three hours. The water was crystal clear and I could see numerous denizens of the deep among the vari-colored coral formations on the bottom of the sea. The worst part of the swim was the intense cold after the first few hours; had I but thought in time, this could have been remedied by a heavy coat of grease. Eight hours and forty-five minutes of constant swimming were necessary to circumnavigate the island—a distance of sixteen miles.

My German friend had promised to explore the Blue Grotto with me, but he again showed conservative good sense by refusing to swim in the unusually rough water. After we had walked for more than an hour towards the cliff of Anacapri, which contained this gem of nature, I stubbornly refused to turn back. Plunging into the foaming surf to swim alone in search of the tiny three-foot hole in the hollow cliff, I floundered along the shore for nearly an hour before reaching the entrance.

I must admit that I was never so frightened in my life as in those brief moments while entering the cavern. The waves dashed high, closing up the entrance which winked at regular intervals. Within, all was dark. A hundred thoughts entered my mind at once. What if this is not the grotto after all? What if I can't find my way out? What if I should catch cramp in this deep water? What if an octopus should be in the grotto?—one was found nearby the day before. What about sharks?

But once inside and facing the small entrance, my fears vanished. Here in this great hollow cliff was the most indescribably beautiful azure water I had ever seen. A transparent, phosphorescent, violet and blue light permeated the calm waters. My body seemed to be made of a substance like glowing blue quicksilver. When I

[35]

swam out of the Grotto the light seemed dazzling and harsh, the water colorless and the cliffs gray and neutral. I waved at my friend high up on the cliffs and churned the waters coming ashore.

A day or so later, I swam to "Hermit Island" and squeezed my way up through the long winding natural tunnel through the center of the island to the top, to visit the ruins of an ancient stone building where, according to tradition, an old monk once lived for years with hundreds of rabbits as his sole companions.

I had already gained twenty pounds in weight, and as Bucephalus was pawing the ground, impatient to hit the trail, we bade farewell to this island of dreams, beauty and color.

CHAPTER VII

See Naples and Die

On the first rainy morning in autumn, Bucephalus and I coasted down to the boat landing, prevented two black cats from crossing our path, and sighed in relief when we were safe in the little boat bound for Naples. The open road beckoned and Bucephalus pricked up his ears, sniffed the sea breeze and exultantly awaited the landing as our boat wove through a score of Mussolini's warships stripped for action.

The sunlight broke through the thinning layer of gray clouds dotting the bay with patches of golden light like spots on a leopard's back. In the distant background a ray of sunlight focused like a giant searchlight upon Capri. I can never forget, and some day I shall go back to Capri!

When I first disembarked into Naples, at least forty or fifty men, women and children surrounded and followed me faithfully unto the end. Not for once did my group of satellites disperse; my every movement was observed.

[36]

When I inquired of my "lieutenants" as to the direction of the Deutsches Wandererheim the entire brigade walked by my side as one man to the very entrance and were loath to see me depart within.

At the "German Wanderer's Home" I spent my first evening "traveling around" maps of the world with a motley array of comrades, and looking at hundreds of pictures which talented young artists had painted at various times and presented to our host, a two hundred and sixty pound beer drinker called "Herr Fatty." He was the subject of most of these paintings and appeared in exaggerated caricatures showing his exhausted greatness being hoisted down from a hiking trip to Vesuvius on the shoulders of a thousand comrades; as a national hero saving the people of the surrounding villages from the fate of the Pompeians by sitting on top of Vesuvius and plugging a new eruption; as the sun which shines with warmth and hospitality upon the people of all nations, et cetera ad infinitum.

There is an old saying "See Naples and Die." A very truthful statement, but the nature of death depends upon what part of Naples one sees. Along the beautiful Santa Lucia bayfront drive are parks with palms, fountains, statues, flowers, bridle paths and fresh air. But if one gets lost in the dusty, or perhaps muddy, old maze of crooked "vias" off the main highways, one sees that death here has not lost its sting. If one can overlook the poverty and distress underlying Neapolitan existence—as the natives themselves seem to do in their wholehearted enjoyment of life—and see only the mask of gaiety put on by these people, one will enjoy the show.

On my second night in Naples, international assault was made on Vesuvius. Two Germans, three Polish boys and I started out from the Wandererheim shortly after sundown. The moon was so full and bright that the color of a person's eyes could be seen. On our way to the foot of the

[37]

volcano, we passed many groups of trembling street urchins, clustered around big fires which they had built on the streets.

A couple of hours later we were zigzagging up the side of Vesuvius through heavily laden vineyards and fig groves. The fruit tasted cool in the moonlight, and the night was cold—like Christmas in Georgia.

The view of Naples from the side of Vesuvius was in itself more than worth the night trip. From Capri, ten miles out in the bay, all the lights had seemed to be in long lines along a straight shore, but from our lofty position everything was now seen in its proper perspective. The contours of the round, almost land-locked bay of Naples were plainly distinguishable; the reflections of the scattered fleecy clouds gave the water the same appearance as the sky with its shades of velvety black and silvery white; the concentric circles of Naples' millions of twinkling lights in the misty grey background of moonlit landscape resembled the red hot ripples of a gigantic flow of lava into the sea.

It was nearly three a.m. when we reached the concrete steps going up the peak itself. It was freezing cold and I wore only sandals; the others, alpine climbing shoes. However, my sandals were really better, even if colder, for climbing over lava, since the hempen soles did not slide like hobnailed shoes.

The moon was now over the western horizon, and the crater was shadowy except for flaming smoke from the actual boiling pot and a few adjacent crevices. Every few seconds the whole mountain top was lit with a brilliant red light by a series of ebullitions of red coals of lava the size of grapefruit, which rained down on the sides of the little inner crater with a thunderous roar and clatter. The sounds emitted by these eruptions were unearthly, different from any I had ever heard, peculiar to a volcano. These eruptions were followed by puffs of sulphurous smoke,

[38]

and the odor of gas was everywhere.

Hand in hand, we wound our way along the trail marked occasionally by splotches of whitewash. We had to watch our step for on the side of the trail were many cracks and fissures in the earth, several feet in width and of undetermined depth. Just outside the range of the lava shower we sat down to watch nature's fireworks and wait until the sun came up, to take a peek down into the crater itself. We could dodge flaming rock better at night, but could not watch our step as well as in daylight. Once when I was looking into the steaming pool of flaming liquid a terrific rumble came up from the bowels of the earth preceding a bombardment of missiles of lava. One piece hit my thumb, burning it rather severely, and I stepped upon another, burning my shoe.

As soon as it became broad daylight, the glowing red color of the lower part of the funnel of smoke and the metallic blue of the upper portion could not be seen. Night is the only time to see Vesuvius—and preferably a moonlight one, too!

We reached the Wandererheim at ten a.m., after almost constant walking for thirteen hours, and I took a well earned rest.

CHAPTER VIII

Italy to England in Six Days via Bicycle

After riding in circles around town, Bucephalus and I struck a "bee line" for Pompeii. (I had purposely seen Vesuvius before Pompeii in order to appreciate more fully that city's destruction.) As usual in Italian towns, the streets were filled with strutting soldiers and loud-mouthed peddlers. From balconies above the street housewives, by means of ropes, lowered baskets for fish mongers to fill. On every corner were Lotteria de Merano

[39]

booths; I passed one where the proprietor was persuading a group of children not more than eight or ten years old to invest their pennies in these get-rich-quick gambling tickets. I felt like wringing his neck.

From Naples to Pompeii, 25 kilometers away, there are two roads. One is the fine strada cut through the middle of lovely vineyards between Vesuvius and the suburban sections of Naples along the bay front, for auto tourists only; the other, for the natives with their big wheeled carts, cuts through the heart of the continuous suburb all the way to Pompeii. The tourist sees the lovely vineyards and exclaims, "How beautiful is southern Italy!" The native driving his cart down the typical Italian street connecting Naples and Pompeii has no remark to make. He is accustomed to seeing diseased, crippled, deformed human things lying around in the filth of the street. Perhaps he has rickets, sore eyes, skin diseases and lice himself— hardly one normal, healthy person did I see on all this winding road. Everywhere children were having a happy time like little monkeys inspecting each other's heads. Several battalions of Italian soldiers passed, on their way to "clean up" other countries and make them nice refined places like Italy!

And so it was from Naples, the city of the living dead, that I stepped into Pompeii, the city of the stone dead.

For two days and nights I wandered as in a dream through this the most complete and well preserved set of ruins I had ever seen, taking in everything from the exquisite murals of Viking ships, of Moors carrying off white maidens, of bull fights and hunting scenes, to the amazing baths with their water pipes, conduit and aqueduct systems.

On the third day I arose again from the city of the dead, cycled up the Apostle Paul's historic Appian Way—on one side a broad fertile valley, on the other, high rolling mountains—on past the bathing resorts and beautiful

[40]

homes of the Italian Riviera, stopping only to eat, sleep and swim at the beaches by the side of the road.

This part of Italy is as beautiful and fine for biking as the central section from Bologna to Sienna is ugly and difficult. Along the sea, the mountains are just as high as the Appenines of Central Italy, but one can easily ride up the graded roads, and coming down—Oh boy! I coasted 36 kilometers down one mountain without either pedaling or putting on brakes...just opening up my lungs and lustily singing to the eerie accompaniment of Bucephalus' musical spokes and tires, which were whirring with a droning buzz as of bees.

Leaving the beautiful shore road at Genoa, I worked leisurely down river gorges, through green pastures, dairy farms, purple vineyards, and yellow cornfields, through ancient, crumbling, walled-in villages, through groves of shade trees, which are almost totally lacking in central and southern Italy.

The only compulsory stop from Naples to northern Italy was at a railway crossing on the outskirts of Rome, near a huge sign written in ten different languages: "No motor horns allowed to be blown at any time in this city." Here I had to wait twenty minutes for a train to cross the highway. The bells of a nearby chapel chimed "Santa Lucia."

But there was no more easy sailing when I bumped into the barrier of towering snow-capped Alps a hundred kilometers north of Turino. The country between Ivrea and Montreux, Switzerland, is the finest part of Italy in every respect, both in regard to people and to landscape. At Aosta I left the beautiful valley, donned alpine shoes, and started up a donkey trail, steep but straight and shady, rather than go the winding highway. The country along this route is delightful with its grassy slopes of different shades of green, caused by various shades of light falling upon them through clouds between the gorges, surmounted by snowy peaks. Huge herds of milk cows showed up distinctly on the opposite hillsides, but because of the distance they appeared as "ant-size."

The trail ended at the last village on the Italian side, St. Rhemey, and I had to take the main highway which at that point is little more than a path.

The last 25 or 30 kilometers up this rocky trail to the Grand Saint Bernard pass were the longest I had ever experienced. Near the top it was bitter cold; the wind howled and clouds swirled around like tornado funnels. During the last four kilometers I took a rest period every few steps and had to be very careful not to fall asleep— once I dropped off to sleep and woke up nearly frozen.

Finally I reached the pass at 10:30, nearly two hours after dark. I spent the night in the hospitable cloister of Grand Saint Bernard. After supper I was escorted under arched walls and over huge flagstone floors of the magic halls of the monastery to the best bedroom in the world. Each bed was piled high with clean downy blankets and each had double mattresses and springs.

The next day was so cold and stormy outside and so hospitable and interesting inside, that I accepted the Prior's invitation to stay until after lunch. The monks are all jovial, good-hearted, intelligent fellows—excellent linguists, and among them are masters of all trades. They have their own resources—dairies, flocks of sheep and goats, shops—and live in medieval simplicity and plenty.

I had a great time playing with the Saint Bernard puppies, each being as large as I, and warming my feet and hands against their shaggy fur. There were about fifty huge pure-blooded Saint Bernards, each weighing about two hundred pounds, roaming through the halls of this grand old monastery.

At noon I had a final repast with the monks, and at 2:00 p.m. started down the mountain. I passed about fifty monks taking their daily stroll up and down the trail, and though it was bitter cold and sleet and rain were falling heavily, each took off his hat and bade me "Gute reise" as I whizzed past.

Everywhere along the road the Swiss farmers—clean, wholesome looking people—were busy gathering and storing the crops. When I waved to the little Swiss girls each would yodel or wave back.

I believe that the natural boundaries and high mountains account for the segregation of the different races and the retention of their own respective customs and language.

Bucephalus stormed through Lausanne, Geneva, and on over the Ural mountain pass into France. In landscape, roads, people, and every other respect, France was much finer than I had anticipated. Bucephalus was very impatient in France and galloped through the magnificent old cathedral city of Dole—over green hills where a lonely little boy or girl, staff in hand, tended cows and sheep—up tree-lined highways and paths lined with hawthorn hedges—past shell-torn stone buildings, grim reminders of the War—through Avalon—Auxerre—Appoigny—Sens— and on to Paris. In Paris, Bucephalus insisted on taking in the city, and that we did, in grand style.

After Paris, we made a rain drenched dash to Calais where we embarked for Dover. As the crossing was cold and rough, I adjourned to the engine room and relaxed by the warm boiler.

Dover was freezing cold, so I sleepily dragged my weary body and faithful old Bucephalus to a youth hostel where we rested for the night.

CHAPTER IX

Bucking Through Britannia

The first and most impressive thing I noticed about England was that everybody spoke and understood— English. Having neither heard nor spoken English for three months, for the next few days I nearly talked myself to death. It was amazingly easy to read the newspapers, advertisements, road signs; and I remember quite distinctly the very peculiar pleasure I experienced in reading such advertisements as "Buy Barbasol tooth-paste—British to the Teeth," or "Harvey's House of Hovis on the Highway to Health Twixt Tweed and Trent!"

The day was clear, warm and peaceful—like an autumn day in Georgia—as I biked from Dover towards London. At noon I stopped at magnificent old Canterbury Cathedral and rambled for two hours through its vast interior.

Along my route into the city, flocks of sheep dotted the hillsides like myriads of stars in a green sky; birds sang in the trees and woods lining the highway; the people were self-respecting—fine—with relatively high standards of morality and of living; and I thought at the time that this small island was the cradle of the civilization that will endure and last through the ages.

As I rode over Westminster Bridge, by Parliament House, Westminster Abbey, through the heart of the city, and down Charing Cross Road to the Youth Hostel at the top of Highgate Hill, my first impression was that London is undoubtedly the busiest big town of little shops I have ever seen. The next few days found me map in hand, meticulously covering the city. The nights were spent at operas, theatres, and watching the mass of homogeneous humanity that is London.

Upon heading north I found the English roads even better for cycling than the French ones. Though we traveled leisurely over rolling plains of oak-dotted meadows and farm lands, Bucephalus averaged over one hundred miles a day with no difficulty.

It was surprising to see pheasants and rabbits out in the wayside meadows and fields, sunning and enjoying themselves just like so many chickens. In one meadow, I

[44]

counted twenty-four rabbits all in a row on the edge of a hawthorne hedge. No wonder every grocer's shop is heaped with wild (?) game. I saw many farmers picking mushrooms—like children on an Easter egg hunt. Since the ground is nearly always moist, conditions are just right for the growth of this plant and many are found. All of the thatch-roofed houses are covered with wire netting. The moist atmosphere has caused moss to grow on the tops of the stone houses until the roof is a mass of green.

Whoever said that England has no fair October weather should have been with me during these days. True, it rained in front of me and it rained behind me; but it never rained on me, as I traveled up the great north road through the heart of England; and as I saw more of the country I became prouder of my English ancestry.

England is a cyclist's paradise, from the chalk cliffs of Dover to the windy moors along the Scottish border: soft green meadows dotted with huge ancient oaks and golden balls of hay—old Roman bridges—deep calm rivers—clean country hamlets with each house named and dated—miles of smoky industrial centers—crystal waters of the lake region—finally the grassy land of the sky over into Scotland.

Scotland was more beautiful than I could ever have hoped for, the portion near England having England's green meadows, sheep, cattle, and rural aspect, minus the smoky industrial plants which were scars in the midst of nature's loveliness. Along the roadside were many lakes teeming with fish, wild duck and geese. My trail wound through several stretches of dark forests, with overhanging oaks, hemlock, spruce and pine, then burst out into dazzling sunlit meadows farther on.

I was amazed to see that the Scotch really wear kilts and talk and sing in the true dialect of Robert Burns. As in England, I passed many fine country estates and old castles. Here, too, cycling is very easy—one has none of

[45]

the difficulties, but all of the pleasures of easy and comfortable traveling in a beautiful and interesting country.

As I sailed out of the little horseshoe-shaped harbor of Stranraer, bound for Ireland, two waves extending in parallel lines across the harbor escorted the ship all the way out to sea. The captain explained to me that this was due to the extremely shallow water in the vicinity, so that every time a ship puts out to sea two big waves accompany her.

Upon landing in Larne, I went to the first house I saw to buy some milk, and enjoyed my first taste of Irish hospitality. The son pulled off my boots and put a pair of moccasins on my feet, warmed his bathrobe by the open fire and put it around me; then before I could catch my breath for marvelling at the warm-hearted nature of these people, the daughter brought me a hot breakfast of oatmeal, ham, eggs, cheese and marmalade. As I started away, I handed the son a large carton of oatmeal flakes, and the last I saw of him he was running after me trying to give them back.

A downpour of rain and terrific head-winds confronted me up the shore road to Londonderry. This road, built on the very seashore itself by famine relief workers in 1850, with mountains and valleys running down to the sea on the left and the emerald waters of the Irish channel on the immediate right, is unequalled for beauty of landscape and sea. The long, flat-topped mountains, bare of trees, but covered with green grass, resemble gigantic alligators with their mouths resting on the brink of the sea, and with colorful little vales winding down between their parallel bodies.

Shortly after noon, the rain turned to sleet, and as the sleet threatened to knock my eyes out every time I looked up, it was impossible to enjoy fully the landscape. For the first time I saw waves put into reverse by the wind. Just as the breakers dashed toward shore, the wind took them

[46]

sweeping out to sea or else lifted them in the form of spray and gave the road and surrounding country a salt bath—at times it seemed as if the whole sea was being blown out onto the road. It was head-winds for me! While going to Fairhead, a little town on the north coast, I actually had to push Bucephalus downhill.

However, it was fortunate that I did not visit Ireland before the rest of Europe, for I liked the country so much that I probably should not have left to see any other.

At Ballycastle, I went through Bonamarge Franciscan Friary and warmed a bit; but by the time I reached the village of Coleraine, I was truly cold from rain! There I discovered why so many composers are inspired to write such songs as "Smiling Irish Eyes," and "Wild Irish Rose," for never in my life have I seen so many fine looking lassies.

I spent the night in the home of a prosperous dairyman on the road fifty miles from Londonderry, receiving the same warm reception as in Larne earlier in the day. I was treated as the Prodigal Son returned. My host wanted to take me in his little Austin over the mountains to "Derry," but I protested that Bucephalus might scratch his car; and besides, he had been too nice, anyway. In parting, he warned me never to mention William of Orange, the embodiment of Protestantism, or the Pope, the embodiment of Catholicism, to any one in Ireland. I thanked him for his advice, shook his hand for the fifth time, and sallied forth into another day of head-winds and rain.

The shores of Donegal county and most of the rest of northern Ireland are very beautiful, and, with a tail-wind instead of a head-wind, would be ideal for bicycling.

I had a tough time zig-zagging through the cattle mart in the city of Donegal. The people were worse than cows about standing nonchalantly in the middle of the road and making cyclists and motorists go around them.

[47]

The Irish jaunting cart is unique; looking like a huge washpot on two wheels, it has seats around the inner rim, thus causing the passengers to face each other towards the center. In Italy I had seen enough of donkeys to last a lifetime, but as I penetrated deeper into the Free State I began to see multitudes of donkey-drawn carts.

Just before twilight, Bucephalus and I passed over the beautiful river Erne which flows through the typical little Irish village of Ballyshannon, with its cold, grey cobbled streets and grey-walled houses blending perfectly with the grey clouds above. We were so intently watching the full moon trying to break through the clouds on the misty mountain tops that we went "on the rocks" several miles beyond Ballyshannon, sticking a brier in the front tire, and necessitating our stopping for the night in Bundoran, a little village built on a few rocks between the high mountains and the sea.

The following day was another great day in the rain. My alpine shoes absorbed water like a blotter; each evening when I took them off, I poured out of them a cup of ice water. The country continued beautiful, with black streams, picturesque glens, singing birds. Now I saw thousands of little donkey-drawn milk carts. Every person I met on the road gave me a hearty greeting—indeed, there are no people like the Irish! As the day grew older the wind grew stronger and I had to spur on Bucephalus or freeze.

We finally had to stop for the night at a poor little house which was all I had recourse to; but one cannot imagine what an enlightening and entertaining evening this proved to be. My hostess had been a cook in Boston before she married and had a dozen bright-eyed children. So fond were her reminiscences of America that she could not do enough for my comfort, while her husband, a poor farmer, told me all about Ireland's troubles, revolving around the high tariff imposed by England, from a farmer's point of view. The farmers can raise enough for actual food, but not enough money to buy shoes for the children—these children were bare-footed in the cold weather. As I sat in my corner and heard the long story of Ireland's hardships, between puffs of smoke from the old man's pipe, I thought of a book I had once read—"Put Yourself in His Place", by Charles Reade.

The next morning I had not gone far when I passed a funeral procession, with the black carriage moving slowly down the road and followed, as was customary, by the relatives of the deceased walking all the way to the cemetery, regardless of distance.

I stopped for lunch in a cozy little cottage, and it was very difficult to leave the warm fire of peat—the cheeriest fire of all—and plunge out into the stormy weather in an attempt to reach Limerick before night-fall. The gale threatened to blow Bucephalus off the road. However, in spite of the weather, we passed Ardnacrucha, the huge electric plant which furnishes electricity for the whole of Ireland, and on over the beautiful river Shannon, to the outskirts of Limerick on the road to Tipperary. From the moment we left the broad streets of Limerick, we ceased encountering head-winds for the first time since leaving Italy.

When at Pallas Green Barrack, seven miles from the famous Glenn Star Belgian Priory, Bucephalus was stopped by a policeman for having no headlight, I took opportunity of inquiring about a night's lodging. We spent the night at the Barrack, and had a great evening with the score of officers quartered there. When I arrived, the cook had left for the night, so the chief of police donned an apron and cooked me a fine supper himself. Until my clothes dried, one of the sergeants contributed a pair of wool socks, another a pair of number eleven, special size shoes, and another—a six-foot-four giant—a pair of his trousers. Thus temporarily accoutered, I dined.

Most of the officers slept in a large common room, but the chief, fearing that their collective symphony of snores might disturb my own peaceful slumbers, put me in his room for the night.

I awoke at six a.m., with the intention of getting an early start, but met with a little Irish obstinacy. The chief, whose snoring had sounded like the air sputtering out of Bucephalus' tire in a muddy road, suddenly awoke and proclaimed that his self-respect and reputation would suffer irreparable injury if he permitted me to leave without a hot breakfast, and besides (so he thought) I needed more rest. Since the cook did not arrive until eight o'clock, I had no alternative except to turn over for a couple of hours more sleep.

It was fine riding beside the beautiful mountains and lakes of the Killarney region. After much criss-crossing through southern Ireland, Bucephalus and I started down the Suir River Valley to Waterford and the sea.

After over one hundred miles of hard riding, I reached Waterford at five p.m., to learn that I must either wait three days in Waterford for a boat to Fishguard, Wales, or ride immediately to Rosslare fifty miles over the mountains and catch the midnight boat from that point. Bucephalus and I went into a huddle and decided on a forward pass to Rosslare. Thanks to a full moon and starlit skies, we wound down the river valley, over several small mountain ranges, and crossed the goal line at Rosslare at 9:30 p.m. After a midnight feast we went on board and were soon sailing into St. George's Channel. The Emerald Isle became only a pleasant memory.

After wandering through Wales—a land of strange names, moated castles, green mountains and queer dialects—we pushed on, through Monmouth, Ledberry, Warwick, Stratford-on-Avon, Tewkesburg, Oxford, London, Canterbury—a land where history speaks everywhere—on to Dover.

[50]

Three and a half days later, Bucephalus had crossed Belgium and breezed into Köln (Cologne) hitting on all fours. Having biked through thirteen countries, I had reached my destination and was settled for at least a few months.

As the days passed, I found the experiences of those months of travel furnishing me daily food for thought. Too, at most unexpected moments, pictures of the trip flashed through my mind. I could plainly see myself riding down the fjords of Norway; basking beneath the Caprian sun; struggling through the snowstorm down Matterhorn; sitting in a hay-loft door, watching the last rays of the setting sun fade away and the first stars peep out; singing in the rain through Ireland. With such memories, and already anticipating a Mediterranean tour, I plunged into new experiences at a German University.

END OF PART ONE

"These are the things I prize
And hold of dearest worth:
Light of the sapphire skies,
Peace of the silent hills,
Shelter of forests, comfort of the grass,
Music of birds, murmur of little rills,
Shadows of cloud that swiftly pass,
And, after shadows,
The smell of flowers—and of the good
brown earth—
And best of all, along the way—friendship
and mirth."

Henry Van Dyke

"Marco Polo" in Venice

se
the
oduct
the
wiss Alps

Bucephalus
enjoyed galloping
up this winding
way from Capri
to Anacapri

Blue Grotto

Grand (?) Canal,
Venice

Neuschwanstein

Through Rheintal on the asc

*Halfway mark
(note snow-covered Knorr
Hutte wherein we spent
first night)*

*Zugspitze trip:
Three-fourths finished*

The Peak

Start

CHAPTER X

Paradise Balls to Paradise Halls

Cologne was once a Roman City named "Agrippina Coloniensis"; the old Roman wall is still in existence. The city is built in the form of a circle around one side of the Rhine river, with the great streets running in semi-circles.

Living with a fine family on the edge of beautiful Grünn Gürtel (Green Belt), the outermost of the semi-circular streets of Köln, and a section famous for its park extending all the way around the city, I had the pleasure of riding Bucephalus at least three times each day up this drive to my classes at the University five miles away on the other end of town. At least seven times a week I would ride into town to attend an opera, Gürzenich concert, or one of the famous Kölner Karneval celebrations. I may forget what Herr Doktor Von der Lyon taught me about International Law from the German point of view, but I shall never forget the night I took a beautiful little Russian duchess to the Bird of Paradise Ball, or the early morning that I helped my friend, Fritz, to a doctor's office, after he had been wounded in a student duel.

Thus with nearly forty miles of cycling each day during the fall months of school, a daily dozen hours of winter sports during Christmas holidays with my German friends in Gotha, and yet another period of intensive physical and mental exercise during the winter term of school, I was in perfect shape when Bucephalus and I breezed out of Köln bound for the Mediterranean. Though February, it was springtime along the Rhine. This was the time to see

[55]

Germans "in the natural" and not smothered with swarms of summer tourists.

All went well along the winding river gorge from Bonn to Bingen—through quaint old villages like pictures from an illustrated fairy book—and on to Worms, but when I started up the Schwäbische Alps to Münich I bumped into Old Man Winter himself. The drop in temperature was so sudden that I stopped every few hours to warm, picking out cottages with the largest chimneys, as they invariably had the coziest fireplaces. However, my stops had to be brief as Bucephalus froze up several times while waiting outside for me and I would have to bring him in by the fire to thaw out the chains and wheels. If old Bucephalus could have talked he would undoubtedly have moaned, "Woe is me! Woe is me! Where are my red flannels?"

Haystacks dotted the broad valleys like Eskimo igloos and everything was dazzlingly white except when the trail flew up and hit me in the face when, temporarily, the outlook was dark. This happened nearly every time Bucephalus became the slightest bit overbalanced in the hard, slick, sleigh-packed snow. In the valleys, the wheels spanked through the soft snow with sounds like successive explosions of small firecrackers.

The greatest danger lay in the icy, frictionless trails down the mountain sides. But I soon became such an expert bike-balancer that I went down twisting and sliding in all sorts of ways, with the rear wheel fore and front wheel aft, sideways, and every other conceivable style except the customary manner of front wheel front. My posture and mental attitude must have been very similar to that of a rodeo bronco-buster. However, mastery of this bike-balancing business solved only one of the minor problems besetting me. Whether I liked it or not, every few kilometers, I would have to dismount and trot along beside Bucephalus, in order to keep from freezing.

Nevertheless, "sweet are the uses of adversity." As it

was cold enough for my own breath to freeze on my face, I bought a little sugar and a few eggs, along with fresh milk from a wayside dairy, stirred them all together in my aluminum flask with the result that in a few minutes I had ice cream to round out my dinner of bread and cheese.

At München it was necessary to add an ice pick to my collection of impedimenta since my hunting knife proved inadequate in coping with the ice and snow which constantly accumulated on the spokes, rim, fenders and chain, and threatened to lock the wheels. Once I struck too vigorously at the ice on the tires and disaster struck; the ice pick glanced and completely penetrated the tire. Luckily the Jugenherberge at Garmisch was in sight and the requisite repairs were made in comparative comfort. Fate laughed ironically at my efforts; later in the night the expansion of ice between tire and rim caused the tire to explode. I ordered a new tire from München, but pending the arrival of Bucephalus' "shoe," I was grounded.

Since I could not travel far in the winter wonderland without Bucephalus, I decided to try my luck at ice skating. I set out early one morning to the Riesersee, a lake not far from Garmisch, where no one could see me making beginner's mistakes. Soon a graceful young woman arrived, accompanied by her trainer. She was rather amused at my skating, and gave me a few pointers on balance and technique. She was from Norway; and I told her about my bicycling there. And then she began to skate! It was like poetry in motion! She went on to win the Olympic gold medal, and became an overnight sensation as a movie star – Sonja Henie!

My interest sparked, I attended several of the Olympic games at Garmisch. I was quite proud to see our American team win the bobsled run, but was horrified when I watched the Italian team captain tragically fall to his death from the high ski jump.

Watching others compete and perform in sports was

exciting for a while, but then I became restless and wished to either join in the sport or pursue my own adventures. Yet I still was without my trusty steed Bucephalus; still was I grounded.

Sitting in the Youth Hostel, I tried to plan some sort of brief foray in the surrounding mountains. What follies I had already committed in the name of adventure! Yet—the follies of youth are the manna upon which the dreams of old age feed. My meditation was cut short by the appearance of Ballard Donnell from the Alpine Hut across the way. Our trails had crossed twice, and this tall vagabond whom I had last seen on the cliffs of Dover, had spent so much time lately in torrid Spain that he was now cooling off and resting for a few weeks in the Bavarian mountains. Spain was still reeling from its civil war.

As we sauntered out for a couple of litres of milk at a nearby dairy, one of the typical midwinter snow flurries set in. Ballard suggested that since the snow storms of the past few days had made farther travel into the mountains via bicycle practically impossible, we make a little skiing expedition over the mountains to Ober-Ammergau.

Our qualifications for such a trip hardly equalled our ideas. Ballard had lived in Florida all his life and had never seen snow until a couple of weeks before. Of course I lived "up north" in Georgia and had seen snow—such as it was. Anyway, after a minimum of consideration we decided upon the trip, which, at my suggestion, was to be stretched to Neuschwanstein, King Ludwig's dream castle sixty-five kilometers farther on.

Two hours later we actually started out in a snowstorm on this "cross country" ski trip of 170 kilometers through the Bavarian Alps with a compass and map, showing the general lay-out of valleys and mountains, to guide us. At first we had thought of taking cameras and sleeping togs, but since the packs would be too heavy and the cameras would probably be ruined in the snow, we decided to

[58]

leave everything behind. Being very amateur skiers, we expected to have many a tumble in the snow before our return, and did not wish to be bothered with any unnecessary baggage.

Snow stung like needles peppering our burning cheeks. It did not fall, but swept past parallel to the ground.

We skied past picturesque old Friedhof von Dlbergen, perched on top of a little mountain, with a path winding round and round the mountain to a little chapel on top. Every few feet along the path there were little shrines covered in snow and icicles. As there was no water with which to quench his thirst, Ballard stopped every few minutes to crunch icicle pops which he broke from the snow banks and trees.

The mountaineers with their frost covered moustaches and beards certainly made a picture. I noticed that the farther one ascends into the Bavarian Alps the longer, more grizzly, more luxuriant and more numerous are these beards. Pipes are correspondingly longer too. It seems that the old boys are afraid that a cigar, cigarette or short-stemmed pipe might singe the whiskers.

We passed through Ettaler village and wandered around the Ettal Cloister. The black-robed monks, gliding about through the arched doorways like so many silhouettes, created the same fantastic, unreal atmosphere about this monastery that I had sensed in others.

After spending the night in the rather airy Youth Hostel in Ober-Ammergau we awoke the next morning to find our top blankets a mass of white frost from the condensation and freezing of our own breath. The haus-mutter brought a pitcher of water, but before we could get out of bed and into our clothes, it had frozen and burst the pitcher. Before I could brush my teeth, another pan of water had turned into ice. It was cold weather. Even so, the clear cold of this day was much better than the heavy snow of the day before.

[59]

We made a quick dash to the little village of Altenau to get the soreness of the previous day's run out of our joints. Here the cold early morning air gave way to warm sunshine; we gradually shed jacket, coat, sweater, shirt, undershirt, and by noon we were toiling in shorts through deep snow. A narrow little timber trail from Altenau to Schwangau, the connecting link to the rest of the world, led through a deep forest, through lumber camps and little out-of-the-way villages. Life was being lived as Ballard and I toiled through these wintry woods perfumed with the smell of freshly cut timber—every little sprig a huge puff-ball of snow—every bridge a mass of snow—winding up, down, around and over the tops of mountains.

We arrived at the Youth Hostel at Schwangau with frozen feet and blistered backs. Though the Hostel was closed for the winter, the haus-vater took us in and treated us with the same genial hospitality that the Irish had shown me in the fall. We were given new socks, bedroom slippers, a huge pot of Frühling soup, bread, and rum and "schnaaps" in our hot tea after we had drunk three litres of hot milk. Fortunately the haus-vater was a dairyman and had twelve cows in the next room.

At dawn, after a good night's sleep beneath a snow bank of goose feathers, we started off in a fine snowfall for the fantastic castle—the paradise halls—of King Ludwig.

CHAPTER XI

Neuschwanstein to Zugspitze

I can hardly believe that my visit to Neuschwanstein was anything but a beautiful dream, too wonderful for reality. The castle carries out the theme of the old legend of Lohengrin and the swan in its every phase of architecture. The artistically designed door-knobs of silver are swan's heads, and everywhere are beautiful

[60]

Nymphenburg porcelain swans, silver washing-fountain swans. The murals carry out the entire themes of Wagner's operas. There are paintings of Tristram and Isolde, Lohengrin, Sigurd, Siegfried, the Valkyries, the old German gods, the Vikings. Especially outstanding is a golden-coated bronze statue of Siegfried killing the dragon, showing remarkable workmanship in the meticulously moulded and shaped leaves of trees, ferns, and vegetation surrounding the combatants. Everywhere are chased, golden embellishments.

In the throne-room is a two-thousand-pound candelabrum suspended by a movable golden chain. Golden columns support the marble stair-case up to the throne, and a blue sky and stars are represented overhead. The sun shining through the colored glass chapel windows cast its rays on the exquisitely carved woodwork, and the rustic beauty of the panelled walls harmonized and counter-balanced to perfection the golden tapestries and mosaic tile floors of some of the rooms.

On opposite walls between the King's and Queen's apartments is a realistic grotto with stalagmites and stalactites as found in a natural cavern. It was quite remarkable to grasp a stalagmite, pull the side of the dark grotto away, and emerge without warning into the splendor of the King's gorgeous apartment.

Outside the entire castle is of rough marble, but inside the polished marble columns are encircled by golden bands containing precious and semi-precious stones. From every side of this castle, perched on a precipice, are beautiful views. On one side, one sees a frozen green cascade of icicles hanging hundreds of feet down from the single arch of Marienbrücke, spanning the deep gorge of the frozen river; on the other side, one looks out through sheets of plate glass in one of the observation parlors to see the entire valley and surrounding country spread in one enormous panorama, with the villages of Füssen,

[61]

Schwangau, Alpsee, Schwansee and others discernible in the distance.

Neuschwanstein is only one of King Ludwig's "dream castles"; but having seen this one, I could understand how he bankrupted his kingdom to build them. Only an insane man would have dared attempt to build such a dream. "The lunatic, the lover, and the poet are of imagination all compact!" Ludwig was all three. It took imagination to build these marble dreams and while he may have been crazy, he certainly taste in two things—castles and women. The portraits of all the paramours of this old boy are "paragons of consummate loveliness and beauty." After all, what is life but a dream? Any one who can materialize a dream has achieved, in a sense, a certain degree of immortality. The castles of Ludwig—his dreams—will be admired by generations to come.

After saluting Ludwig and bidding him farewell, I started on the trail again with Ballard—on to Austria. We wound up through a gigantic forest, following a frozen creek bed, past frozen waterfalls and cascades, rocks like polar bears, and up through a ceiling of clouds into a clear blue sky to the very top of Oxenkopf mountain.

We did some real skiing up this precipitous mountain, in herring-bone style with our skis turned outward in a V-shape; or when the going was too steep, we went up sideways altogether. Near the top of the mountain the snow was so deep on the plateau that we skied over several unusually symmetrical snowbanks before discovering that we were skimming over the roofs of submerged houses. There the snow was fifteen, twenty, and twenty-five feet deep. Many huts and larger houses, filled with hay and provisions for the use of lost skiers, were scattered over the mountainsides.

As the trail stopped at the top of Oxenkopf, we had to back-track down the steep mountain to Hochplatte. Here we found a mountain ranger who informed us that no one had attempted the descent into Austria since fall—before the heavy winter snows fell.

From Hochplatte over into Austria there were no ski tracks, and as the summer mountain path winding down the gorge lay beneath twenty feet of snow, there was no trail. Cliffs, avalanches, chasms between snowdrifts, and hundreds of other dangers confronted the reckless wayfarer down this icy gorge. However, we decided that it could not be much worse than the descent down the precipitous mountain.

The foot-wide trail, past powder-puff bridges, ravines filled with snow, and frozen cascade-filled gorges produced the most dangerous beauty that I had seen as yet. There is an old saying "See beauty and die," but my motto is "See beauty and live." On the way we became lost and wandered up and down Oxenkopf for three and a half hours. Several times we fell and snow covered us from head to foot, within and without, filled our shoes and gloves, making it absolutely necessary to find Ammerwald before night set in—or else!

The sparkling snow against a blue sky, the delicately frozen waterfalls, the ski tracks through the virgin snow leading into the pass, the dainty, patterned trail of the chamois, the last rays of the setting sun shining through the hoary trees overhead—the entire beauty of the scenery was exhilarating—all this, combined with the seriousness of our situation, keyed our senses and made the danger fascinating.

We skimmed down the mountain zigzag fashion, sitting on the ski sticks to put on brakes. This method of skiing may be unorthodox, since it is considered unsportsmanlike to ride the sticks like an old witch on a broom; but the exigencies of the occasion made anything excusable, and we safely flew down the length of the frozen valley with-out more than half a dozen falls against the side of the mountain. These falls were usually intentional, as several

[63]

times, we would whiz around a bend to find suddenly yawning space in our immediate path. Being very inexperienced skiers, we did not attempt to perform any of the roulades and cadenzas but stopped in a method that has been effective from the time that the memory of man runneth not to the contrary—we fell.

A fuzzy old Austrian mountaineer, watchman at the Alpine Ammerwald hotel, had heard us crashing down through the valley and had just started up on skis to meet us when we zoomed past him. This tough old fellow said that he and his niece were taking care of the hotel, which was closed for the winter. Though we had been coming down at express-train speed for the last two hours, we were still nearly 4,000 feet high between towering mountain ranges.

Since we were the first people whom the old man and his attractive niece had seen for months, they were quite glad to have company, and the hotel was ours for the night. The electric stoves were immediately put into action thawing out our socks, shoes and weary bodies. My socks, being frozen, stood upright and there was ice between my toes. We were hungry as wolves, and oh boy! could that girl cook!

Early the next morning we started down the river valley to Griesen. The color of the violet blue sky was comparable with the waters of the Blue Grotto. The atmosphere was filled with millions of frost particles glittering like silver dust in the sunlight.

Near the end of the cold, sunless gorge—sunless because of high white caps on either side—we passed a large grotto in the side of a cliff. Water had dripped from the ceiling and frozen, resulting in icicle formations on the ceiling and floor of the grotto. The huge icicles hanging from above almost touched the big mushroom-like icy creations rising from the floor.

Skiing across Plansee, Tyrol's second largest and most

[64]

beautiful alpine lake, was a unique experience. We passed by excursion boats frozen in the water, and under diving towers. What a beautiful picture our skis left across this trackless, frozen shore! What a picture, the towering white caps soaring above the sun at the end of the trail! The trees along the lake's edge were covered with frost, and our clothes were white with frost. Beards, of four days' growth, were white as snow, eyelashes white, hair white. This was the coldest cold I have ever felt.

We soon slid into Griesen, near the bottom of the valley, hit a good road, opened the throttle and landed back in Garmisch in short time. Garmisch was thawing out, and the comparative warmth of the day on our return was quite different from the stormy, frigid weather in which we had left the village.

We decided to conclude our sojourn in Bavaria by climbing the Zugspitze, the highest peak in Germany, soaring 9,730 feet up into the air. After this I expected to be ready for a little sunny basking and bathing in the Adriatic along the Dalmatian coast.

Early the next morning we started out for the sunlit peak which was smiling at us bewitchingly and sardonically. The trail led through tunnels, beneath frozen waterfalls and along dark gorges full of natural caves. At the foot of cliffs there were huge mounds of snow several hundred feet deep. the warm midday sun brought avalanches down the sides of the gorges which poured over the cliffs like waterfalls.

After climbing upward all morning, we finally reached Anger Hütte 4,098 feet up, where we ate our lunch. For three hours we struggled, digging our skis in the sides of the cliff, before we reached a ledge half-way up where the wind blew fine icy snow over us from a glacier above. Here was a sign directing us to the top via "Knorr Hütte über den Sau Weg" or else to the other side of the ledge "durch das Brunntal." Both ways looked the same to me,

[65]

namely, straight up. We chose the one to the right via Knorr Hütte.

As the sun began to set, the scene of our struggle became coated with ice instead of soft snow crust. The midday sun had melted the surface somewhat, and the evening cold was turning it into ice. Occasionally we would have to take off the skis and climb up the rock wall in true alpine fashion, linked together with a rope. We were so tired that our tongues were hanging out like red bow ties when we clambered in the "door" of Knorr Hütte at 7 o'clock. This "door" happened to be a window in the second story as the snow was a little deep.

After sleeping in my clothes before the fire I awoke next morning as stiff as an old maid. Every bone in my body was aching from that strenuous climb.

When we finally reached the peak at noon, we decided that enough was enough, and came down via the "elevated." This trip down was certainly a sky-ride. Although it had taken us fourteen hours to climb up the Zugspitze, it took only seventeen minutes to get down to Ehrwald, sailing "through the air with the greatest of ease" thousands of feet above ravines, valleys, and snow; the giant cables stretch across from one mountain peak to another on gigantic steel towers. It was more like a ride in a balloon than anything else. At Ehrwald we stopped long enough to surround ample victuals and then proceeded on through the forest to Garmisch.

Poor old Bucephalus was overjoyed to see me, and I promised not to leave him behind again.

CHAPTER XII

Crossing the Kreuzberg

Bucephalus and I left Garmisch in company with an American bicyclist, Harry Espenscheid, a young Harvard

graduate who was also headed south and lacked a
traveling companion.

It seemed queer to be going over the Alps in the dead of
winter in our shirt sleeves as though it were a hot summer
day. The snow was several feet deeper here in the
Tyrolean Alps than in the Bavarian Alps, and the warm
spell of the past few days had made the roads comparatively more dangerous. If the roads had been consistently
glazed ice, or else melting snow, we could have adjusted
our travel;, but going up hill in the shadow of tall forests,
the road would be cold and ice-covered, whereas on the
other side of the hills in the sunlight there would be slick
mud and slushy snow. Several times I did "swan dives."

At Zirl we coasted down the beautiful valley of the Inn
river to Innsbruck, then puffed and pushed for eight hours
up the winding road of melting snow over Brenner pass.
The electric train shoots up the gorge through scores of
tunnels to cover this same distance in only a few minutes.
However, it was a fine bike trip up to the pass. Along the
way we passed several streams roaring down from the
mountain tops, in well-built, cement channels. These
channels prevent soil erosion and facilitate the production
of power. Near the top of the pass, the spring-like landscape and atmosphere gave place to a deep, snow-filled
highway with barrier walls of snow ten and fifteen feet in
height.

We lost two hours in Steinach trying to spend the rest of
our Austrian money before entering Italy, and listening to
strange stories told by the mountaineers. A typical one was
of children being lost in these great mountains for years,
and being wild savages walking on all fours when found.

Harry and I awakened early the next morning in our
little hut atop Brenner Pass to discover that it had been
snowing heavily all night, and that it was still snowing
thick and fast while the wind howled in loud wails. Our
road was entirely obliterated except for a few road signs

and the barest outlines of the road walls of snow blocks.

However, we pumped safely down from Brenner Pass through many little villages perched on the edge of the gorge, the spires of their church steeples soaring up suddenly into view out of a halo of boiling clouds. During the day we went down a gorge into a downpour of rain, over the slushy snow, and up another from rain to heavy snowfall again. Layers of cloud would slice off the mountain-tops from view, making their bases resemble plateaus, tablelands, and valleys.

We kept noticing signs giving two sets of figures referring to distance, and discovered that the first set represented the number of kilometers to Rome, while the second gave the distance to the nearest village. All roads still lead to Rome!

We were in the region belonging to Austria before the World War, and most of the people in this section boasted of Austrian blood. The cows here were not tested for tuberculosis and we did not drink milk. However, there was plenty of pure frozen water. Lower in Italy, even the water is not fit to drink, and wine is the only alternative. Our diet consisted chiefly of orange juice, figs, bananas, cheese, honey, raw vegetables, and chocolate candy.

We spent the night with a huge family of peasants, and while the father was busily talking to Harry, I wrote in my diary. Before eating a supper of bread and potatoes, the family mumbled "grace," the unusual feature of this ritual being that the Italians say grace before sitting at the table, mumbling out the long phrases with a sound like the buzzing of insects. At the first and last call to dinner, they say grace in whatever position they happen to be in, standing, sitting, playing cards, lying down or sewing, and then after making the sign of the cross, make a dive for the table.

In general, the people in this region are ignorant, uneducated and superstitious. The country is most

[68]

*All sorts of snow figures
adorn the wintry streets
of Bavarian alpine villages*

*he farther one ascends
nto the Bavarian Alps
the longer, more luxuriant
and more numerous are
these beards*

*This is the picture
that saved my life*

*This little alpine boy
curiously watches me
make ice cream*

Before we had left St Candida
more than a half-dozen kilometers
behind the great highway had turned
into a lumber trail

(Note Harry gets hot as
he starts up Kreuzberg)

As dusk
deepens,
so does the
snow...
"Woe is me,
where
are my red
flannels?"
cries
Bucephalus

Greek monk

"I've got them on,"
replies the
well-dressed Greek

beautiful, with its gorges of green, clear rivers, symmetrical mountain peaks, little tableland valleys with church spires peeping out of every cove, and an old castle on each hill-top and precipitous brink of a gorge, a thousand feet above the roaring stream.

Two days later we struck the Dolomites at Toblach and pushed on to St. Candida, a quaint old village with unusually picturesque, antique architecture. The village was full of Italian flags, and huge snow statues of Mussolini were being sculptured on every corner preparatory to a big celebration. While eating a light lunch, we were told that it was considered impossible to go over the pass without skis or snowshoes. We were beginning to tire of Italy, which, in general, was not friendly to Americans; and, as Kreuzberg was a short cut to Jugoslavia, we decided to tackle the pass, anyway.

Before we had left St. Candida more than a half-dozen kilometers behind, the great highway had turned into a lumber trail. The lumber trail lasted only a few kilometers and soon came to an end at the upper edge of the forest just when we needed a trail most, where the ascent became steeper.

Up the unblazed trail we started, miring up to our knees, waists, and at times even up to our necks in the deep snow, with our bikes and packs over our shoulders. Harry, who was not so reckless as I, suggested that we turn back and catch a train to Trieste rather than freeze up in these snow-bound regions, but I argued him into following on.

The Dolomites have the most fantastic shapes, cut out by nature in the jagged rocky cliffs, of beautiful cathedral spires and other architectural resemblances. The summits are one hundred per cent rock, with no trees, and for this reason, fine ski country in the deep snow at their bases.

Although it was almost impossible to imagine that a road had ever been along our route, we followed a general direction to the top by means of road signs which helped

[71]

us to ascertain where the highway was supposed to be. After wading up through snow for four hours, we reached Montecror, a little village of days gone by, at the very top of the pass.

Like the summer road over the pass, this little village seemed to have met a mysterious death. All the buildings were desolate and in ruins, only the bare walls of roofless houses standing.

A half-dozen soldiers stationed in this ruined village had dug a tunnel-like path, from four to six feet deep in the snow, all the way down to Padola on the south side of the pass where they obtained provisions. The only trouble with the path was its narrow width of one-and-a-half feet, not nearly broad enough for the bikes.

It was the perfection of pathos to see Harry and me painfully trying first to push the bikes ahead of us and falling all over them every other step; and then trying to carry them horizontally at arm's length over our heads. We were beginning to think it impossible for matters to be worse when, for no reason at all, except the passing of time, darkness swooped down upon us. Woe was us! Woe was us! Eternity seemed to stand still while we looked at the big snowy Dolomites with their jagged spires silhouetted against the dark violet sky.

Wedged in as we were, in this "rut," there was no danger of losing our trail. Our only light was the golden mass of stars above. Our only danger was from exhaustion.

We were becoming a little discouraged at floundering through the darkness eight kilometers from Padola, having come only a few kilometers since dark. It was nearly midnight. Several times we fooled ourselves into believing that we saw lights of some mountain cottage just ahead. When we really did see the lights of the village of Padola a few thousand feet below us, we stopped and, like true sons of Israel arguing over the genuineness of merchandise, we debated the genuineness of the "good fortune."

[72]

Suddenly we fell across a pile of logs freshly cut and strewn up and down the "road." From this point downwards the "rut" evolved into a log slide—a trail on which we could not only walk, but ride. We mounted our bicycles and whipped them into action. The logs had packed the soft snow into a tube-like tunnel down the mountain sides. Putting on brakes was out of the question—the bikes held the bit and we held on. Going around a curve we would be at right angles to the bottom. We had only one light between us, my dynamo light, which burned only when biking fast, and it was necessary for Harry to follow close behind in order to see the trail.

Just as we shot out of the tunnel like skyrockets, we ran head-on into an array of gleaming bayonets. After calming down Bucephalus, I asked the men behind the guns where we might find lodging for the remainder of the night. They assured us that we need not worry about such small matters, for Mussolini, the Keeper of the Peace, would provide. We were promptly escorted into army headquarters. In order to facilitate our progress, a few bayonets were judiciously carried only a few inches from our backbones, and occasionally we were gently nudged by these fingers of cold steel.

Upon reaching headquarters, our worthy sergeant announced our title in a loud voice: "Spies." We bowed and entered.

The captain—a true servant of Il Duce—ordered Harry to remove his hat while standing in the presence of him— the representative of the power that was Rome. Through force of habit, I had already removed mine upon entering the headquarters. Harry hesitated—but I whispered that now was no time to stand our ground upon such a fine point of honor. The valiant soldiers surrounded and pointed their guns at us.

Just as the captain was ordering us to be handcuffed and thrown into jail, I interrupted his orders by presenting a

[73]

passport, International Student Identity card and letters proving that I was no spy. The captain looked at the passport upside down, proceeded likewise with the Identity card and a portion of the letters. I was still guilty. Justice was not blind—just couldn't read. Finally I provided a clipping from an article in a newspaper in which was a photograph of me in a ship's ventilator. Ah! this was evidence worthy of consideration! No true spy would allow himself to be photographed! With a gesture of condescension and generosity, he ordered us released. We were expelled from our worthy potentate's presence in little better fashion than we had entered.

We hurriedly widened the space between this post and ourselves as quickly as possible. However, in Padola, three different hotels refused to admit us as they considered us spies. Finally, we found lodging in a smoky old tavern owned by an elderly Swiss widow. As we ate supper in the midst of a noisy group of soldiers and other idlers who were drinking, gaming, and carousing, our meal was interrupted every few minutes by various officials who had to examine our passports.

With practically no regrets, we departed early the next morning. By noon we had eased over Sappado Pass in ten feet of snow and had come down on the other side of the pass into a spring-like climate. For the first time since leaving the Rhine valley, nearly three weeks before, Bucephalus trod on solid dirt.

CHAPTER XIII

Dancing Daughters of Dalmatia

After crossing the Regina River bridge from Italy into Jugoslavia, we inquired of two white Russians (exiles), Konrad Grastovisky and Ovalostine Graditely, where cheap but clean lodging might be found. We were escorted to an imposing granite building on top of a hill commanding a panoramic view of the coastal towns and islands.

Though the interior of our mansion for the night was spotlessly clean, it was filled with quite a variety of tramps. We discovered that the name of the place was "Rodnicky Put," the local home for poor workers and wanderers. It was quite an experience to be with the motley group of companions, most of whom could speak English, German, or French as well as their native Jugoslavian tongue. All of us marched into the dressing room, deposited our clothes into laundry bags which were hoisted up to the ceiling, and then marched to the showers for a hot bath.

Harry and I were not familiar with the regulations in such institutions; while revelling in soap suds and hot water, the time limit was called and the water was cut off. We had to get special permission to have the water turned on again to wash the soap off our bodies.

Every one was then given a clean night shirt—one of the type that grandfather must have worn—and sent to bed in one of a score of bright snowy-walled rooms. This grand old institution "Rodnicky Put" certainly has class!

At dawn we began our dash down the rocky, barren, fjord-indented coast, winding up and down the cliffs hanging out over the sea, and around the miles and miles of land-locked arms of the sea with a little fishing village on the tip of each "finger."

We swooped down the rough donkey trail and ate dinner on a quay at Bakar, basking in the warm sun and watching the sailing vessels skim gracefully in and out of the harbor. On our menu was sauerkraut, which was made of the whole instead of grated or sliced cabbage. I bought a pound for one dinare (2 cents), a pound of butter for six dinare, a litre of milk for four cents, and three eggs for less than one cent.

How strange that so much food could be grown and obtained in this poverty-stricken country—enough to supply in a large measure the surrounding countries! All the eggs I saw in Germany had "Jugoslavia" printed on them. The country has a warm-year-round climate, but I do not know what inspiration the hens on this rocky coast have for laying eggs. Rock, rock everywhere, and not a cock in sight.

It seems customary all over the world for young people to become engaged or married on holidays. Since this 25th day of February marked the first and most important date of the annual carnival season, it was my good fortune to stop at an engagement feast in a peasant home near Susak.

The future bride and groom were seated on crudely constructed thrones of boxes on top of the dinner table. The groom wore a hat made of a cabbage with the heart out and with as many goose quills stuck through the top as possible. The girl wore a red shirt, white shawl over her head, a necklace of real oranges, and potato weights tied all around the bottom of her black silk skirt—a symbol of future prosperity. (Both were children of farmers.) The guests, also appropriately dressed, were lounging around the table, singing in "close harmony," over their wine kegs. The songs and singing were very similar to those of devotees of Bacchus the world over.

Harry and I were invited to tarry and help finish the barrel of wedding punch—an orange-colored concoction reminding me of the "bowla" I tasted at a Christmas feast in Gotha.

Every few miles along the way we met gay processions of clowns, bag-pipers and drummers, hundreds of boys, girls, old men, women and young children, dressed in the native costume and waving the Jugoslavian flags. Others were arrayed in all sorts of original outfits draped with cow-bells—cow-tails—sheep hides—cock feathers— cone-shaped hats of roses. In one procession the King of the Karneval was carried in a sedan chair on the shoulders of four native-costumed bearers. To the delight of all, Harry and I led many processions for several kilometers. In every village there was hilarious celebrating, the town folk dancing and singing on the Piazza. No wonder it was 4:00 p.m. before we reached Novi, the center of this great yearly festival.

We obtained a room for the night in a peasant cottage by the sea, and rushed up to the city Piazza on top of the hill, reaching it just in time to witness the mock-serious ceremony of beheading "Musopust," the effigy of the Evil spirit of the carnival. By relegating this villain to a timely death, the good, happy carnival spirit could reign supreme for the ensuing year. On the next day, the people of all the countryside would gather in the Piazza at three o'clock, march three times around the city in their native costumes, then convey Musopust's remains to the top of the mountain adjacent to the city and bury him with all the usual rites and ceremonies of a funeral.

All the men, from baby brother to grandpa, wore the traditional red skull cap with a beautifully embroidered black lace band around the side, embroidered with a coat of arms design on top, and a black cockade flowing down one side. The women wore the traditional costumes that were probably used hundreds of years ago, consisting of a black skirt, large white lace collar and cuffs, as in the dress of the Elizabethans, a bouquet of flowers in the bodice, with green springs of boxwood instead of fern, velvet straps, long, flowing, white lace headdress, gold earrings and gold and silver coins sewn all over the front of the dress from neck to waist.

It was a wonderful color scene as these people, young and old, did the hop-skip steps in a frisky, graceful movement round and round, to the rhythm of the song of a score or more stentorian-voiced "callers," who were in a small circle of their own in the center of the Piazza. The callers put their heads together and shouted the same verse over and over with such entrancing rhythm that every one danced like an African savage hypnotized by the thud of the tom-tom.

Harry and I were almost danced to death when it was whispered around that we were Americans. We were given quite a rush by the village girls, but at ten o'clock—after four hours of dancing—we sought safety in flight, and took refuge in our little room above the splashing waves.

With an early start southward next morning, we climbed like Rocky Mountain goats, up and down and around the jagged coast line, stopping at noon to catch our second wind at Senj. While the barber was giving Harry a shampoo, I explored the town and sunned at the old fishing docks. A large passenger ship bound for Split, stopped for a few minutes and Harry could not resist the temptation to get on board. I climbed on Bucephalus and started down the trail again alone.

CHAPTER XIV

From the Pearls of Dalmatia to the Isles of Illyria

Any one desiring dream-like scenery should take a boat trip down the Dalmatian shore. Myriads of islands furnish an absolutely sheltered channel all the way down the coast, and from the mainland, the numerous isles hide the open sea from view. It is a perfect setting for sailing in and out of beautiful isles on mirror-smooth water.

But tourists traveling by boat have no idea whatever of the life of the people along the shore. They see barren, rocky, island-cliffs transformed into soft, purple beauty by the distance—beauty in all directions. For me, plugging along one of the world's worst roads, there was immediate stark barrenness on one side contrasting with the grand panorama on the other. Yet the view was always changing:

one moment I looked up at the distant island mountains across the channels; an hour later I looked across the tops of a hundred islands from my perch two or three thousand feet above the sea. Somehow, the distant beauty was richer because of the barrenness of the immediate landscape.

The road became so terrible at Jablanac that farther cycling was impossible. Road workers had put large stones in the rain-washed road and had not yet broken them up into the usual baseball sized lumps. I pushed Bucephalus the remaining twenty-five kilometers to Karlobag. There I ate a supper of mutton, sauerkraut, goat milk, and cheese with a peasant family, around an old home-made clay oven. There were no extra beds, no hay, no hotel, so I slept in my sleeping bag on the smooth rock sloping up from the sea.

I was up at dawn, and after a swim in the warm sea-water, started pushing Bucephalus to the top of the 3,000-foot pass over to Gospic. Near the top of the pass I stopped at a peasant cottage for two hours out of the rain, and, while watching an old grandmother and her neighbor spinning wool, drank hot milk. The floor, full of holes, gave conclusive proof of years and years of spinning. Since all the clothes worn in this section are of home-made cloth, the women and girls are kept constantly spinning.

I took a fancy to these wholesome Jugoslavians. One had to admire their proud mastery of fate and circum-stances, their cheerfulness in the face of great poverty. They make a living by fishing and raising sheep and goats, and even conjure up little gardens a few feet square out of the rocky cliffs. Many build walls around the roof edges of their houses, haul dirt to the house tops, and plant little gardens on the roofs.

While rivers of water boil out of the sides of the road into the sea, and gigantic springs bubble up into the sea along the coast, all this water is salty. The natives have

[79]

only rain or snow-water to drink. Large, walled-in, concrete drains act as reservoirs for rain-water, but in the summer months there is no rain and then water is brought in by ships to which peasants go for water, just as we might stop for gasoline.

It is natural for one to like people who are friendly. In marked contrast to some countries, especially Italy, here the American flag is respected and the people admire America and Americans.

On the way up the pass, I had to stop a dozen times to conceal Bucephalus behind boulder walls on the sides of the road so that pack-trains of ponies and donkeys could pass on their way down to coastal markets with provisions and home-made rugs. Occasionally a donkey became frantic at the sight of old Bucephalus.

Although it was only 1:00 p.m. when I reached the top of the pass, it was so cold and wet and the road was so bad that I stopped for the night. My host had a large family of bright-eyed, intelligent children, and while the wind howled outside, I entertained them with animal shadows on the walls by manipulating my hands in front of the light. They easily learned the tricks and as I left the warm hearth for my hay-bed in the rafters above, they were busily engaged in creating new images on the walls.

All night the wind blew, the rain and sleet fell, the floods came, but our little house stood. At daybreak the wind, sounding like a huge cataract roaring down a mountain gorge, still tore at the little house. At 7:00 a.m. Bucephalus and I left with storm-clouds literally falling from the sky in the form of sleet and rain, and though we traveled until 7:00 p.m., bucking through the worst storm I had ever encountered, we made only 48 kilometers. Twice the wind played a joke on me, once throwing me in the muddy road, and again into a deep drain ditch filled with water. The joke was on the wind though, as it did not make me any wetter. Though it was downhill most of the

[80]

way, I had to walk against the wind and three punctures added spice to the situation. By dark, poor old Bucephalus was exhausted and I wearily dragged him into a barn, made him comfortable for the night, and then hit the hay.

Having finally struggled down the 3,000 feet to Gospic, we started up the broad, green valley. Though the coast is rocky and barren, inland Jugoslavia is a comparatively sheltered land of green pastures and farms.

We passed hundreds of peasants on the way to the monthly cattle market in the town. Ninety-nine in every hundred, including women, wore the typical shaggy sheepskin jackets, many of them with vari-colored embroidered patterns along the front of the jacket, and with the wool dyed brilliant colors. All the males, from baby boys to old men, wore the conventional red and black hat, while the women crowned their heads with colored shawls. The men carried vari-colored woolen knapsacks on their backs. Tufts of dyed wool were tied to the donkeys' ears. All of the animals in this section were very small in contrast with the giant work-horses of northern Europe. Some two-pony, home-made carts were to be seen. Not a single animal would pass Bucephalus and me. It would either stampede off the side of the road, or stand trembling until we passed by. Most of the people had not seen a bike before. One man told me he knew of a "rich" fellow over in a nearby village who once owned one. There were many little girls carrying new-born lambs in their arms;, boys driving calves; tall, wild, cossack-looking men dashing down the road with yokes of ponies.

Near Biloj I was amazed to see a gigantic kneeling figure cut in the solid rock on top of a mountain. Peasants say that this statue is as old as the hills and was made by the Romans. One young fellow told me of a large collection of coins he had found three years before, with "Caesar Augustus" stamped on each.

Though lacking the color and romance of our assault on

[81]

Kreuzberg, my second pass of the day, via an ancient Roman road from Croatia over into Dalmatia, was probably a greater physical and mental strain than that climb: here there were a blinding downpour of sleet and snow, strong head-winds, and cold, ugly mountains not at all inspiring.

Gliding down to a little village of rock-slabbed houses, perched against the rocky mountainside and as difficult to distinguish from the background as quail in brown sage, I stopped the first passerby with this query, "Malim, Tkogovori ovete Engleski jasom Amerikanski." He soon located a peasant who had been in America three years and who was so happy to display and slay the English language before the entire populace, now quickly gathering to hear the conversation, that he at once informed me that the whole village would be mine for the night. Furthermore, I might sleep in his brother-in-law's barn—his own was not good enough.

As in Ireland, I was treated like the Prodigal Son returned. The entire family ate from a common plate and in deference to me, the plate was placed nearest my position at the table. Father-in-law and a few cronies came in later with a few bottles of wine, and the celebration continued on into the night.

It is strange how these Jugoslavs can live in the United States for several years and then return to their country unchanged. There was nothing American about any I met.

At Sibenik, Bucephalus and I burst out upon the warm Adriatic. The storm had blown itself away, and the sky was clear for the first time in days. We stopped under an olive tree a thousand feet above the emerald isles—not like the barren, rocky islands farther north—and gazed up the green valleys stretching out to the feet of Split, which seemed to be only a couple of miles away, though in reality about twenty. I drank in the balmy breezes, and as Bucephalus was beginning to get drowsy, I whipped him

[82]

down the trail through the old excavated Roman metropolis of Salona and on to Split. I reached the post office at sundown and found Harry waiting for me there.

Now the capital of the province, Split has been the center of Dalmatian life and history for more than two thousand years. Here is the great palace of Diocletian, the slave's son who became master of the world, and, for the years of his retirement, built this palace on the shores of his province. During the passing of years, the palace resolved itself into a maze of 268 dwellings, and at present more than 3,000 persons live within its walls. The beautiful mausoleum was turned into the cathedral of Split. This great palace represents, with the ruins of the ancient city of Salona, the most notable Roman remains on the eastern Adriatic.

I bought a loaf of bread at a baker's named "Bettiza Sin"; then we pulled out of this most interesting city, passed the excavated city of Salona again, and sped down the fine beach road that took us all morning beside the very water's edge.

There was a variety of scenery. The trail would plunge suddenly from the rocky, barren cliffs into the cool shade of green forests of wind-blown pine trees growing down to the very brink of the waves; the vineyards and olive and fig groves were planted down the slopes to the very beach itself. The high surrounding islands prevent high water, and the waves are never more than ripples which do not wash away the vegetation.

All the little villages along the coast, perched high upon the sides of the cliffs or else nestled down in a snug little harbor filled with colorful fishing boats, had the rock tops of their houses whitewashed, though the sides were unpainted, retaining the natural, dull grey color, like the grey mountains along the shore with their peaks splashed with white snow.

Our good road ended at the popular seaside resort of

Markarska, and we had to leave the edge of the unending array of little crescent sea-beaches, and start up a 37-kilometer road zigzagging more than 4,000 feet up the Alexs Dom mountain.

Upon striking the rugged mountains of old Montenegro, we bumped into bands of wild looking men in short knee-breeches, colored sashes about their waists, artistically embroidered jackets and Turkish fezes, turned-up-toed shoes, and long crooked knives gleaming under their belts. I was growing a beard and I tried to look as tough as these old boys—for among them were some who had no scruples against knifing a harmless-looking individual for whatever of value he might possess.

The women wore white woolen breeches buckled below the knee, just like the men, and a short poncho-like skirt used for carrying vegetables and yarn. Since the women did all the work, I suppose that they were entitled to wear pants.

Fifty kilometers before reaching Ragusa, "The Pearl of Dalmatia," we saw the lights of the city, but to reach it that night we had to bike four hours by moonlight. Three kilometers from the city as the crow flies, Harry and I struck a fjord around the edge of which the road wound, making almost a twenty-five kilometer detour—very typical of the entire Jugoslavic coastline. Bucephalus snorted around enough fjords in Jugoslavia to circumnavigate the globe!

We stopped long enough in our dash down through Albania to sail out to Corfu and back to the mainland. At least I returned to the mainland, but Harry stayed to explore the island for a few days before continuing via boat to Greece.

CHAPTER XV

Athens, Georgia—Athens, Greece

Bucephalus and I sauntered into Athens in early spring—the most beautiful time of the year—when the air is filled with the fragrance of almond blossoms and aloes, with the songs of birds, the chatter of cylinder-hatted monks, the splash of fountains—all a wild symphony of temperate beauty.

There was something springlike even in the costumes of the national soldiers and peasants. The men seemed to have on nothing whatever except their long winter under-wear, short coat, garters, profusely cockaded hat, and a pair of black soft slippers with a powder puff on the toes. Some wore very short "thigh-high" pleated skirts and seemed to have forgotten their trousers. In the vernacular of a modern debutante: they certainly were cute!

The more I saw of Greece and the Greeks, the more I liked both. Whenever I stopped to look at my maps—either of city or country—I was immediately surrounded by a crowd that became intensely interested in the map. At each such stop the spirit of old Demosthenes would hover over the group and heated debates would result among the sons of Athens regarding the locations of the University, museums, cities, and universe.

I started out to view Athens in my customary manner when striking a big city, namely, by biking at random, giving the whole town the "once over" from the outside; then, with the aid of a map, following a systematic course of sight-seeing as completely thorough as one of Cook's tours. I was fortunate in obtaining from the Minister of Education a pass to all the places of interest in the whole of Greece.

My first night in Athens was so beautiful and clear, with the moon shining in her full glory, that I could not sleep indoors. After a dinner with Spiro Horocopus, a wealthy young Athenian, who had entertained me the previous summer in his villa on the Isle of Capri, I checked out of the Hotel and cycled up to the Acropolis to sleep in the Parthenon. This is the only building in the world so perfectly constructed that its perspective eliminates the defects of the human eye. I noted, too, that the beauty of the old Greek buildings lies not only in the artistic and faultless construction, but also in the beauty of location on commanding hill tops.

The Parthenon gates remained open for awhile after dark so that the visitors might drink in the beauty of the immediate surroundings, and the panoramic view of the moonlit Attic plain, in whose gently rolling slopes is spread out the violet-crowned, classic city of Athens, the city of Theseus, of Hadrian, and the modern city that has grown up in recent years, with Piraeus—the port of Athens—in the distance.

When Bucephalus and I reached the entrance shortly after midnight, the gates were locked, but it was quite easy to scale the wall at the right of the gates. I took my sleeping bag over first and then came back for Bucephalus. It was very difficult to get the bike over, but as it was a long way from Cologne and I expected to cycle back there in time for my last term of school, I could take no chances of having it stolen. The noisy scramble woke the big German police dog at the watchman's cottage just outside the walled-in summit of this sacred hill; but in spite of his barking the watchman was not aroused—only my fears were!

This was a night to remember. I had previously thought of ruins only as pieces of a broken and forgotten past; but on this night the old temple itself seemed alive and the shades of the ancient Greeks—Socrates, Plato, Pythias and Phidias—walked about with me. All the Greek history I had ever studied came flashing back in vivid pictures as I

[86]

walked for more than two hours among these noble ruins high above the moonlit slopes of the sleeping city. The ancient Greeks must have lived close to the gods to have been able to create, in stone, such perfection.

If they came as close to perfection in person as in stone, I can readily understand why a thousand ships were launched across the briny Aegean in pursuit of Helen, that likeable little lady.

At the crack of dawn I arose from the marble slabs in the middle of the Parthenon, went over the wall and down to earth again before the watchman came around to open the gates for the usual stream of tourists.

That morning I ate fried devil fish and raisin bread with the captain of the port of Piraeus and a couple of sailors who had been around the world a dozen times, but unfortunately had never heard of Georgia, the fairest of the Southland.

Our meal was in one of those hundred per cent Greek restaurants with groaning loud speaker "music boxes" sticking in a window, to the music of which several devotees of Bacchus cut some fancy native steps, while vendors passed back and forth with wares which they never seemed to sell. Some one occasionally passed around the hat to take up enough tribute to warrant playing the same tune again. How different was this meal in the atmosphere of the fowl, fish, fruit and vegetable markets of Piraeus from that with my cultured and wealthy friend! The rich and the poor, the good and the bad, the beautiful and the ugly, are always present, but too many tourists and travelers see only the one or the other and return from their travels with a lop-sided outlook on foreigners.

It's carniv
season in
Jugoslavia

Our trail wound up and down the
cliffs hanging out over the sea...

and around the miles and miles
of land-locked arms of the sea
with a little fishing village
on the tip of each finger.

ploring Egypt

Water pipes and water boy

I helped cheer on the American
Bobsled team of the 1936 Games,
and was saddened when the
Italian team captain was
killed in the ski jump

Pretty Sonja Henie of Norway
gave me a lesson in figure skating

Biking the broad British
boulevard of Cairo

CHAPTER XVI

Mediterranean Misadventures

I was the only deck passenger on the Vesta, an Italian freighter bound for Egypt, but considered myself first-class compared to the other passengers piled down in the fo'castle with no way of getting out. There was such a large herd of cattle on the ship, both below and on deck, that it was impossible to go from one end of the ship to the other except by climbing along via cables.

The ship was so heavily loaded that she glided smoothly, and seemed to take off for a good voyage. We passed hundreds of little islands as we rounded the lower edge of the Ionian Sea and headed for Candia, the capital city and chief port of Crete, where we would have a twelve-hour stop.

At three o'clock in the afternoon we sighted the gleaming, snow-covered peaks of Crete, and reached Canea, the northwestern seaport town of the island, at sunset. There was a three-hour stopover here in this interesting place of monks, monasteries, and industrious native artisans; we pulled up anchor at ten bells, embarking on a stormy sea. The waves rolled high and the salt spray soaked me on my high perch on the left bridge, while the wind nearly blew me into the sea before I awoke at 2:00 a.m. and moved my bed to the wind-protected starboard side.

We reached Candia at daybreak and anchored in the outer harbor. I went ashore in a small boat through the old ten-foot thick wall-gates surrounding the inner harbor, which contained only sailing vessels.

Here, as elsewhere, the first typically Greek sights were the saintly, long-bearded, stove-pipe-hatted monks. Most of the natives were in picturesque costumes, the men wearing boots which were nearly hidden beneath their

[90]

baggy balloon breeches, a sash around the waist, kerchiefed headgear in pirate fashion, gold embroidered jackets with a double row of blue buttons running to a point at the waist in the form of a V, a large cutlass in their waist band, and all the other accoutrements of real buccaneers. The Philistines, who made life miserable for the Hebrews in Bible times, were a race of pirates who emigrated from Crete.

Crete is a semi-tropical, heavily wooded country, but from the looks of the snow-capped mountain ranges towering in the background of the coast, it might also be a land for skiers. Certainly it is an interesting place historically. A new building was under construction for the museum at Candia, and, because of my letter from the Greek Minister of Education, I was permitted to see the museum although it was closed to visitors. I found all sorts of queer and ancient relics not to be seen in other museums I had visited: a terra cotta disk from Bhaestos with the impressed alphabet of an unknown script, supposed to be the world's oldest example of hieroglyphics; a large number of images of double apes, the most sacred symbol of the Minoan religion; bronze mirrors, stone lamps, and bone-carved figures of bull-fighters.

I was back on the ship in the late afternoon to find it four hours behind schedule in sailing for Cyprus, as the Italian sailors did not seem to know how to load the goods taken on at Crete. They had carelessly let one load crash down through the hatch, nearly knocking a hole in the hold of the ship and scattering soap and raisins all over the floor.

We took on a shipment of soap, Golden Sultan raisins, several kegs of sea snails for Cyprus, several hundred metal barrels of olive oil for Alexandria, where it would be transferred to a ship bound for Yokohama, and a new load of sweet, clover hay for the cattle aboard ship. There was no room below, so this cargo was piled high on deck.

[91]

I promptly climbed on top and watched the waves sweep the deck, drenching each passenger as he dashed across by the open hatch.

I spent the next morning in the prow of the boat, having great fun ducking beneath the spray as each big wave splashed over the bowsprit. It was just my luck for the wind to cease blowing for a few seconds as one voluminous wave hovered over my head and, instead of sweeping harmlessly across deck, dropped like lead upon me, imparting a drowned-cat look to my physiognomy. Hanging my clothes in the engine room to dry, I read the rest of the day in my sleeping bag on the aft hatch as the stiff north breeze and ocean waves spanked the front deck.

All of the passengers were sea-sick, and no wonder, as not one of them would stick his nose out in the fresh air and get a whiff of the salt spray. But the poor cows and beef cattle had my sympathy. This ship was tossing about so much that the poor beasts could not get their "sea legs" and most of them were sea-sick in a big way.

As we rounded the peninsula into beautiful Akrotiri Bay on the Ides of March and headed for the port of Limassol, the little village nestling in the middle of a crescent-shaped harbor on the southern shores of Cyprus, hundreds of gulls glided overhead, and three large dolphin appeared at the prow of our boat where they remained as honorary escorts until we dropped anchor thirty minutes later.

Artistic minarets, the blue, triple-domed cathedral, a palm and pine-lined sea-beach, the rich velvety-green rolling plains of tropical fruit, flowers, and vegetation in the background, the bracing balmy breezes over the bright blue waters of the bay—these are my memories of this dream island.

After leaving Cyprus, the cows, crew, Bucephalus and I had the ship practically to ourselves, as all the poor passengers had packed their worldly possessions in large wicker baskets and disembarked at Limassol.

As there were more cows than the milkman and his three helpers could handle, I ventured to trade with him. In return for all the milk I could drink, I was to give a bucket of water to each of the sixty-four cows on the fo'castle twice a day. The milkman, thinking I was making a bad deal, grinned amusedly at my eagerness to become a waterboy. He did not know that I could drink a gallon of milk any day! After watching me drain the contents of a couple of milk pails, he decided that I had not made such a bad trade after all.

Shortly before sighting the African shores, we zigzagged through a large white fleet of fishing vessels manned by swarthy Arabs in their vari-colored robes. As we glided close by one boat I noticed that in order to keep their "night shirts" from flying over their heads these husky fellows tied strings from the ends of their robes to garters around their legs.

Swerving sharply from our course to keep from crashing head-on into one of these tiny sail-boats, we swung too far over into the blue and green shallows of the fishing reef. Schranch! With a sickening, scraping sound, like a dentist's drill upon a sensitive eye-tooth, the Vesta spliced off the top of a coral reef, shivering and groaning from stem to stern; then after a final moment of thunder, the old boat eased off into the deeper waters, and Bucephalus sighed with relief.

CHAPTER XVII

Entree Into Egypt

For the first time from the ocean, I approached a great metropolis at night. As we sighted the delta of the Nile at Rosetta, and glided past the red and yellow lights lining the shore, I watched a dozen giant search-lights around Alexandria make all sorts of patterns in their play to and fro across the sky. Once they located and concentrated their combined rays upon a great north-bound air-liner soaring high above the city. Immediately the silver sides of the plane sparkled with clearer brilliance than if seen by ordinary daylight.

The pilot ship coming to usher us into the harbor resembled some strange sea-monster bouncing over the waves with its green eye on one side, red on the other, and yellow above in the center of its forehead. We wound through the entire British fleet, finally anchoring beside a great airplane carrier in the middle of the harbor. Hundreds of lights in the immense ships made them glow like huge phosphorescent bugs or caterpillars.

As usual, I slept on deck, and was awakened next morning by the strange sounds emanating from these monsters of the deep, as they began coming to life. First was a bugle call from the flagship of the fleet, followed by all sorts of "barnyard" noises. The siren whistle of the airplane carrier sounded like the mellow mooing of a melancholy cow, while other noises were like the cackling of hens.

My first glimpse of shore, at 6:30 a.m., was of two Arabs in solemn prayer in a coalyard, one clothed in a red turban and black gown, the other in ghostly white, with their heads and hands on the ground towards Mecca and the rising sun.

When we landed, Bucephalus and my knapsack were grabbed and thrown into a horse-drawn coach before I could say anything. I immediately retrieved my possessions, informing the surprised driver that I was neither millionaire tourist nor invalid.

The mile ride around the docks to the customs house was a memorable panorama. I saw more baggy-trousered and night-shirted, sinister people than I had ever seen in my life—such was my first ill-omened impression of these swarthy sons of Ham.

[94]

Alexandria reminded me of Miami, Florida, with its palms, parks, flowering trees and bougainvillea covering the houses.

Licorice tea vendors were everywhere in brilliant outfits of red shirts, purple turbans and white blouses, with a brass jug of tea swung carelessly around their waist, and brass cymbals held in one hand. All the men sitting in the doorways were smoking huge water-pipes with puffs and gurgles like the rumbling of a distant waterfall.

I zigzagged to Cairo up different mouths of the Nile, past little villages of goat hair tents and mud. Hay and corn were piled out on the roofs of the houses, for the thicker the roof covering, the less heat penetrated into the house.

This was the richest land I had ever seen—fields of vegetables, purple sugar cane, wheat, cotton spread from horizon to horizon. Everywhere was color and life in action. Against this background of luxuriant growth were polychromatic-costumed peasants busily engaged in scores of different methods of irrigation.

Every type, means, and method of locomotion were to be seen. Simultaneously within my line of vision, as I biked alongside one of the mouths of the Nile between Alexandria and Tanta, were a giant air-liner overhead, freight and passenger trains on the railway, long-robed natives on bicycles, donkeys, camels, Arabian horses, water-buffaloes, mules, goat-drawn wagons, and automobiles. But most popular of all seemed to be water transports of every type. Gracefully fashioned sails towered above many boats, but in the absence of wind, men or donkeys pulled from shore or else the boat was poled along.

Most of the women I noticed along the way ruined their natural beauty with red and purple designs tattooed on their faces and necks, and with antimony coloring around their eyes. Even so, I can more readily appreciate the

[95]

accomplishments of Cleopatra.

Not liking the looks of men I constantly passed on the road, I stopped for the night several hundred yards off the highway in a clover and alfalfa field, in the middle of the Delta about seventy-five miles southeast of Alexandria.

At three a.m. the light from the last quarter of the moon made the sky so bright that it waked me and I discovered that though I had put a raincoat around my sleeping bag, the dew had soaked through from the outside as if from rain. However, I went back to the land of Nod, to wake again at sunrise after ten hours of refreshing sleep.

CHAPTER XVIII

A "Cracker" in Cairo

As dawn dissolved the darkness on the great Delta of the Nile, and my bed of purple clover and alfalfa was transformed into a field of sparkling emeralds, I beheld a magnificent cathedral looming up out of the fog banks above the rising sun. A few kilometers of cycling in that direction proved this vision to be a reality, and not a work of magic or the "stuff that dreams are made of."

It was a marvelous mosque with needle-like minaret and bubble-topped roof soaring up through the heavy layers of fog into the golden sunlight. As the fog rapidly disintegrated and evaporated before the piercing sun-beams, the mosque, actually appearing to take flight on the wings of the dawn, was more like an incarnate dream walking than anything I had ever seen.

For two hours, I nearly froze while cycling through the early morning air. An endless stream of camel caravans driven by night-shirted natives rose up like an army of ghosts from the receding fog. I would have spent the previous night at the campfire of one of these caravans along my trail, had I not decided that safety lay in solitude

[96]

rather than in numbers, in the case of a stranger among strangers.

Strings of women were wending their weary way to market with clay jugs of milk, baskets of camel and goat dung pancakes, vegetables, pigeons and ducks balanced atop their huge pillowed headdresses, and little Junior or baby Cleo, or both, astraddle mother's shoulders. This was my first visible evidence of the great burden carried by women of the East. Though starving, these women would never think of parting with the bejewelled veils, gold earrings, silver bracelets and anklets adorning their own persons and those of their children. What gaudy artificiality! But little wonder, when we consider their heritage as daughters of the dark-eyed damsels of the days of the Pharaohs, who, not satisfied with their refreshing schoolgirl complexions obtained through the use of their little alabaster vases of perfumes, oil, and cosmetics, wore false eyebrows and false eyelashes, and concealed the natural beauty of their hands within golden gloves!

At many wayside mud homes, women were busily pounding corn into meal in hollowed stone vessels and sifting it into great copper caldrons while men were spinning thread from goat and camel hair.

Egypt is not a country for impatient motorists; cars are stopped every few kilometers by police patrols. Once, my bicycle was held up and appropriately labelled with my name and address. It had been difficult enough to recognize my name in Greek letters, but in Arabic script it was shorthand of an unknown tongue to me. In the best pidgin English he could muster, my patronizing policeman explained the beauty and richness of Arabic, even its ordinary words and names having symbolic double meanings. His own name was Errian Wahba Effendi (Mr. Naked Gift) and that of his cohort was Wahba Habib Nakhla Effendi (my beloved palm). "'Effendi,' the Arabic for mister," he explained, "is affixed at the end of the

[97]

name instead of at the beginning as in English. Only the Intelligentsia—wearers of the red tarboosh—are given such title. The 'fellahin'—farmers, most of whom wear uniform blue dress—are jailed if caught wearing the red tarboosh."

"When in Rome, do as Romans"; thus, native fashion I stopped on the roadside at high noon, dropped my feet into one of the Nile's many mouths, and enjoyed my lunch of dates, orange-colored camel cheese, and a big bouquet of peas—pods, stems, and all!

Living is said to be very expensive for foreigners in Egypt. However, as most Egyptians are quite poor and thus unable to pay much for food, the only problem confronting the economically minded tourist is the location of cafeterias catering to the better class Egyptian. Accordingly, my first Egyptian meal, of delicious fruits and vegetables, cost only five millemes (two and a half cents) for a gigantic pancake filled with beans, tomatoes, lettuce, rose petals and spices!

Near Tanta, I caught my first glimpse of the Sahara, rolling like a great yellow sea, in striking contrast to the green vegetation of the Delta of the Nile, the richest spot on the globe. Everywhere in the canals natives were busily performing their ablutions, and washing carrots, cabbages, horses, and water buffalo.

After a record morning run of 169 kilometers up the flat Delta in rather zigzag fashion via the city of Zag-a-zig, I reached the American Express Company in Cairo at 2 p.m. All of Cairo "knocks off" for siesta from noon until 4 p.m. While waiting for the Express Company office to open its doors, I met a young Arab, who cycled around town with me. We gave the "once over" to old Cairo, Coptic churches, Island of Rodah, Mosques of Amir, Mohammed Ali, and Sultan Hassan, Citadel, Tombs of the Mamelukes, and finally brought our day of rambling to a close beneath the four graceful spires of the Mohammed University at El

[98]

Azar Mosque. Nearly ten thousand students gather at this great institution, coming from all parts of the Moslem world to study theological points far removed from practical affairs of every-day life. In one room, I found a group of black Nubians from the Sudan, squatting on their haunches in a circle around a grisly-bearded old son of Ham, who sat in the same monkey-like fashion as his pupils, and entranced them with his monotonous chanting of the Koran, sounding far more like the babbling of a baboon than the sagacious sayings of a University professor!

I would have prolonged my visits in the many other rooms of the mosque where the Moors, Persians, Iraquians, and other tribes and races were segregated in their respective classroom circles; but the muezzin call of the faithful to prayer just as the last rays of the dying sun vanished from the skylight broke up classes until another day.

I polished off the end of my first perfect afternoon in Cairo by cycling over to a great African Exposition then in progress on the western banks of the Nile. By far the most interesting single feature of the fair was the crowd itself. It was a rare treat to see Bedouin and nomad families fresh from the desert examining for the first time in their lives such modern mysteries as the telephone, radio, moving pictures, and other marvels, which either had the effect of frightening the amazed audience nearly out of their wits, or of charming them into God-like adoration.

After a day of exploration in the agricultural and industrial palaces of the Exposition, dodging sprays of attar of roses from real perfume-factory floats on wheels, witnessing a spectacular goose step, fox trot, and buck dance by a riderless Arabian horse to the tune of a snake charmer's flute, I cycled out to my "headquarters" on top of Cheops pyramid.

I reached the Giza pyramids at midnight after a fine ride

through the flower perfumed night air, and amid the soft patter of droppings from the thousands of kites and other birds roosting in the overhanging trees. I had originally intended sleeping on one of the great slabs near the base of Cheops but the more I thought of the terrible snakes I had seen at the Exposition, the higher I climbed until my sleeping bag lay on the very peak of Giza's highest pyramid. Even here my slumbers were interrupted by frequent visits from some of the multitude of giant scorpions, which swarm over the pyramids by the thousands in daytime, to bake on the granite slabs in the hot sun. However, one accustomed to a bed beneath the stars can sleep better even under such trying circumstances than in a downy bed within the four walls of a palace.

With the dawn came my full awakening, just as the sun peeped over the distant desert plateau between Suez and Cairo. It gradually spread its rays across the beautiful Nile with its rich valley of fruit, flowers, palms, vegetables, and glistening green fields of grain, studded sporadically with minarets of roadside mosques, or other beautiful works of man, which harmonized so perfectly in the natural setting. This magnificent panorama, unfolding before my eyes as I sat atop Cheops, stretched out between the yellow seas of sand like a giant belt of precious jewels.

To the west were the endless sands of the Sahara; to the south stretched the long string of golden pyramids on the edge of the desert beside the Nile valley; to the north spread Cairo and the Nile Delta in burnished yellow and sparkling green, beneath the high plateau on which my pyramid was situated; and to the east lay the golden glow from the not yet risen sun.

The silent spell of the desert was soon broken by the arrival of a party of American tourists riding donkeys and camels out to view the sphinx and pyramids before the

[100]

unbearable heat of day. As I clambered down from my bed to the base of the pyramid and started cycling away, all produced cameras to take a picture of Bucephalus. Several offered to take a few pictures of me as I rode their camels, but I emphatically declared that as Bucephalus, and not a camel, had brought me to the pyramids, I would not insult my trusty steed in such a manner.

Before the sun was an hour high, I had breakfasted with a party of Chicago archaeologists seated on the paws of the 5,000-year-old Alabaster Sphinx, bade farewell to "Old Glory" waving in the breeze above the dense thicket of date and coconut palms of ancient Memphis, and again headed southward, on a trip which would take me to the forks of the White and Blue Niles at Khartoum, before putting Bucephalus in reverse and flying back down to Cairo.

CHAPTER XIX

The Nile

Egypt is an ideal country for cycling in the early spring when the atmosphere is cool and dry, even though the sun is alarmingly penetrating to one unaccustomed to the tropics.

That great green artery, the Nile, is not merely the lifeblood of Egypt, it is Egypt. In this country, all the countless millions of living things, both animal and vegetable (except for a few scattered Nomads, wolves, and hardy cacti blossoms eking out an existence in the Garden of Allah), live and thrive along the banks of the great river. As this green life line is never more than ten miles wide above Cairo, and is more often only a few yards wide, where the great oceans of sand roll up to the very banks of the river, a traveler up the river sees the whole country at a passing glance.

[101]

Along the road, I passed great armies of "human ants" carrying baskets of top soil from barges in the Nile to the highway, building it up above the surface of the Delta. Flies were so terrible in this region that every mother with any regard for her child, enshrouded it completely in veils.

While cycling along the flat road near Elayat at noon, I noticed all the natives and their water-buffalos bathing in the river. Pulling off my own clothes, I dived into the old Nile for one of the most refreshing swims in my life. The water was surprisingly cool, like that of a mountain stream.

While I was drying on the sunny bank, my feet dangling in the water, and my mouth crammed with raw turnips and carrots, several curious native boys crept stealthily to Bucephalus and began to purloin our belongings. One grabbed my thermos flask, another, my buckskin shorts; another, Bucephalus' pump. Without causing serious damage, I retrieved everything and resumed my journey up the river.

As night began to fall across the desert, I noticed several Arabs encircling their tents with an odoriferous shrub (resembling pennyroyal) to keep away beasts and snakes. Because of the heavy dews, so characteristic of the country, Egyptians seldom sleep beneath the open sky. Everywhere they marvelled that I could sleep outside without contracting pneumonia.

The finest way in the world to kill time on a hot spring day up the Nile is to chew sugar cane on the shady river bank and watch the myriads of great barges sail by with their cargoes of golden grain, green bananas, purple onions, white goats, and black sheep. The Nile valley is luxuriant with sugar cane, olives, grapes, dates, and other kinds of fruits. Away from the immediate vicinity of the Nile, practically all the natives raise is sand.

During the first few days of cycling up the river I spent most of the broiling day time in sampling these luscious products along the cool banks. I cycled at dawn and twilight hours, and slept at night along the same old snaky bank of the Nile.

The best things in life are free—a bed in God's great out-of-doors, fresh air, sunshine, moonlight raining down from a cloudless sky, wind rustling in the palms, waters lapping the river banks, frogs croaking, birds singing, the laughter and gaiety of children, the joyous companionship of Bucephalus! Loneliness loves company. Nothing is finer in a foreign land than a friend to share your joys and make them double; and your sorrows and make them half. This is true, even though your "friend" be only a bicycle.

Every one of the 1345 milestones up to the forks of the White and Blue Niles was marked by exquisite monuments of days gone by: the highly carved pillars of Sethos Temple at Abydos, and Humor Temple at Denderah; the Ramesseum, Memnon Colossi and Tombs of the Kings at Thebes; Ptolemy gateway at Karnak; the magnificent Temple at Luxor, chief tourist center of upper Egypt; the weird Temple of Horus at Edfu; and at Philae, the beautiful temple of Isis, called "the Pearl of Egypt."

Since the construction of the Nile dam at Aswan—the largest dam of its kind in the world—the holy island of Philae with its wonderful temples is partially submerged. I swam part way out for a closer inspection of the island, but when several uninvited guests in the form of crocodiles met me halfway, I decided that it would be just as well for me to return to shore, and be satisfied with a more distant perspective of this miniature Venice.

Crocodiles, snakes, hippopotami, and other denizens of the Nile became more numerous after passing the second great cataract.

One day as I sat eating "sun-bread" (this delicious yeast bread rises and cooks in the sizzling Sudanese sun) in a little oasis village south of Wadi Halfa, a country bride passed on her miserable wedding march, in a

[103]

cashmere-covered litter swung between two camels, fore and aft. The rear camel, with his head tied beneath the litter, seemed to be even more sea-sick than the bride.

At Khartoum, I was nearly knocked from my bicycle seat at sight of a glaring corpse, propped up in a sitting position atop a hearse, parading the streets for all to see— it was an uncanny but not unusual funeral for one of the few Greek patriarchs in the city. To think that I had traveled throughout Greece, yet had to come far up to this out-of-the-way place to see a Greek funeral procession!

One night as I lay in my sleeping bag in the moonlit desert near Khartoum, a weird, monotonous, drumming sound reached my ears. Out in the desert to the southeast, I saw the glow of campfires with shadowy forms flashing in phrenetic movement around the flames. Creeping closer, I noticed that two black Nubians were frantically beating a maddening rhythm upon their tom-toms, while a half-dozen others were dancing as if they were stepping upon coals of fire each time their feet touched the ground. So strenuous and exhausting were their movements, that several of the dancers finally dropped senseless upon the ground, only to arise, upon reviving, and continue their epileptic dancing where they left off. When I left the sickening performance several hours after midnight, the dancers were still going strong. The last sound that reached my ears as I dropped off to dreamland, was the beat of the tom-tom. It was my first, and I hope, last, dervish dance.

In my dreams, the maddening music of the Upper Nile was replaced by a Viennese symphony orchestra playing the waltz of the beautiful Blue Danube. Then I was singing once again the rollicking old stein songs with my Cologne University comrades! Dawn came, and with it nostalgic awakening. How far, far away seemed my cozy little room in Cologne! It was a long, hard road from Germany down to Africa, but it would be much longer and harder on the return journey through the Holy Land, Asia Minor, up the Danube, and down the Rhine. Here I was penetrating deeper and deeper into the Dark Continent, every foot taking me farther and farther from my college friends—and only two months before my summer session of school! Like a bat out of Carlsbad Caverns, Bucephalus about-faced, and headed north as fast as my legs and his wheels could carry us.

The Nile

*At dawn
I beheld
this
needle-li
minare*

"Me and my pal"

*Baby Cleo
rides to
Zag-a-Zig
market
with Papa
Tony*

Egyptian husband goes to town with two of his wives veiled against flirtatious oglers and baby enshrouded against insects

In Massarah quarries

Lighting effects in lower picture are furnished by Mother Nature through huge holes in the quarry roof

CHAPTER XX

The Closed Gateway to the East

After my long trip back down the Nile, I turned Bucephalus toward Suez, the gateway to the East. On March 21, I passed through old Cairo of the bazaar brass shops and fruit markets on the road to Heliopolis and Suez. Twenty-five years ago, Baron Em Pain, a Belgian nobleman, invested a small fortune in real estate seventeen miles out in the desert east of Cairo. He paid one mill per meter (half a cent per yard) for the land, irrigated and transformed the desert into a Garden of Eden, and later sold it at five pounds per meter ($25.00 per yard). Today the Baron's Cinderella desert is the new Heliopolis, a beautiful city of palatial homes and hotels for rich Orientals.

At Heliopolis, the asphalt road came to an unwelcome end, and I pushed out into the desert road—a mere sprinkling of sage and straw over the sand, marked on each side with trenches and an occasional stone slab to indicate where the "road" was considered to run.

Though hot, dry and devoid of human life, the desert here is not one endless ocean of monotonous sand. My trail was a veritable Egyptian Switzerland of full-bloomed flowers. Nature makes it possible for these plants to grow by giving them protective, waxy leaves, and tuberous, bulbous roots.

On my second morning out in the desert, I discovered fauna as well as flora. Stopping beneath the shade of a rock pile, to drain the last drop of water from my flask and to snatch a few moments of rest, I was just dozing off to sleep when a hissing sandsnake glided out of the rock pile and proceeded to wend his way across my stomach. Although the snake was only about ten inches long, I at once decided to find another resting place before the rest

[108]

of the snake family emerged from the rock pile to join their little brother as he swam about in the cold perspiration on my stomach.

Before crossing the dangerous desert country across Sinai to Petra, and then on to Palestine, it was necessary to obtain a special permit from the Port Inspector. As I arrived in Suez on Sunday, all offices were closed and I spent the day sight-seeing. I noticed from railway station and post office signs that there is no such place as "Suez" in Egypt—the proper name is "Suez Town." Nor is Suez a seaport—it is a mile down the causeway from Port Tewfik. When I cycled down for a dip in the sea, I was surprised at the beautiful blue color of its water, in spite of the fact that it is called the Red Sea.

That night I slept too soundly on the beach. The Red Sea put me in the "red" financially, and I really found that "there ain't no ten commandments there." At the American Express Company in Cairo it had been necessary to convert into cash $300.000 of the $600.00 I had with me in travelers' checks, as the Palestine border officials required such deposit from all residents of Germany. On this, the only night when I ever risked more than a few cash dollars on my person, I waked in the cold hours of darkness just before dawn. In reaching for an extra shirt in the knapsack under my head, I discovered that the knapsack had been neatly slit open from end to end. Tooth brush, diary, and maps lay scattered on the beach around my head and extra shirt and shorts were still intact, but my money-belt containing the $300.00 cash, travelers' checks, passport, and all other important documents had vanished!

Snow, wind, hail, rain, and sand storms had failed to stop Bucephalus; now a technicality had stopped him dead in his tracks. I had no passport and my Egyptian visa had expired; I was no longer lawfully within the country, yet without a passport I was not authorized to leave.

[109]

The spring rush season for Mecca was now in full swing and pilgrim ships were departing every day, amidst the loud wailing of the women, as their husbands sailed away.

After a week of fruitless searching by the native police-men, I realized that efforts to recover passport and money were futile. If there ever was a man without a country, it was I! Wherever I stopped with Bucephalus, I was imme-diately surrounded by scores of goggle-eyed natives, who touched my clothes and bicycle, and jabbered excitedly to each other that I was "the American searching for a million dollars which had been stolen from him." Living mainly upon imagination and without any hope of retrieving my lost valuables, I decided to return to the American consulate in Cairo, secure new passport and recovery of funds on my travelers' checks, and leave the country before losing my wits.

In dire distress financially, without one cent of money in my pocket, I made the mistake of trying to sell all unnecessary personal effects at public auction, to the highest bidder for cash. So far as I have been able to ascertain, public auctions are unheard of in Egypt; the Oriental prefers a lengthy battle of wits over the purchase or sale of an article, and the auction was too much for them. I first exposed for sale my highly prized University of Georgia silver-buckled belt. An enormous crowd gathered and continued to gather. Before I was able to go very far in receiving bids the crowd became too excited; the police came to the rescue and cleared a trail for me to cycle away from the surging mob and dart into safety in a small hat pressing shop. Here, the silver buckle caught the eye of a tall, bearded Egyptian and I quickly accepted his offer of two dollars. This was enough for railroad fare to Cairo, so I immediately dashed off to the railway station. I did not have the heart to make Bucephalus retrace his steps across the desert.

The gateway to the East had been abruptly closed to me,

almost at the point where Moses had led the children of Israel out of Egypt. The Red Sea had opened up for Moses' triumphant exit, but some distant descendant of old Pharaoh had unceremoniously stopped my flight. I hoped that I would not have to wander in the wilderness forty years before reaching the Promised Land!

I had intended crossing the desert back to Cairo on the fast Diesel-engined train, but I was misdirected into a stuffy old third-class pioneer train, which was going almost to Port Said before circling back to Cairo.

It was my first and last experience on a local Arab train. My third-class car was packed like sardines, as in Germany. However, this is the least of all troubles in Egyptian trains, whereas it is the only unpleasant feature of German ones. People are reasonably human and clean in Germany; too, all students and many economically minded business men travel third-class in Germany, each minding his own business, or joining whole-heartedly into song or conversation.

Arabs, on the other hand, are a prying, worrisome people. Not less than a dozen swarthy natives peered curiously over my shoulder as I sat on the hard wooden seat, writing in my diary while the train lumbered frantically across the desert.

Some of the Arabs were cleaning their long rifles; others smoked their water-pipes, putting the home-made coconut-shelled water containers in the train aisles. Not only was every seat well filled with five or six natives, some of whom squatted on their haunches in true Oriental fashion in the seats themselves, while others perched like monkeys on the backs of the seats, but even the pack-racks along both sides of the top of the car were filled with snoring followers of Mohammed. The already over-crowded train gradually increased its human cargo at each station along the road. I could hear the throb of the engine: "Cairo or bust—Cairo or bust—Cairo or bust."

However, I was soon to look back gratefully upon the human cargo on my train for giving me an insight into human nature that would enable me to go alone, yet in safety, through the wildest tribal regions on the globe. Only because of my own destitute position, was I enabled to learn what great reservoirs of kindness lay hidden in the hearts of even the poorest and hardest-featured—hard faces, because life had not used them well—of my companions.

When word was passed around that I was not really one of those brain-cracked millionaires, "roughing it" for the novelty, but was actually broke, like the rest of them, I was immediately showered with sincere sympathies and offers of material gifts from all. Poor little fruit vendors urged me to accept gifts of oranges, bananas and nuts. Even the timid, hooded Moslem women crept up and insisted that I accept a loan of their meager one-or-two piastre fortune. Everyone—especially the poorest and most wretched looking—was eager to share his only possessions.

I no longer saw the scars, sores and deformities of the diseased, poverty-stricken heaps of humanity; I saw only the gleam of kindness in their eyes, and felt the indelible impression in my heart of a redoubled faith in mankind.

Far out on the rim of the desert I would occasionally see caravans of camels floating over the horizon. Times, like people, rarely change in the Orient.

The engine breathed a long sigh of relief as the passengers scurried onto the station platform in Cairo.

CHAPTER XXI

Street Children of Colorful Cairo

While waiting for my new passport, I whiled away the time, ambling along the streets of the fashionable garden city of Gezireh Island in the middle of the Nile, or sauntering with Bucephalus through the slimy slums and Khan Kalili bazaars of old Cairo.

In street shops natives make polished glass beads by fitting glass on a rod which is rapidly revolved, by running a bow string across it (like playing a violin) with one hand, and applying a chisel to the rotating glass with another. It is uncanny what beautiful wood-carving natives do, by spinning wood on a revolving wheel, and with the same bow-string mechanism used in glass work, cutting all sorts of designs in the wood while it is in rotation.

There are many ivory shops where artisans, with the simplest of tools, busily saw, chip, and sandpaper pieces of rough ivory tusks into intricately designed boxes, figures of elephants and camel caravans. There are also brass, iron, gold, and silver craftsmen. Coppersmiths, too, make all sorts and sizes of vessels, from huge 25-gallon wine and olive oil jugs, to diminutive one-inch coffee sets.

Other shops look like the dens of necromancers, with their dozen or more wash-tub-size, earthenware bowls of vari-colored liquids half filled with sand, in which the big fat Arab soaks and scrapes his handful of metallic ornaments until they glisten like rays of the new day sun (like rubbing Aladdin's lamp).

There are also shops where all sorts of ivory-handled Sudanese knives, some crescent shaped, some crooked like a snake, with a hook at the end, may be purchased for only a few piastres. In one shop, I found the knife of a Belgian Congo tribesman. Near the hilt, the blade was flat; but the point of the knife was thick, sharp and corkscrew shaped, so that the wielder could easily pierce to the vitals of a victim's body and drag out his intestines when withdrawing the knife.

In the motley stands of the street market there were on exhibit, not whole fowls, but only the most popular Arab choices: gizzards, necks, and half developed eggs.

[113]

The only unpleasant feature of browsing through bazaars is the constant annoyance of shop-keepers, who assure you that you must buy their goods. One fellow was so persistent in trying to sell me a fountain pen, clinging to me for a half hour like a leech, that I gave him two piastres for his pen. The pen was no doubt a stolen one as he readily accepted my offer, though he had set three shillings as his price. Another fellow had me in his shop and clad in a night-shirt, turban and sandals before I had time to convince him that I needed only shorts for cycling. However, we compromised, and I proceeded to give him an order for a suit of clothes to make myself presentable at a dinner party at the American consul's home. But alas! I found it quite a job buying a tailor-made suit in Cairo, as one shop sells the cloth, another makes the buttons, a third makes the thread, a fourth the braid, a fifth the lining, and finally a tailor is found to put the pieces together. Needless to say, I went to the dinner party in my shorts, as it would have been two weeks before I even reached the tailor!)

As I renewed my journey down through the maze of carnival-like streets, another bicyclist was busily riding from shop to shop and lighting gas lamps by means of a combination blow torch and auto pump.

In little hole-in-the-wall salons, children were waving palm leaves over the heads of barbers and customers, to keep off flies while shaving. Outside the barber shop doors were large vases of water filled with green leeches, which are rented and universally used to bleed patients.

Dusky damsels sat on the sunken hearths of their homely dens and pulled bread and pies from huge ovens by means of flat fifteen-foot-long paddles.

With so many distractions, I almost ran unseeingly into a little ten or twelve-year-old child walking on legs only five or six inches in length. His legs had evidently been cut off above the knees one night as he slept in the gutter, in the pathway of a heavy vehicle, and the fat stubs of his legs now spread out like camel's feet as he walked, or, rather, dragged himself down the street. Many other legless people were running about on roller-skate platforms or else walking on their hands and dragging the rest of their bodies after them. An old blind man was leading another poor fellow whose diseased eyes had gone totally blind such a short time before that he had not yet learned to walk about in the dark like his companion.

On the curbstone nearby, sat a toothless old hag, with her naked baby balancing across her leg and letting nature take its course in the gutter. Farther down the filthy lane, a group of three and four-year-old children were huddling against the mud wall to snatch a little sleep on the cold sidewalk, before the chill of night should turn their pleasant dreams into nightmares. Their "bed"—the side-walk pavement—was naked and bare save for a few piles of manure, rotten vegetables, and tin cans. These were just a few of the hundreds of poor children neglected in infancy by their mothers, to go through life alone. In another corner, I saw an old wreck of a man, stark naked but for his long fuzzy beard and a rotten loin cloth. He was the living picture of what these children will be sixty or seventy years hence, unless somebody does something about these terrible conditions.

In writing of this subject, one could correctly name his book "Children of Cairo Streets," because they are born actually on the streets, live their miserably ignorant lives on the streets (nature is kind to them in that they never know a better life and accept their hard fate as a matter of course), and finally die on the streets. Everywhere through these older quarters of Cairo, these poor dregs of humanity lay in the gutter, stretched out across the side-walks, or crowded in window sills, doorways and dark corners.

[115]

The most pitiful sights were the broken bodied eleven- and twelve-year-old mothers begging for bread for their little babies clinging to their shoulders.

My sympathy did not go out to these poor people so much because of the physical discomforts of sleeping on bare rock—since I did the same thing so much in my travels that I knew one could harden oneself to such a point that the discomfort was negligible. The pathetic part was that these poor wretches knew nothing of a home or of the better things of life that we Americans, too often perhaps, take for granted.

My journey through old Cairo carried me out to the waterfront, past endless strings of houseboats, sailing vessels and river steamers, and I looked across the shadowy waters to see a crescent moon smiling down through the towering palms and turreted mosques silhouetted against the sky. Twilight was turning into starlight and moonlight. The heavily foliaged trees along both banks of the Nile were being rapidly transformed into solid masses of white, by the thousands of snowy egrets going to roost in their branches. No wonder so much has been told of Arabian nights; there are no more beautiful sunsets, dusky twilights, transparent starlit and moonlit nights, luminous dawns, and dazzling sunrises than those of the East.

In the reading room of the Anglo-Egyptian Y.M.C.A. I met the American Exchange Student to Rome. He, too, was on a holiday and wanted to see Cairo from the filthiest back alley dives, to the royal palace. He asked me to join him, and though I felt that there was nothing in the slimy slums of the city which I had failed to see, I soon learned that I was sadly mistaken.

After attending prayer meeting at the American Church, and the evening band concert in the park, we left the Y.M.C.A. at 10 p.m., bound on one of the most unusual adventures of our lives. An elderly English professor in

[116]

the Cairo University had agreed to act as guide. He led us up Sharia Ibrahim Pasha to Bab El Hadid Midan (Sharia means street and Midan means square), where we turned from the Great Central Railway Station down through collonaded Sharia Clot Bey. Turning into what at first seemed to be a blind alley, we suddenly found ourselves in the midst of the Wasa district of Red Light and underworld fame. I had seen St. Louis Street in New Orleans, strange sights in the slums of New York, London and Paris, but nothing was comparable with these horrible haunts of Old Cairo. The narrow, snaky lanes were crowded with prostitutes standing in long lines outside the doorways and grabbing at every male passing up the street. The greatest difficulty lay in breaking safely through the crowd of women at the entrance to these narrow streets; here were congregated those who wanted the first chance at men entering the district.

Fortunately, I did not look so promising in the suit of clothes my six-foot American companion had lent me for the occasion. My Bavarian outfit was impossible here, since it attracted too much attention. As it was, I managed to navigate through the crowded streets with comparative ease and safety; but my two companions were continually beset by swarms of girls, attempting to drag them by fair, foul and effective methods into the houses. Other females, reclining practically naked on couches just inside the doorways, beckoned and called to all passers-by.

At nearly every other house several natives were seated cross-legged on tables, and puffing away on snake charmer flutes. Men and women alternated with the snakes as dancers. Children of the streets wailed and cried pathetically as we passed them, but their cries turned at once into grunts of disgust and dissatisfaction as soon as we passed them up unnoticed. Old men and women seated in windows, or on steps of mosques, sang the Koran in a monotonous chanting manner. Nerve-wracking Egyptian

[117]

music screeched through radios and phonographs in shops along the streets.

This district is largely owned by the Coptic Church, so I was informed; and most of the resorts of ill-fame are licensed by the city.

While advancing down a dark alley of the Wasa district, we suddenly burst upon a different type of wailing, emitted from the throats of several dozen people sitting in gilded chairs in a well-lighted room lavishly decorated with tapestries and Persian rugs on ceiling, walls, and floors, in striking contrast to the dark, poverty-stricken appearance of all the rest of the neighborhood. A large oblong box in the center of the room was covered with golden embroidered cloths; gazing whimperingly into the box were a few small rag-a-muffin children and a score or more bedraggled women of the streets. In one corner of the room an iron kettle of soup was slowly boiling over a camel-dung fire.

I soon learned that this was a "sitting up" party, in honor of a deceased prostitute. Such parties last for three days and nights. Regardless of how rich or poor the relatives of the deceased may be, the gilded chairs, tapestries and other princely interior decorations are considered necessary features of such occasions. Therefore, these articles are rented from undertakers. Many funerals are held in tents, rented and pitched across the street in front of the house of the deceased; occasionally a large number of deaths entails serious traffic difficulties.

Constant reinforcement of friends and relatives who drop in for coffee, cigarettes and a few hours of mourning, make it possible for this moaning to be continuous.

Perhaps Isaac Watts had such people in mind when he wrote lines of philosophy that:

"Some of us creep into the world to eat and sleep
And know no reason why we are born
But only to consume the corn,
Devour the cattle, flesh and fish
And leave behind an empty dish.

If our tombstones when we die,
Be not taught to flatter and to lie,
There's nothing better can be said
Than he's 'et up all his bread,
Drunk up his drink, and gone to bed."

Pessimistically the old professor replied that the epitaph
of this poem could not apply to these people; he pointed to
a group of half-starved waifs huddled in the shadowy
street corner.

We had seen too much for one evening. It was three
o'clock in the morning when we returned to the Y.M.C.A,
a sane, sober and solemn trio.

CHAPTER XXII

Mother of the Pyramids

On my last day of cycling through Cairo, I was
pleasantly surprised when Vivian Crippe, a young Oxford
graduate "at large," rumbled up behind me in his rattle-
trap, topless "tin lizzie," christened "Jessica", and invited
both Bucephalus and me on an afternoon cruise up
through the shady banyan, locust, sycamore, and palm
groves on the eastern bank of the Nile, to the great
Massatan Heights near Heluan.

We spent all afternoon exploring the marvelous
Massarah quarries which extend for miles beneath these
great cliffs. It struck me as strange that these quarries had
been worked constantly for their limestone, sandstone and

[119]

alabaster for more than 5,000 years, and now workmen were still busily sawing limestone slabs in the snowy-white depths far below. They conveyed the stone to the railway terminus several miles away, by means of camel caravan, which reached the quarries through long, subterranean, beautifully arched tunnels. It was an unforgettable experience to follow a caravan of a hundred camels through one of these alabaster and limestone tunnels to the quarry where the Arabs were at work.

Climbing several miles over the top of the Heights, to the soft sinking sands covered with volcanic rock and lava formation, we beheld the Nile valley spreading out below us like a long strip of green only a few hundred yards in width. We descended Massatan Heights through a huge canyon penetrating like a wedge into the cliff. Along the high levels were the sandstone quarries, with limestone and alabaster farther down. For two hours we wandered through these old man-made caves from which the rocks of the Pyramids were cut. All sorts of designs and inscriptions of the ages past were carved upon the square or arched caverns. In many places smooth columns and colonnades were left in the sides of the walls, where the great blocks were cut, floated across the flooded Nile on huge rafts, and dragged on sleds to the Pyramid site.

Although we went hundreds of yards from the main entrance of one of the caves into branch caves extending in all directions, we seldom needed a flashlight, as light radiated through numerous shafts in the deep ceiling, illu-mined the interior with a soft yellow twilight color, which added much to the natural beauty of the smooth walls—the same walls that were hewn out by the slaves and workers of the old Pharaohs.

Night traveling in this part of Egypt is very dangerous, as the whole plain in front of these cliffs is hollowed out by the network of underground quarries which have been worked for ages. Scattered over the plains are hundreds of shafts, from three to thirty feet in diameter, extending a hundred or more feet downward. It is almost impossible to see these traps until within a few feet of them. I dropped rocks down some of the deeper ones to hear them strike the bottom a few seconds later, sending melancholy echoes ringing through the endless network of caverns. However, I almost threw one stone too many. Just in the act of dropping my last stone, I heard rumbling, sawing noises and perceived a man with a torch in the depths at the end of the deep hole down which I was about to toss my "sounding stone."

Strange, that these ancient and exquisite caverns are almost completely unknown to tourists. Not only do they have a history more ancient than that of the Pyramids, but they are also far more interesting. As evening shadows were creeping across the plains, we decided to depart from the fascinating chasms before falling into one of the pits.

It was a fitting close to my six weeks' sojourn in Egypt that I was destined to leave this land of the old Pharaohs on Easter morning. While impatiently waiting for a new passport I had bicycled several hundred miles through the streets of Cairo and vicinity.

Cycling through the cool, picturesque bazaar streets, ablaze with colorful commerce, and protected from the hot noonday sun by overhanging roofs, was an experience smacking of real adventure. At night, as I went gliding down the narrow lanes, every shop presented a real pageant of life. Truly memorable were the many hours of cycling at random, emerging at every corner from beneath the shadowy, overhanging, upper stories of houses, to catch a view of towering minarets and domes silhouetted against the transparent, dark blue, midnight sky, with the full moon peeping up from behind one of these graceful, ethereal spires. Cairo is beautiful in the daytime with its cosmopolitan color, but it's a hundred times more beautiful at night when the moon peeps over the dome between the minarets of the citadel.

The loss of my old passport had meant more than the loss of an unusual collection of visas; it meant the parting of the ways for me. My plans to return to Cologne in time for the second semester of school were blasted, and I now, for the first time, decided to make my trip Around the World on a Bicycle, instead of merely around the Mediterranean.

END OF PART TWO

gyptian dignitaries

Who would have believed a maiden in purdah would have been so flirtatious

Schoolchildren of Cairo

With V. Cripper, and "Jessica" of the Massatan Heights

I cycled out to my
"headquarters" on top
of Cheops Pyramid
(in background)

I met Spiro
on the Acropolis

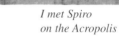

Alabaster Sphir

I sang "Auld Lang Syne"
with this laddie guarding
the Citadel Gate

Heliopolis
Mosque

Cairo craftsman
– his brains are
his feet

Water pipe puffers

"Only to say this, and this is the chiefest thing:
Never let your dream be taken from you."

Donn Byrne
Messer Marco Polo

PART THREE

CHAPTER XXIII

Sunrise on Sinai

All the bakers of Cairo had piled their shop-windows with huge doughnut-shaped loaves of bread, dotted and designed with layers of gaily colored Easter eggs, shells and all. On Easter morning, with several of these strangely decorated cakes in my knapsack,. I set out on the long trail to Jerusalem via Petra, the mysterious rose-red city of rock in the Arabian Desert.

Life was a path of roses (without the buds) when my rear tire was punctured in a half-dozen places by large rose-bush thorns, even before I reached Cairo city limits. Except for this little delay at the start, the Winds of Fate were with me as I "breezed" out to Suez, singing "I am bound for the Promised Land."

Everything was closed at the scene of my earlier disasters, as I rushed down to Koubri to cross the Suez Canal and strike out across the Sinai wilderness where Moses and the children of Israel had wandered for forty long years before reaching the Promised Land. Powerful winds swept Bucephalus down the canal highway with such force that he needed no encouragement from me.

At Koubri, I bargained for a dozen limes. Like all Egyptians, the native vendor enjoyed the bargaining as a game of wits, to see how much or how little I should pay. Though insisting that I pay twenty piastres for the limes, he finally agreed that one piastre was more than a fair price for them! The sliding scale of prices has always been in vogue in the East.

[126]

With the aid of my International Identity card and other important documents, I bluffed the subordinate officer in charge of the canal to let me cross into Sinai, even without making the usual sixty-pound deposit. Had it been any other day than Easter Sunday, when all the chief border officials were on a holiday, I would have never obtained permission to take the trip.

Equipped with compass, black goggles, tropical cork helmet, water canteen, limejuice canteen, sleeping bag, and a gallon of almonds and raisins packed away in the saddle bag around Bucephalus' back, I was ready to plunge into the unknown. In fact, I felt as safe with my few dollars' worth of trappings as if I had purchased the usual elaborate outfittings for such a dangerous dash. An air mattress, more varied assortment of foods, clothing, and other accoutrements would have added to my ease and comfort, but these were luxuries. I had yet to see an American tourist who did not almost ruin his trip by overloading himself with unnecessary baggage.

Of course, when traveling in a rather thickly populated country, I could indulge in a few luxuries. But when undertaking a serious journey such as this, across the absolutely desolate wilderness of Sinai, where life depended upon my physical endurance and the ability of Bucephalus' balloon tires to stand up under my weight—which was really enough without added encumbrances—I was determined that my equipment be reduced to the barest necessities.

Without the sun helmet, my brains would have literally fried in the fiery heat waves of the desert; without the black-lensed goggles and their close-fitting rubber rims, my eyes would have been blinded by the first sandstorm or by the first day of brilliant sunlight; without sufficient quantities of food and drink in a dry desert—well, the result would have been all too obvious.

Fortunately, one of my canteens was of the finest French

Foreign Legion pattern, of heavy pewter, and capable of holding a half-gallon of water. I considered myself lucky when I found this useful flask in a junk shop of old Cairo. The other, not quite a quart-volumed aluminum canteen, was Hitler's regulation army flask, which every German soldier is required to wear on his belt, and which had already served me well in my travels through Europe. It was quite a versatile old can, having pleased my palate the previous summer with Norwegian goats' milk, Italian wine, English ale, and Bavarian "Dunkel Bier." The past winter it had gone even so far as to produce ice cream to tickle my epicurean taste as I cycled over the icy Alps. And now, after carrying me contentedly up and down the Nile on its contents of olive oil, it was sending me out into the wilderness with trustworthy assurance that its luscious litre of limejuice would keep the old "power-house" from perishing.

Over Sinai, the air was yellow with flying sand. Although it was only 1 P.M., the dazzling daylight had faded to twilight. A terrific gale was threatening to dash the ferry boat to pieces against the bank so that the ferry-men would never have consented to take me across the frenzied canal stream but for the timely arrival of a water truck answering an SOS from perishing nomads stranded on the opposite shore, on the edge of the desert.

The only car crossing the desert that day was a specially constructed Ford bearing the family of the Secretary at the American consulate in Cairo. They all looked dazed, as if just awakening from a horrible dream. They had been waiting three hours for the ferry to cross over and take them off the Sinai Peninsula. For four days they had motored across the wilderness before reaching the canal and civilization. They seemed on the verge of nervous collapse as they told of their breakdowns, mirings in the sands of the desert, and other harrowing experiences. The secretary begged me not to start out in the blinding sandstorm, as I would surely get lost and end up as food for starving wolves.

At the canal patrol office I signed my death-warrant intention of cycling across the desert, ducked my head, and plowed forth with the last words of the secretary's warning ringing in my ears: "It's already the worst storm in three years and still brewing stronger."

My efforts to sing were short-lived. I could hear nothing but the singing of the sand as it roared like ocean waves across the desert, and every time I opened my mouth I was choked with the tiny stinging particles. My ears and eyes also were soon filled. At last I could truly appreciate the usefulness of the great sheets of cloth with which all Bedouins enshrouded their heads. Frantically, I tore rags from my shirt and stuffed them in my ears before the driving sand had time to burst the ear drums.

Every few kilometers I had to stop and clean the driving sand from the axles of my wheels. Several times I was forced to stop suddenly and carry the cycle on my shoulder through deep sand dunes freshly piled across the hard-surfaced trail. They were almost identical experiences to those among the snow-blocked alpine passes, which I had surmounted the dead of the previous winter! In fact, the sand whistled across the desert with the same stinging, blinding effect as that produced by the snowstorm I had encountered while on the ski trip to Neuschwanstein Dream Castle in the Bavarian Alps.

In spite of obstacles, numerous stops, and poor visibility (farther than ten feet in every direction was yellow nothingness), I made record-breaking speed riding on the wings of the gale, which swept me across the desert at a thrilling, terrific pace.

By nightfall, I succeeded in scaling Mitla Pass near Nekal on the great gravel plain high above sea level. Here I spent the night at the last outpost, a camp of workers who were beginning to build a real road across the desert

[129]

to Palestine, thus forming one of the last links in the chain of paved roads completely encircling the Mediterranean.

After riding with the storm all day, I enjoyed the evening as guest of the Italian roadmaker and his family consisting of wife, two children, a chicken, and a dog. The night was freezing cold, and the howling wind continued to pile sand inside the tents and cover the beds and tables beneath thick layers of the fine particles. Although our vegetable-spiked egg omelets were also filled with sand, we all seemed happy and glad to be alive. Our hostess was short of bread, but I remedied the situation by producing the last two loaves from my knapsacks. In less time than it takes to tell it, we had filled our stomachs with the Easter cakes and our "gizzards" with sand.

Before going to bed, my host proudly exhibited several of his latest trophies picked up around the camp. He showed two huge snakes, one of which he had killed three days before, and the other which had just been killed when it entered the tent in search of its mate. I was also interested to learn that the little desert scorpions which he had pickled in olive oil were deadly poisonous. Several times during the past few days, I had sat nonchalantly beside these little crawfish-looking creepers, thinking them to be perfectly harmless. My host assured me that the only way to save one from immediate death after bite of such a scorpion, is to brand the wound with a hot piece of metal and soak the wound for several hours in the pickled scorpion juice. He was surprised that I carried no weapons. Having no weapons of his own to spare, he gave me the next best thing, a box of matches, and warned me to buy a gun and never sleep in the open without my campfire blazing all night; otherwise, wolves would attack me.

Pointing to a large wolf-hide stretched as a coverlet on his bed, my friend calmly told me of a Bedouin killed by the wolf earlier in the spring as he slept on the edge of the encampment. The cries of the victim had immediately aroused the entire group of road workers; but before they could kill the wolf with their long knives, the poor Bedouin was dead, his neck eaten almost completely in two. My host was about to give me some friendly tips on how to deal with lions in the wilds of Trans-Jordan and Palestine, when I informed him that I could sleep just as well if he deferred the story-telling until morning. He consoled me by stating that I probably need not worry at all about lions of Trans-Jordan, as the wolves would surely put the finishing touches to me before I got that far. He certainly was a comforting fellow.

Next morning I was underway at dawn, with a basket of pretty colored Easter eggs hanging from my bicycle handlebars, and a bottle of olive oil added to my diminishing supply of lime juice. The children had refused to turn me loose without first accepting their Easter eggs, and the parents were equally persistent as to the oil.

For several kilometers, the trail was quite passable with its foundation of chicken wire covered with gravel, but it soon became so rough that I found cycling to be better in the open plain alongside the road.

The entire desert was covered with beautifully colored, queer-shaped stones. In Cairo, I had met a young Egyptian whose hobby was collecting stones of all shapes and varieties. How he would revel in the little ship, animal, human and other figured stone moulded here on Sinai by Mother Nature's own hand!

Sinai presents a perfect picture of erosion. The hills here are masses of crumbled rock, predominately yellow, which look as if they might be blown away by one strong puff of wind. So crumbled and sliced away by the hand of Time are the hillsides, that all the various strata of earth and rock stand out in bold relief, most of the strata running parallel with the general contours of the earth's surface, but many shooting up in vertical ridges. Many hilltops are

[131]

splashed with limestone resembling whitewash. Others are capped with beautiful black and purple agate stone, as though drenched with ink.

Espying caves on one mountain top, I climbed up to discover that they, too, were examples of Time's erosive powers. The limestone inside the mountain peak had crumbled away, leaving paper-thin sun-baked walls on the outside of these natural caverns. A few tons of pressure upon this hollow mountain-top and it would crush like an eggshell. There were many tracks and other convincing evidence that wild beasts used these caves as dens, but what held my speculative attention most, was a smooth, cement-like cannon ball perfectly fashioned and imbedded in the limestone sides of the cave, as if placed there by human hands—could this perfect sphere contain a letter written by Abraham or Moses?

From my commanding hilltop, I gazed across the great gravel plain dotted sporadically with strange little flat pieces of table-land. In the middle of one of these tiny plateaus, far up the trail, I saw a Bedouin caravan camp hidden behind a brush fence, hastily erected to keep sand-storms from engulfing the goat-hair tents.

Ten minutes later, I was seated inside the main tent, in the family circle, around a large "wash pan" containing the juicy pulp of uncooked mashed tomatoes. In this common bowl, we dipped our freshly cooked bread and ate with the gusto of those enjoying their last meal. Outside the tent a small child was giving a camel's legs an olive oil rubdown. I could hardly believe my eyes when I noticed that a real bicycle was strapped to the side of one camel. My hospitable host reassured me by saying that the bicycle was a sort of spare tire in case one of the camels sickened and died. On his journey across Ettih desert to Beersheba two of his camels had died and the poor fellow had been compelled to walk for three days without food and water. At Beersheba, while recovering from his narrow escape and preparing for a return journey to south-western Sinai, he took a fancy to the British-built bicycles in the city and purchased one from a local owner in exchange for a camel.

As my Bedouin host heartily agreed that the bicycle was the most reliable of all vehicles and capable of going anywhere that the rider was willing to take it, we parted like two old friends who had much in common.

Heat waves rippling across the desert gave the effect of rolling billows of an ocean. The bracing "sea breeze" was still sweeping me across the desert in much faster fashion than Moses traveled. Little wonder that Moses followed a "pillar of cloud" by day. It seems that winds constantly blow across the peninsula toward Palestine. Thus, clouds are a good natural compass to the traveler headed from Egypt toward the Promised Land. The "pillar of fire" which Moses followed by night must have been a brilliant planet like Jupiter or Venus, which actually resemble blazing balls of fire down here on the desert horizon.

All day the unearthly beauty of Sinai's weird painted desert of all colors and textures had inspired me to sing "Valley of the Moon." Under the purple cloak of a real Arabian night, it was even more like a strange, far-away planet. As I lay in the heart of the desert plain, listening to the wind rustling through the pure, crystal clear night, and watching the great orbs of stars and planets twinkling in the midnight blue of the sky, I felt at peace with God and the universe.

I thanked my lucky star that I had been unable to sleep when, several minutes later, a large black form glided motionless across the top of a sand dune in the direction of the rugged mountain range lying only a kilometer north of my trail. For several minutes I lay watching the form as it stood statue-like on the sand pile, the clear-cut contours of its body plainly discernible against the horizon.

So great was my relief when the figure suddenly melted

[133]

away behind the sand dune that I was about to drop contentedly to sleep, when a half-dozen or more similar figures emerged from the gully to the south of the sand dune and crept stealthily in my direction. They were desert wolves. Although I stopped their advance with a shower of rocks, they held their ground even when struck. Hunger seemed to have deadened all other senses, including their sense of fear.

When a stone struck one of the foremost brutes in the forehead, he did not utter a sound, but merely changed his tactics from a direct attack to circling round and round my sleeping bag. Such procedure would not have bothered me so much had I been able to rest. Yet, every time I settled into a comfortable position for a few moments' rest, one or more from the encircling pack broke ranks and started toward me, evidently thinking I had fallen asleep. The entire night was a restless one spent in shooing off my affectionate pets, which kept stalking around like ghosts, with the savage joy and anticipation of Indians doing the war dance for the benefit of early Colonists tied to the stake. About 3 o'clock the wolves grew tired of their vigil and vanished.

Several times during the night I had attempted to ride away from my adversaries; they opened a pathway before my headlight, but closed in from the rear, nipping at the hind legs of poor old Bucephalus, so that we had to stop and defend ourselves from that quarter with rocks. Now that my erstwhile close friends had evidently lost their nerve and were retreating to the hills, I saw no reason why I should try to entice them to return. With the half moon still hanging brightly over the western horizon, I was astride Bucephalus and well along the narrow caravan trail to Petra before sunrise.

CHAPTER XXIV

Petra to Palestine

Though I could have easily reached the mysterious city of rock by nightfall, my fourth night of cycling east of Suez was spent in the desolate little plain on the Akaba road, just south of Petra. I did not relish the idea of sleeping in Petra with the tombs of the dead staring down at me from all sides. It was much more fun browsing through Petra in the bright morning sun than in twilight shadows.

Because of its inaccessibility, its colorful setting in a painted desert, the beauty of its rock-hewn tombs more exquisite and awe-inspiring than the innermost of the old Pyramid quarries, and the secretive character of the Arab race of Nabataeans, who made it the fabulously rich capital of a prosperous trading empire, Petra, the rose-red city of mystery, has a fascination which no traveler ever forgets, once he lays eyes upon it.

For centuries a mysterious race of robbers held the narrow Musa River gorge (so called because the Arabs believe it was made by the rod of Moses) through the City of Rock as the only pass by which the perfume, pearls, spice, silver, silk, and gold laden caravans from the Orient could cross the impregnable mountain barriers into Palestine and Egypt.

Down to a depth of twelve hundred feet the winding gorge sinks and narrows to a width of only five feet. Little wonder that the City of Rock let no caravan through unnoticed, or let armies enter unwanted. Little wonder that the City of Rock took toll of all commerce between the Mediterranean and Indian Ocean, and, unmolested, drowned itself in wealth, while on all sides great civilizations rose and crumbled. With its perfect natural fortifications, the City of Rock could defend itself with

[135]

only a handful of men.

So powerful did these Nabataean inhabitants become in the course of time that they were able to help the great Augustus Caesar against Mark Antony and Cleopatra, by wiping out the entire Red Sea fleet of Egypt. It was not until 106 A.D. that Petra finally lost its power and became a Roman province under Emperor Trajan. Later it was a stronghold for Arab thieves and murderers.

Though today this once-proud city of a glorious past is stripped of material wealth, a hollow shell of splendor still exists in its magnificent temples and tombs cut in the solid-rock mountain sides. Today the traveler may climb the rock-hewn stairway to the blood basin and altar, but he will no longer find the Nabataeans here offering human sacrifice to the glory of Duchara, chief of their race, who, in Egyptian fashion, took to wife his own sister.

The exquisitely sculptured temple of Isis still graces the living rock wall facing the exit of the city, but no longer does a priest stand here to receive the thanks of a safely returned traveler or his prayer for protection as he sets out again for the desert. At the foot of the Great Place of Sacrifice, the thirty-three tiers of sandstone seats of the Greco-Roman open air theatre may still be seen; but there are no actors upon the stage, nor spectators in the seats.

Only in the hundreds of tombs, carved in close tiers on the iridescent mountain flanks, is the scene today just as it was in the days of Petra's glory. Where these hill-folk lived, they have been buried. Like the ancient Arabs, they believed that one of the several souls of a mortal would remain as a guardian spirit by his well-preserved corpse. As it would revenge wrongs done to its body, it was presumed to have sufficient tribal feeling left to help in guarding the store place for tribal plunder. This, the shadowy arm of the dead was supposed to have done in the first Macedonian and Roman invasions; and encouraged by such achievements of their forebears, the

Rockmen settled permanently under their protection, and very cheerfully lived with the spirits of their dead. Working, playing, fighting, and trading, the Rockmen liked the protecting, inspiring company of the souls of fellow tribesmen.

The palatial tombs of kings, the magnificent mansion tombs of rich merchants and even the working folks' small, plain-faced tomb-caves, modelled on the style of their small, square cottages, all stand out today as among the greatest wonders of antiquity.

Nevertheless, one morning of lonely wandering among the spirit altars of these tombs was enough. Bent upon bicycling far from this city of the dead before nightfall, I left the Wady Moressa ("Valley of Moses"—local name for the place), cycled past Jebel Haroun (Aaron's Mountain—the Mount Hor of the Bible, where Aaron was buried on the journey from Kadesh), and struck out across the dangerous and desolate Wadi El Araba on my rugged trail to El Kossaima. It would have been much easier to follow the Trans-Jordan route up to Jerusalem, but Bucephalus seemed to prefer unbeaten paths and new trails.

From a historical point of view, the Trans-Jordan route would have carried me through much less interesting country; and even if I should lose the trail to Kossaima, only a hundred miles away, following my compass in a general northwesterly direction, I was bound to run across the great caravan route, or the old Turkish railroad stretching from Suez to Beersheba. By keeping direct to my course I would strike the trail near Kossaima around sunset.

However, I had not anticipated a three-hour delay in repairing tires studded with desert brambles and thorns. It was almost midnight before I crossed the purple depression of the Jordan and struck the well-beaten trail which led unmistakably to Beersheba. Tired but content, I

[137]

pushed to the peak of a perfect cone-shaped mountain of pure white limestone shooting its symmetric majesty above the little broken plateaus beneath the higher mountain ranges. Here I spent the remainder of the night, unaware and unconcerned as to what dawn should bring.

Imagine my embarrassment upon awakening next morning to find that I had slept in a graveyard after all!

Encircling the mountainside below me were hundreds of graves, covered with clothes and other personal effects of the deceased Bedouins buried here. Less than ten feet from my sleeping bag, on the top of the mountain, was a small rectangular tomb with plainly visible figures of tea pots and other utensils carved on the solid rock front of the tomb. These symbols I later learned were indicative of the gracious hospitality of the deceased, who was always known to entertain royally his guests.

Sitting nonchalantly in the broiling morning sun, at the base of the mountain graveyard, just as if it were a cool shady day, a group of Bedouin women and children were busily baking bread on a thin copper sheet placed over a camel-dung fire. Surrounded by their chickens, turkeys, dog, goat, and water jugs, they seemed perfectly at home here in the middle of the desert. I tried to take a picture of one of the little jewel-bedecked girls, who had offered to fill my canteen with the cool, fresh water of her earthenware jugs; but each time I started to click the camera she and the other women covered their faces and shoulders, so that the exquisitely designed necklaces and headdresses of gold and silver medallions were concealed behind masses of black cloth.

Before I had pedaled a dozen feet, one of the little girls came running towards us, one hand still carefully covering her face with a shawl, but the other holding out at arms' length what looked like a giant cone of ice cream, but which turned out to be a huge pancake rolled up into a funnel—cornucopia-fashion—filled with pounded almonds, spliced dates and raisins, and a cup of camel clabber.

Arabian artistic taste was manifest along the trail by all sorts of geometric designs of stars, wheels, flowers and other carved figures, outlined with rocks or merely drawn in the sand. I had little time to look at these oddities of the wayside landscape, as my attention was almost wholly taken up with flies which clung so stubbornly to my legs and arms that I had to pick them off with my hands. The heat was also so unbearable that I nearly melted away before reaching the little oasis of Kossaima. There I stretched out on the icy stone slabs of the custom house beneath the shade of the first little cluster of trees I had seen since leaving Suez.

Several kilometers farther up the trail at Auja Hafir, I officially passed into Palestine. Unthinkingly, I insulted the border police by asking them to pose with a group of Bedouins. The latter were clad in brilliantly colored robes, girdled with large, colored leather belts which were decorated with metal designs; their long chased daggers gave them the finishing touches of real "moving picture" sheiks.

While waiting for the border officials to examine my passport, I made the acquaintance of members of the Colt Archaeological Expedition who, for the past four months, had been excavating an old Roman Byzantine citadel built in 400 A.D. on the little mountain overlooking the modern village.

One of the English members of the party told a detailed account of some of the obstacles which had to be over-come. While he was digging on the citadel, a cloudburst suddenly dropped from the sky to transform the dry gully at the base of the hill into a raging torrent, marooning him for three days before the flood subsided and he could cross over to the camp. No wonder I had marvelled at the washed out appearance of the peninsula! Yet, in spite of

[139]

heavy rains, it was still a desert country devoid of vegetation. I could truly appreciate the frequent Biblical reference to the wilderness, since the people in those days must have known little country that was not wilderness.

Climbing up the great wall encircling the crown of the citadel hill, I went on a self-conducted exploration tour through the two old Roman churches and about forty rooms of other houses which Mr. Colt had already unearthed. My hour trip through this old city of the buried past was one of the most interesting and enlightening of my experiences.

It was not like viewing the empty insides of the Pyramids or other such places where the contents have already been removed to museums. Here at Auja Hafir, nothing had been removed from its natural setting, as excavations were really just beginning. When I raised the marble slabs beside the beautiful, flower-designed altar screens of the old arch-windowed, Corinthian-pillared churches, grinning skeletons saw the light of day for the first time since 400 A.D. I also discovered scores of such human skeletons inside rock-hewn vaults in the floors of these churches. In rooms of other buildings were jugs and vases of glass and earthenware material, charcoal, wooden stools, and many household implements unknown to me.

By far the most beautiful feature of the city was the great rectangular courtyard spread out on top of the mountain, its mosaic floor in vari-colored metals and stones of all types, sizes, shapes and designs. Larger disks of red marble, triangular and square and rectangular-shaped pieces of white, yellow and black marble, were placed artistically to form a smooth polished floor.

I was scurrying over the top of the citadel with the fervour of a real discoverer when the mountain caved in beneath my feet and left me clinging for dear life to a marble slab, while my feet dangled helplessly in space. Pulling myself upon this slab, I looked down to see that I

[140]

had unintentionally and unknowingly discovered the citadel well! As I peered down the chasm, I heard the dislodged surface stones rumbling against the sides of the well and finally, with a sickening thud, striking the muddy pit several hundred feet below.

My delight and desire of discovery and exploration had fallen irretrievably into the well, and I was glad to leave them there and cycle up the sunset trail to Beersheba. Though almost ugly beneath dazzling noonday sun, the shadowy eroded gullies scarring the distant rolling hills of purple and gold seemed to add a touch of beauty to the twilight landscape spreading out on both sides of the broad plain.

As the sun sank out of sight over the western horizon, my trail suddenly dipped from the beautiful plain into a sinister red gulch, and finally emerged at the bank of the river before Beersheba.

Local custom-house officials had seen my bicycle headlight in the distance; they had run down to the river and were wading across the shallow water to help me carry Bucephalus into town. They all breathed sighs of relief when I was identified as the strange young American whose solo cycling across Sinai had caused so much excitement up and down all the wireless stations along the route. For centuries, native nomads had crossed the desert on camels. Of late, tourists had made the trip, crossing by airplane, or even by desert lorries, but to make the trip, alone, and on a bicycle, was unheard of.

A week beneath the beautiful, cold, clear, starlit sky of the lonely desert had cast its fascinating spell upon me, just as it had done to shepherds of old, who studied the stars as they watched their flocks by night. Declining the royally extended invitations to rest in Beersheba's best beds, I climbed to a quiet hilltop above the medley of noises in the city below, placed my sleeping bag on the windswept heights beside an old mud-walled camel enclosure, and drifted off to dreamland.

[141]

Passport entry:
"Last seen at Suez"

Bucephalus marks spot wh
wolves waged war

A wanderer
in the wilderness
(Note one of
"Ten Commandments"
I found here
near Mount Sinai)

Bucephalus saunters
down the oldest street
in the world

"Bull" session after
Arab wedding

Garden of
Gethsemane

A certain man
went down from
Jerusalem – on the
Jericho road

One of "1001"
Arabian knights

CHAPTER XXV

Marching to Zion

Before bicycling up to Jerusalem from Beersheba, I took
a short sight-seeing trip through the one main street and
down the half-dozen alleys projecting from its sides.
Today this oldest living city is exactly as I would picture it
in Bible times when Abraham spent his last days here and
Jacob made it his home for the first sixty years of his life.
The little mud and rock buildings are the same style as
those built centuries ago.

After all these years, Beersheba is still only a small
town. Colorfully-robed and knife-bedecked Bedouins sit
in circles on the sidewalks in front of fruit, vegetable, and
bazaar shops. The streets are crowded with men, women,
boys, and girls riding camels or little donkeys, which are
still the chief means of native transportation. In the
Moslem fashion, the women conceal their faces behind
thin black shawls. Many of them, especially those fresh
from the desert, wear great pendants of coins hanging
from the forehead over the whole face.

While I was drinking water at Abraham's old wells,
which still furnish the water supply of Beersheba, a young
Bedouin offered to take my cycle up to the custom house
and have the tires tested at the air pressure pump. When
the lad did not return within the hour, I ran to the custom
house and found him writhing in pain on the porch of the
building. Instead of pushing my heavily packed bicycle,
he had tried to ride. The result was that he fell, broke his
own ankle, and slightly bruised the sturdy old vehicle
which had just carried me safely through the wilderness. It
was the first and last time that I trusted my steed to the
care of another.

The trip up to Jerusalem was one of the most memorable
milestones of my life. Having been warned that Palestine

was an ugly, barren, rocky country, I had already painted a picture of desolation and ugliness in my mind's eye, so that I would not be disappointed.

However, all pre-conceived notions faded before the beautiful reality. I started out from Beersheba across a great rolling "Shenandoah" valley of billowy oceans of green grain and red and white clover, dotted everywhere with all kinds and colors of wild flowers: crimson poppies, purple and red hollyhocks, fragrant honeysuckle, morning glories, daisies, thorned dandelions, lilies, wild lilacs (the sweetest perfumed of all), phlox, and forget-me-nots of the same deep shade of blue as the clear Canaan sky above. There were at least a dozen other types of red, yellow, and purple flowers which I could not identify.

It was the quintessence of a spring day. Great flocks of field larks, smaller in size, but sweeter in song, than our U.S. lark, filled the air with melodious music. I drank in also the rich beauty of both color and song of the numerous pigeon-sized, brown-winged birds, whose blue bodies glistened like the radiant light pouring through a transparent blue crystal.

So numerous were the flocks of sheep that many were often unavoidably mingled. It was entrancing to hear one shepherd give his sheep call and watch his stray sheep lift their heads from a foreign flock and then run bleating and baaing back to their master. The shepherd on the opposite hillside would then give voice to his own peculiar call and whatever of his sheep had wandered into his neighbor's flock, would immediately respond by raising their heads and running in the direction of their master's voice.

In front of the caterpillar-like brown and black goat-hair tents, scattered across the green plains or crouched cosily at the heads of the valleys, women were busily shearing sheep and goats, or weaving their new spring costumes.

In the fields, colorfully robed peasants were industriously plowing with pairs or combinations of

[145]

camels, donkeys, and oxen. All the plowshares were roughly hewn, crooked, home-made wooden ones. Attached to each of these one-handled plows, I noticed little cone-shaped goat skin sieves through which the peasants poured and planted the grain directly behind the freshly made furrows of the ploughshares. This same crude method was perhaps employed satisfactorily by Jacob when he tilled this same soil as a boy.

Silhouetted against the clear blue skyline, shepherds with long crooked staffs led their herds of goats and sheep across the hilltops. Great herds of camels also grazed loose with their newborn babies in the mountain-side pastures like herds of cows and calves on a Georgia dairy farm.

As I cycled up through this gorgeous morning pageantry on the road to Bethlehem and Jerusalem, I thought of another fine morning several years before when Father and I were riding from home in Athens, Georgia, to the Blue Ridge Mountains, and singing lustily as the sun rose over the Oconee, the old hymn: "We're Marching to Zion."

After emerging from the wilderness of Sinai, a veritable valley of death with only the soft, funereal dirges of the desert birds to break the silence, this interesting parade of life along the Jerusalem road was dazzling. On that early April morn, as I looked across the purple mountains fading into the hazy horizon, and breathed in the air perfumed with blossoms of flowers, oranges, pears, cherries, and olives, and vibrating with the buzz of a million bees, I knew that I was in one of the garden spots of the world, where life was vivid, and beauty rampant.

Several kilometers before reaching the little sun-baked village of Dahrieh, the road left the broad plains, wound up narrow, green gorges and over rolling mountain ranges into other little valleys rich with grape, grain, olive, orange, and fig. At Dahrieh, I stopped to rest, and eat a grapefruit-sized Jaffa orange, with shepherds under the cool shadows of a beautifully arched, bridge-like flight of steps leading up to the city mosque.

At Hebron, where Abraham and Lot made their division of land, I ate my lunch of figs, cheese and bread dipped in olive oil. In hot countries olive oil serves as an excellent substitute for butter. As I watched the motley crowd of people amble past, I noticed that many old men and young girls were carrying water and wine in hog-hide bags neatly sewed up at the leg and neck ends.

Being a rather large village, Hebron possessed a slightly more cosmopolitan atmosphere than Beersheba. It was a strange spectacle to see German Jews of our modern civilization mingling with peasants whose development was still in the past ages. Although peasant and old town life in Palestine seemed to be, generally, in the same state as in the time of Christ, I occasionally saw shocking and disappointing indicia of the march of Time: peasants balanced empty gasoline tins instead of traditional old earthenware jugs on their heads as they walked to wells for water!

On the outskirts of Bethlehem, I was attracted by a large gathering of Arab peasants in front of a nearby mud-roofed, rock-walled house. A fat woman sat on the doorstep and hammered out a tom-tom beat upon a huge drum, while all the other women clapped their hands and sang as they encircled a young maiden who seemed so weighted down with metal coins and other trappings that she could hardly stand. Upon cycling up to the group of men, I was told that a wedding had just taken place and that I was welcome to remain for the wedding feast which was to be given that night, as soon as the women finished the traditional all-day singing.

I would have tarried, but the beautiful spires and bell towers of Bethlehem's mosques and churches peeping over the hill just a half-mile away, called Bucephalus on.

[147]

Near the entrance to the little town of Bethlehem, I stopped to wander among the long, arched colonnades of the inner court of a French convent, where the air was filled with the odor of orange blossoms and lilacs, and the sound of music as white-hooded nuns sang hymns in the little chapel beside the courtyard.

In Bethlehem, the old narrow cobblestone lanes winding up and down the hillsides beneath beautifully arched, cavernous stone doorways recalled to mind the streets which wound so picturesquely beneath the houses on the Isle of Capri.

Descending the long flight of steps down to the market square, I crossed over to the Church of the Nativity, built in 326 A.D. over the supposed spot where Christ was born. Entering this old church through a tiny, cave-like stone door, I emerged into a beautiful room with red, green, silver, and golden Christmas crystals hanging to the candelabra and a mosaic floor, partially revealed beneath a few uncovered blocks of stone flooring.

From the belfry of the Church of the Nativity, the Dead Sea and the great purple desolate depression of the Jordan valley spread out in a magnificent panorama to the east while the walls of Jerusalem glistened in the golden sun-light to the north. Though nine kilometers by road from Jerusalem, Bethlehem is almost a suburb; only three miles of rolling hills, of waving grain, and groves of olive and fig separate it from the city limits of Jerusalem.

During my first few days in Jerusalem, I lived in the million dollar Y.M.C.A building opposite the King David Hotel. My magnificent residence, built with the money of an American philanthropist, is the most beautiful structure of its kind in the world. With its long, arched corridors of vari-colored marble, fireplaces and mantles of purest white alabaster, mosaic ceilings studded with lapis lazuli and trimmed with gold leaf, this veritable palace deserves its imposing position on the topmost hill of the Holy City.

[148]

From the lofty observation tower of this edifice, which stands 3,782 feet above sea level, I looked eastward down the twenty-five-mile trail to Jericho and the Dead Sea, 1,200 feet below sea level, toward the lavender-colored mountains of Moab rising majestically in distant Trans-Jordan. Far up to the north wound the serpentine road to Sechem (Nablus). Immediately beneath my tower lay Jerusalem, like a strangely overgrown village with a few majestic domes and spires soaring gracefully above the slumps of misshapen rock buildings, with the fantastic, serrated walls of the Old City on one hillside, and the red, tin-topped houses of the modern city standing out in sharp contrast on the other.

Ignoring the modern city, I wandered up and down the ancient, cobblestoned, stair-step streets—beautifully arched hallways—lined on both sides with all sorts of bazaar shops, which were dark in the innermost recesses of this great network of cavernous lanes. There were blacksmithies, fishmongers, and many old carpenter shops where wooden plow shafts and pitchforks were fashioned and assembled by means of wooden pegs instead of nails.

It was no place for cycling. Even walking or riding a donkey was barely possible in the crowded chaos along the arched vaultlike stores hewn in the sides of this City of Rock.

Here every race and religion is rampant in a riot of cosmopolitan color. One week of wandering on these streets and one is not shocked at anything one sees—not even at the strange costume of a group of local monks who wear sportsmen's tropical hats to counterbalance their somber-hued, brown robes.

While in Palestine, I was almost constantly inconvenienced by the large number of holidays. In addition to celebrations for saints and other holy men, the Moslem, Jewish, and Christian Sundays (Friday, Saturday, and Sunday, respectively) assured at least three more holidays each week.

[149]

Although one will always find a few weepers at the wailing wall, the Jewish Sabbath is the time when the wailing reaches its peak. On Saturday, while on my way down to the oldest section of the city, I passed many long-bearded, apostle-like men clothed in shiny black robes and broad felt hats which set off their grisly mien in remarkable fashion. A single long curl hanging from the ear of each of these solemn sons of Abraham completed the unique appearance of the Jerusalem Jews who were also on their way down to the wailing wall. All the way along both sides of this winding way were long lines of beggars, young and old, tearing at the clothes of passers-by and crying "Baksheesh!"

Several minutes before reaching the wall, I heard a droning noise like that of a nest of disturbed hornets; and as I approached nearer, the noise grew gradually louder. Suddenly turning the last corner of the wailing wall, I ran into a scene which I had never expected to see. At one end of the wall a group of Jewish women jammed their heads against the giant slabs of stone, sobbed as if their hearts would break, blew noses, wiped eyes, and intermittently read aloud from their prayer books. Scattered the full length of the wall to the opposite end, were scores of queerly dressed men singing, chanting, and bending toward the wall as if taking gymnastics. The expressions on their faces, and the sounds of their voices, indicated that they too were in misery.

At the extreme lower corner of this historic old wall, one group of men who had evidently stood and moaned until exhausted, now sat in a circle and rested. Several had propped their feet against the wall and were reading their books over tear-smeared spectacles.

Leaving this scene of lamentations, I polished off the end of an eventful morning with a walk all the way around the top of the massive walls encircling the old city. From this point of view, I saw Jerusalem in all its ugliness and

[150]

beauty, from the "tin can alley" of huts, made entirely from gasoline tins, to the exquisite Temple of the Rock, built over the site of Solomon's Temple.

CHAPTER XXVI

On the Jericho Road

At noon, when muezzins from the minarets of mosques all over Jerusalem called the faithful to prayer, I sat eating oranges beside old Jaffa gate and watched the interesting crowds in their beautifully embroidered costumes pass by on their way to market. An endless stream of peasant women was carrying large baskets of fruit and vegetables in true Oriental style. Old Abraham, Isaac, and Jacob-looking men were riding on the extreme rear ends of their little asses or else tossing to and fro on camel humps.

Hurrying down the Jericho road, I stopped for a brief rest beneath the cool shade of cedars and ancient olive trees in the Garden of Gethsemane, so near and yet so far from the confusion and noise of the city. In addition to the Greek Catholic church, there is a Roman Catholic church in this beautiful garden. Each of the many domes of the church was contributed by Catholics of different countries of the world. The church is built over large boulders which project out of the floor in their natural, untouched state, for here Christ is said to have rested on that memorable night when He prayed: "Let this cup pass from me."

In less than an hour's time after leaving Gethsemane, I had cycled the twenty-five kilometers down Jericho road to Khalia and the Dead Sea, 5,000 feet below the city of Zion. On the way down the snaky incline, I had passed several old pedestrians and donkey riders who could have fitted perfectly in the Bible story of "a certain man who went down from Jerusalem to Jericho and fell among thieves." So long was the constant grade that I had to stop

[151]

more than once to let the brake bands of my bicycle cool.

For the most part, the way wound down a wild, barren, yellow, sun-baked gorge. Only near the bottom did I run into a strip of vegetation in the form of green grass and flowering bunches of beautiful yellow blossoms, appearing to be a cross between hyacinth and snap-dragon. I could easily understand how one could be inspired to write the twenty-third Psalm near this lovely spot.

It took me thirty minutes to accustom myself to the water of the Dead Sea which was so dense that I could hardly keep my feet submerged. Floating like cork, equally well on back or stomach, I nearly broke my neck when diving in vain for the bottom. So sticky and stinging was the salt water that I found it necessary to make a hundred-yard dash to the river Jordan and bathe in fresh water, before my skin had pickled in brine. I swam across Jordan at the famous place of John the Baptist and sunned for a half-hour on the banks of Trans-Jordan, before floating back over to the "Promised Land." Being a "dyed-in-the-wool" Methodist, I was rather chagrined and disappointed that the Jordan was so deep, even to the very edge of the bank!

On my trail back to Jericho, on the edge of the plain beneath the Mount of Temptation, I stopped and lunched at one of the many old Greek monasteries on the banks of the Jordan. It seems that all monasteries must indulge in some sort of animal or bird hobby. Just as the St. Bernard dogs were famous pets in the Swiss Alpine monastery before they were exiled to a Tibetan Lamasery for killing a little French girl a short time after my visit there, here beside the Jordan I found the monks catering to great Persian cats. There was also a large aviary of pigeons and doves around the cool, inner, rectangular-walled enclosure.

While cycling through New Jericho, I met my second wedding procession in as many days. The whole country-side of Arabs was parading the streets and shouting like a

group of college boys at a football game. Whirling round
and round in front of the procession was a veil-enshrouded
dancing girl, followed by four gaily dressed horsemen.
Next in the crowd were Arabs waving swords and canes in
the air as they chanted and sang. Women and children
brought up the rear of this noisy group as it wound for
nearly two hours up and down every street of the village.

Upon reaching Old Jericho, two kilometers up the valley, I was dismayed to find only a misshapen mound of
mud and crumbled clay beside the cool waters of the
fountain of Elisha. When "Joshua 'fit' the battle of
Jericho" the walls of the old city really came tumbling
down, so that not a stone remained unturned. Perhaps
there is a mite of truth to the song that the blowing of ram,
lamb, and sheep horns, and of trumpets caused Jericho's
walls to crumble. The acoustics are so perfect down in this
deep valley that noises reverberate like an earthquake
against the engulfing mountain sides. Picking up remnants
of all that was left of the old walls (stony lumps of clay), I
had my picture taken as I held them on my shoulders.

Half way up the gigantic Canaan cliffs hanging over old
Jericho was Krontal, the most fantastic-looking old Greek
monastery I had ever seen. Plastered to the living rock
halfway up the Mount of Temptation, it commanded a
panoramic view of the Jordan valley and all points east.
No wonder the Devil picked this lofty place to show
Christ all the kingdoms of the world and to tempt him for
forty days!

It was more difficult to reach this haven of rest than I
had surmised. Darkness settled over the deep valley before
I had even found the narrow trail cut zigzag fashion up the
precipitous side of the mountain to the monastery.

Luckily, I ran into one of the many caves carved into the
base of the cliffs as homes for Arab farmers. The old
"cave dweller" readily consented to guide me up the
perilous perpendicular path to the monastery. As it was 10

[153]

p.m. when we finally reached the monastery, all the monks were asleep, and the soft chimes of the bells as I pulled the bell rope at the massive arched iron door, failed to get response.

Reluctantly, I followed my guide back to his own home where we sat on the floor with his four children and sopped barley bread in our common dish of olive oil. Bananas and dates, from the sub-tropical garden surrounding our cave beside the ruins of old Jericho, were thrown in as dessert, with individual pots of sage tea as a final "chaser."

We then went to bed on our mats beneath the open sky outside the cave entrance. In spite of the fact that we were perched nearly 1,000 feet above the lower Jordan valley, we were still several hundred feet below sea level and the night air was stiflingly hot, especially as it was necessary to cover my face completely to keep mosquitoes from feasting upon it.

I was back at the monastery next morning in time to see the sun rise above the purple peaks of Moab, and cast its radiant glow just above the monastery, before gradually creeping down the sides of the cliff to awaken Jericho, the Dead Sea and the green fringed River Jordan. The smiling sun grew brighter as it rose higher and higher, slowly wiping the cob-webs from the hazy horizon and shadowy valley as it changed from red to flaming yellow.

Before I had time to protest that I had already breakfast-ed, one of the old Santa Claus monks had brought me a stone stool, tray of tea, goat cheese and home-made whole wheat bread (such as only monks know how to make), and sat me down beside him in the parlor-kitchen, which was nothing more nor less than a great cave carved into the solid rock cliff.

Even the kitchen oven was hewn and hollowed from the rock cliff. Three other monks were busily wrapping stew of ground mutton, rice, tomato, and spices in grape leaves and putting them in the oven to bake for dinner. I soon discovered a queer sense of humor in these solemn-faced old antiques. With a pride equal to that of Georgia's champion tobacco spitter, one of them showed me how he could flip off one of his slippers and make it land on the tip of the tail of a big Maltese cat seated on the hearth on the other side of the cave. He performed this feat much to the dismay of the cat and the delight of the rest of the monks.

All day I wandered through the long corridors of palatial tile plastered with rough stone blocks to the natural roof of the overhanging cliffs, which were arched out for picturesque passageways to the little domed chapels, belfries, and bed-rooms hanging precariously over the valley. In addition to the inner passageways, there was a railed promenade around the outer walls of the monastery actually hanging in space. There was even a miniature garden of green veg-etables and flowers thriving in a little niche cut in one end of the cliff.

When I was ready to resume my journey, the old Abbot jumped astride his little donkey and accompanied me down the mountainside to Bucephalus, who had been left in old Jericho.

Unfortunately, I had reached Jerusalem just a little too late for most of the festivities of Holy Week. The Moslems had begun their celebration with a magnificent sword dance all the way down to Jericho and back again, while in different chambers of the Holy Sepulchre, groups of all nations held simultaneous services. People had bought ten-dollar admission tickets and camped in the church twenty-four hours before the colorful ceremonies took place, in order to obtain standing room to witness the Foot Washings, Holy Fire races, and other fascinating rites.

I was well pleased, upon returning to Jerusalem, to obtain entrance into the Holy Sepulchre for the last of the Latin Easter services. The cathedral was resplendent with

[155]

candle light. As in the Feast of the Passover ceremony in the Greek Orthodox Church of St. George in Old Cairo, every member of the audience now before me held a lighted candle.

First in the long procession were two richly garbed priests who set the chanting rhythm by beating the ends of their maces upon the floor. Next in line were red-velveted children bearing crosses, followed by choir and audience.

In the solemn three-hour march about the church we stopped at Calvary (where Christ was crucified), the Unction Stone and finally, the Holy Tomb in the middle of the floor directly beneath the central dome of the church (where Christ was buried). After marching three times around the Holy Tomb, each of us was allowed to pass through the tomb itself.

Easter and the resurrection of a new day—a day of terror and torture for the Jews. As I emerged from the church a sinister group of street Arabs sneeringly cried "Jahoodi!" (Jew) and unceremoniously threw verbal oaths in my face. News of the first Arab uprising against the German Jews in Tel Aviv on the previous day had just reached the Arabs in Jerusalem and was spreading like wild fire throughout Palestine.

With my German bicycle, Bavarian buckskin shorts from South Germany, goose-feather sleeping bag from Cologne, and black University of Georgia sweater with red "G" on the front, I was a marked man by the Arabs. The German Jews in Palestine wore similar shorts on the streets and in the fields, and rode the same type, heavy-built, balloon-tired German cycle, and slept in the same sort of schlafsac (sleeping bag). Unfortunately for me, the University of Georgia not only has the same colors, but also the same initial letter as Germany—that blazing red "G" on my black sweater spelled "Germany" to the Arabs! It was the beginning of the end of my brief stay in Palestine. Verbal expressions were soon to be replaced with more violent forms of persecution and during the rest of my sojourn in the Holy Land, I was destined to dodge bullets, knives, and stones as I cycled up the road.

Already news bulletins warned tourists to travel from the country by train as quickly as possible. However, Bucephalus had brought me into the middle of the Arab-Jewish disturbances and could carry me out again. For my last night at Jerusalem, before setting out on the Damascus Road, I chose the Garden of Gethsemane as the safest, most restful spot for my sleeping bag.

My sleep in this beautiful garden on the Mount of Olives was the sweetest of all, with birds singing all night in the pine, cedar, and olive trees, which swayed in the breeze with the soothing sound of waves on a sea beach. It was not only a beautiful place in which to sleep, but also, what wandering Arab would ever think of finding me in such a spot!

CHAPTER XXVII

Dodging Arab Devils to Damascus

At daybreak Sunday, April 19, the bells of Pater Noster Church waked me in the Garden of Gethsemane, and I led Bucephalus out on the road toward Sechem. Already colorful streams of peasants, and flocks of sheep and goats were flowing down all the paths and streets into the picturesque, beautiful old city of Mount Zion.

Whether the peasants were in sack clothes or red, yellow, orange and purple embroidered veils and dresses, their heads were heavily laden with fowl, vegetables, or great clay bowls of sour milk and cheese.

Even though it was Sunday in the Holy Land, road workers were busily repairing holes in the asphalt highway; and nearby farmers were industriously and expeditiously plowing by holding the plow handle in the

[157]

left hand, leaving the right hand free to prod, with a long wooden staff, the caudal appendages of the balking oxen, donkeys, or camels, as the case may be.

Dotting the countryside were all sorts of local saint shrines, from white-washed, oval-roofed monuments to old sacred trees and caves. Thousands of wayside caves with no particular sacredness attached to them are used as shelter from sun and rain in this almost treeless country. The sacred caves may be identified by palm branch emblems hewn above the cave entrance.

I did not realize the height of this mountainous region until, in cycling over a pass near Nablus, I pierced through the ceiling of clouds. The hills of Judea may be barren and savage looking, but their ugliness only intensifies by contrast the rich beauty of the valleys of green and golden grain, and the groves of olives, oranges and pears, which nestle between these gloomy grey hilltops.

It was such fine cycling up the gently sloping gorges and around a hundred hairpin curves to another valley spreading out on the other hillside that by noon I easily covered the seventy kilometers between Jerusalem and Nablus. Here I visited Joseph's mountain-top tomb, and "tanked up" on the pure, cold water at Jacob's well in the bottom of an ancient church, just south of the city. The old Greek monk stationed at the well kindly lowered three lighted candles in a silver bucket, to let me see as well as taste the sparkling water.

My dinner in Nablus consisted of liver cubes barbecued on iron needles, placed over a charcoal fire; also, small squashes stuffed with rice and mashed potatoes. Unfortunately, the native word "Jogurt" (sour milk) is pronounced almost like "Jahoodi" (Jew). Thus, when the vendor dubiously queried, "Jahoodi?," I answered, "Bali" (yes), meaning of course that I desired sour milk and not asserting that I was a Jew!

Already children had showered me with rocks while

older people hurled sinister taunts and looks. After my unconditional "confession," the elderly people joined the children in their playful pastime and were about to rid the world of one more German Jew, when I suddenly realized the seriousness of my error, and pointed to the American flag adorning my bicycle. This discovery of my mistaken identity so shocked some of the Arabs that they took to their heels in terror. Others fell upon their knees and begged me not to turn them over to the British authorities.

At least I could continue my wanderings in safety through Nablus, but what would happen in some of the smaller villages around old Samaria where the Arabs had never seen an American flag, or even heard of America?

One advantage of Eastern cities is that by leisurely strolling up and down the streets one can see everything that is happening within and without the open fronted shops, where the human hands of industry are busily turning out copper pots or woven rugs. A worker in one Nablus shop was earnestly plucking a huge iron-stringed bow, as if he were playing a bass violin. In vibrating, the string struck a pile of raw, unspun cotton to disintegrate the small masses of fibre and send the nicely separated particles flying through the air to an opposite corner.

It is interesting to note the change in dress and manners only a few miles will make in all parts of the world, except America. I began to run into unusually colorful camel caravans as I climbed up the gnarled and twisted road over a high pass and down again to the palm-fringed village of Jenin. In these long trains, both natives and camels wore necklaces and nose pieces, those of the natives being in the form of metal disks and bejewelled rings, whereas camels wore bells and beaded bands.

All afternoon I crossed the beautiful Plains of Esdraelon, one solid ocean of waving grain, dotted sporadically by great herds of sheep and black goats which were being led to hillside pastures. Large droves of white storks and red and purple-robed peasants stood out against the background of the unbroken field of green rye. Behind this soft landscape, fairylike undulating mountains graced the distant horizon. Across the plains, I had a wonderful view of Jezreel, and of Mount Gilboa, Nais and Mount Tabor.

Shortly after emerging from an ancient Arab city of mud and stone buildings and goat-hair tents, I suddenly found myself among modern wooden structures in the northern end of the rich plains. In the fields, a big tractor was doing in five minutes what the old native peasants I had seen could not do in five hard days of primitive ploughing. I was stepping from the world of Arabs (which is the same as it was 2,000 years ago), to the twentieth century village of Affula, one of many such Palestine settlements sponsored by British and American philanthropists in behalf of German Jews.

Twenty years ago the first Jewish colonists found the Plains of Esdraelon to be nothing more than malarial infested swamps. Many died while draining and transforming the country into one of the most fertile spots of the world. Now, huge fruit orchards, dairies, poultry and agricultural farms cover these plains.

The Arabs resent the industry of the Jews in reclaiming this land which they had been content to let stand idle. They also protest violently against all other indicia of cultured civilization introduced by the Jews.

Three young Jewish boys cycling outside the city limits of Affula had been attacked and killed by a band of Arabs only a few hours before my arrival, and I found the town in the sort of excitement depicted in a moving picture scene of an American pioneer village preparing for an Indian massacre. The old Jewish farmer and his family with whom I spent the night, were very frightened, but nothing serious occurred, except that one of the night watchmen was found about three o'clock in the morning with a knife through his heart.

[160]

At dawn, I was on the north road up the high overhanging mountains to Nazareth, one of the beauty spots of the world, commanding a wonderful view, not only of the broad sweep of the Plains of Esdraelon to the south, but also in all other directions. It was luck to strike Nazareth on Monday, the great market day.

Although I reached this little city of 9,000 inhabitants shortly after the sun rose over the side of green-sloped Mount Tabor, the market square at the lower end of town was already teeming with hundreds of donkeys, camels, horses, bullocks, sheep, and goats, each type of animal being segregated in different parts of the market place.

For two hours, I sat on the old rock wall and watched an endless stream of peasants pour into market with their herds of cattle. Some were seated on little donkeys, leading a long procession of other donkeys and camels, while others rode Arabian horses with gaily colored, woven knapsacks on each side of the saddle. Still others walked, staff in hand, as they led their sheep down the cobbled street.

After rambling through all the streets of this mountainside village, and visiting the chief places of historic interest, such as Mensi Christi, Jewish Synagogue, and Chapel of the Carpenter's Shop, built on the site where Christ is said to have worked, I filled my canteens with the cold, pure mountain water of Mary's Well inside the Church of Annunciation (so called as it is here that the angel prophesied to Mary the birth of Christ), and started across the hills to Galilee, in spite of warnings by local police that, in view of the recent Arab uprising, it was suicidal.

So exquisitely beautiful was the country-side, with its myriads of purple and pink flowers, red poppies, ripening figs, blooming olives, fertile, freshly plowed soil, and new-mown spring hay, that I regretted having to cycle so rapidly through this lovely landscape.

Bucephalus and I presented a very dashing picture. I

[161]

gave him the reins, the whip and the spur. Riding like an early old Wells-Fargo scout with Indians at his heels and in ambush all along the way, we tore through Palestine.

To a large extent, my time was divided between dodging rocks, bricks and bullets of pursuers and avoiding contact with adversaries expectantly awaiting my arrival farther down the highway. Between rounds, I cautiously caught fleeting glimpses of the scenery.

Dressed like modern Davids, most of the shepherd boys carried slings at their waists and flutes at their lips. Girls and women seated, or sowing seed in the fields, wore big, baggy green or red balloon breeches with their equally brilliant-colored dresses tucked up around their waists to give them the appearance of tulips or other budding flowers.

At Cana, only a few kilometers over hill and dale from Nazareth, I stopped long enough to peep into the red-domed Church of the Wine Miracle and the house of Nathaniel.

I thought no other place on earth, or in dreamland, could equal the landscape of Galilee as I slid down the great green slopes and sheep-covered basin where Christ fed the five thousand, to the pure azure gem (Sea of Galilee) of Palestine, resting in the depths of the world's deepest depression.

After a swim in the cold, crystal clear waters of Galilee and a nap among the shells and smooth rocks on the shore, below the ancient walled-in city of Tiberias, I cycled down to Kinereth, Beganya, and Samakh at the lower end of the lake and back again to the opposite end. Everywhere along the shore shepherds were driving their cattle down for their noonday drink in the sea.

Many saintly bearded old fishermen, like the apostles of old, were pulling in their huge nets from the shimmering sea. Multitudes of ducks and other birds dotted the surface of the sea, while hundreds of great cranes were flying in well-ordered flocks overhead, or were sitting on rocky

[162]

*Krontal, plastered in the living rock
half-way up the Mount of Temptation*

*'olding up all
't remains of
walls of
'cho*

*"Unpickling"
in the fresh waters
of Jordan*

Krontal gardener

*Don Quixote rides again
(beside the Sea of Galilee)*

*Market day
in Nazareth
(below)*

Woodman, shave that tree!

cliffs silhouetted against the sky.

In my wanderings around the Sea of Galilee, I passed Magdala (birthplace of Mary Magdalene), and crossed the Plain of Gennesareth to Bethsaida, birthplace of Peter, John and Philip.

At the site of old Capernium of Bible times, I found only a jumble of ruins resembling those of old Jericho. Christ's prophetic warning, "Woe to thee, Capernium!" had certainly been fulfilled.

The streets of old Tiberias were only two feet wide, bordered on each side with sidewalks three or four feet wide. These streets really seemed to serve better as drain ditches than as thoroughfares.

Many Arab tent villages were scattered over the sea-side slopes, while queerly shaped Jewish settlements (houses built in circles, rectangles, et cetera), lay in the broad basins, verdant with orange, grape, and other tropical fruit and vegetables. However, not a Jew was to be seen. All were waiting and watching for Arab raiders from their house windows.

Upon learning that a new Arab raid in the villages of the Plains of Esdraelon had resulted in the deaths of a score or more Jews just after my departure from Affula, I immediately went into a huddle with Bucephalus and we decided that, in the future, our greatest safety lay in solitude, rather than in Jewish settlements. Like Julius Caesar, we sought safety in flight. High above the water of the northern shore of Galilee, near the great Hospice which commands a wonderful view of the lake and entire countryside, I found an ideal resting place in an old cave whose walls were covered with drawings of animals.

However, as my cave was still below sea level, I realized the necessity of climbing higher, or else of remaining in the sea breeze by the very water's edge. To remain in my then present position meant a night of miserable torture by mosquitoes. I settled the question by climbing into one of

[165]

the small fishing vessels tied to a deserted spot of shore-line. Here I spent my last night in Palestine in comfort, rocked to sleep on the cradle of the deep blue waters of Galilee.

I was thankful that I did not "wake up dead" at dawn, and that I was able to lead Bucephalus across the Jordan into the beautiful cedar country of Lebanon and on to Damascus, before Arabs had time to impede our progress permanently.

My personal experiences in Palestine were now only pleasant memories. The Arab disturbances had merely added spice to the venture. Of course, on more than one occasion, Palestine had seemed too full of rocks, but I had managed to dodge the rocks and ignore the curses. There was no room for self-pity, as mine was temporary tran-sient torture, ending at the borders of Syria. I left all my sympathy for those poor Jewish farmers and merchants who seemed to be subject to permanent persecution.

CHAPTER XXVIII

Delving Through Damascus

Since cycling at such steadily strenuous speed through Palestine's Arab-Jewish conflicts had made protracted dinners impossible, it was natural that during the first few days in Damascus, I lounged around the long caterpillar-like bazaars where all the colorful, exotic dishes known to Europe and the Far East were blended into food combinations fit for the gods.

As the cost of living was very low, I found Syrian food to be cheap, yet wholesome and delicious. With a single Syrian piastre (1 1/4 cents U.S. money), I purchased large perfumed fruit or cream pies, together with a litre of joghurt (hot milk poured into great copper cauldrons to congeal into a form of clabber), and a vegetable dinner of rice, meat, and tomato wrapped and cooked in cubes of young grape leaves, like the similar dish made by monks on the Mount of Temptation.

Cooked grape leaves soon became palatable, but in my sojourn in the Near East I never acquired a taste for attar of roses and other such perfumes used in flavoring foods in similar manner as we in America use vanilla, almond, or lemon extract.

In little arched holes in dark stone walls throughout Damascus, one is entranced by the artistic industry of bakers of bigger and better bread. As if by magic the baker, using deft fingers, spread a small chunk of dough into a large, thin pancake, flapped it on a great round cushion, slapped the cushion against the inside walls of a blazing hot, hollow, spherical-shaped clay furnace, where the pancake stuck for a few moments before it was removed, a crisp, brown disk.

Easterners are fond of brittle bread. They eat crackers, strings of large and small doughnut-shaped loaves, beaten biscuit, and a number of other similar types, each of which is prepared in its own unique oven. Shredded wheat, enjoyed by both peasants and townsmen of the Near and Far East, is cooked on the six-or-eight-foot-in-diameter disks of copper, which serve as lids for huge hollow clay ovens. Like streams of water playing from the perforated nozzle of an old-fashioned sprinkler, the shredded wheat batter is sieved out in fine strings of concentric circles around the entire surface of the hot copper sheet. In a few seconds, the wheat has attained the same calibre as that made by machinery in America.

As I walked or cycled through the bazaars, word was passed to shopkeepers and customers on both sides of the streets that I was "Le Americani Bichiclete." I heard many whispered remarks that I was "Allemagne Jahoodi" (German Jew) fleeing from Palestine Arabs. For some reason the local Jews seemed to believe that I was one of

[167]

their persecuted brethren. I argued vehemently that such was not the case. The argument was not convincing as they would wag their fingers, and smile. Ah! I thought, I would offer conclusive proof! I took some of their leaders to a cafe and ordered pork in a loud voice. I began eating the pork, but when one or two of my companions did likewise I realized the futility of further evidence.

Everyone soon knew what and how much I ate for breakfast, and where I was each minute of the day. If I sat, the cynosure of attention, on a park bench, traffic was at a standstill. Natives gathered on every surrounding street corner, and four-horse drawn carriages stopped in the middle of the road to let their occupants peer out the windows at the strange foreigner. Once, when the crowd had assumed enormous proportions, I wheeled around, dashed toward the crowd, and said "Boo!" The ensuing confusion and hejira were stupendous.

However, my popularity (or rather, notoriety) was bearable, since the Syrian natives were all good-hearted courteous and considerate in confining their curious questions to each other instead of directing them at me. Even bazaar shopmen let me browse in peace through their shops. Instead of annoying me with sales talk, they merely offered me a chair in which to rest and drink a cup of tea with them. These clever clerks had discovered that the secret of good salesmanship lay in letting the customer peruse for himself and make known his wants.

I spent many hours cycling through the fruit groves and rose gardens of this beautiful city, which rests like a miniature Delta of the Nile, in the midst of barren desolation. Roses were rampant everywhere. Even butchers stuck bouquets of roses in the mouths of the skinned and drawn sheep and goat, hung on display in front of their shops. Donkeys heavily laden with pot flowers, shrubbery, and great arched blossom-bedecked lattices, paraded the streets like walking hot houses.

Cedar-sloped, snow-capped mountains furnish a refreshing background and also send sparkling streams of water down through Damascus. One of the finest features of the city is in the thousands of water streams, bubbling up from the great rock fountains at dark bazaar corners, or from iron-grilled crevices cleft in the rock walls, with iron-chained silver cups at each fountain.

With the aid of their toes, native artisans exercise uncanny skill in weaving beautiful, world-renowned, Damascus cloth, and in fashioning wooden sandals, leather boots, saddles, and pocketbooks. Sea shells and coral beads fringe most of the leather work.

In the silver and gold smithies everything imaginable is made, from gold thimbles to silver-cylindered letter containers. For hours I was fascinated as the silversmith made such delicate work that no tools were fine enough to fashion the chased designs of his handicraft. Placing a flaming torch before his unfinished work of art, the smithy blew through a hollow ivory tube, the air forcing the jet of flame against the white powder-covered silver to mould it into beautifully chased goblets decorated with lace work of such fine silver threads that I almost needed a magnifying glass in order to see the minutely embroidered tracings. Though I watched closely, and marvelled, I still don't see how he did it!

As in Egypt, many of the Syrians enjoy their long water pipes, which are so inconvenient to carry that they are customarily retained for rent in the walls of the downtown shops.

Many of the bazaars boast of upper stories, little open-fronted shelves, on which the native artisans work nimbly with hands and toes at the spinning wheel, smith's hammer or glass blowing tube. Like monkeys they occasionally stop work for a few recreational moments to assist in locating little bugs in the heads of their companions.

In the streets, mothers were similarly engaged in

constantly removing lice from the raven black locks and paint splotched faces of their infants.

Beneath these covered bazaars, camel and donkey caravans seemed to be walking through a house! These camel caravans are colorful affairs as they jingle along heavily laden with vari-colored clothes, carpets, silks, and perfumed spices. Equally picturesque are the orange-draped donkeys, which are driven by seedy old Arabs, strikingly similar in appearance to their beasts of burden. In addition to animal and human "vehicles," long "stretchers" were the usual mode of conveying cut-glass vases and miscellaneous articles from one street corner to another.

Three-weeks old peaches, plums and crab apples—all green as gourds and as unappetizing as possible to the American palate—are seemingly popular with the natives, since vendors at every street corner keep up a lively trade with these stomach-aching delicacies.

Moslem women add variety to the scene in their solid-hued robes of white, black, purple, orange, or green with mysterious mask-like veils over their faces and long drawers extending to their ankles, where they culminate in comical-looking fringes.

Many young native boys may be seen showing off their richly embroidered arabesque-designed jackets.

Perfecting the Damascus street scene is the French Foreign Legion, often referred to as the celebrated Legion of the Damned because of the large number of murderers and other desperate fugitives from justice, of all races and nationalities, which fill its motley ranks. Whether Algerian blacks, native Syrians, half-breed Chinese, or hundred per cent Frenchmen, all are stocky, sturdy-built specimens of humanity.

Not only does every bazaar shop present one aspect of the educational drama of Life in Action, but nearly every other narrow hallway, extending from either side of the street, is a peep-show into a beautiful courtyard garden of some well-to-do merchant. One looks through these gracefully arched entrances into the colonnaded rectangular arcades, shaded by flowering fruit trees and vari-colored, glass-domed roofs through which the dazzling noonday sun is enchantingly distilled. These gardens are examples of the wonders man can accomplish by working in harmony with nature. In this calm, quiet retreat, so near and yet so far from the noisy hurly-burly world outside, the business man may be seen at prayer, or performing his ablutions in the beautifully tiled fountain adorning the center of the courtyard.

In the Syrian National Museum, I accidentally bumped into the American Exchange Student to Rome. It was our fourth chance meeting in as many weeks, as we had run into each other on the streets of Cairo, Jerusalem, Nazareth, and now Damascus. Although he traveled by boat and train, Bucephalus seemed to get me places with equal facility.

After four days of sight-seeing, I was beginning to think that Syria was the exceptional country wherein I should see no funeral procession, when suddenly the tom-tom tattoo of drums and the clash of cymbals directed my attention to just such a sight as I had expected to see. Heading the funeral marchers were two men carrying long poles entwined with flowers and green vines. They were followed by two banner bearers on each side of a lidless coffin. The rear was brought up by a motley crowd of mourners who were keeping perfect time, in step and speech, with the maddeningly monotonous music of the native band immediately behind the coffin.

The funereal atmosphere of the neighborhood was in keeping with the March of Death. Though not in the bazaar section, the shadowy streets were almost subterranean passageways; the upper stories of the houses projected so far out over the street as to shut out practically all light of day. Without exception, every house door was decorated

[171]

with brass hands as knockers to ward off evil spirits. Huge black and yellow cats stalked slowly through the dark alleys, or ran howling before the street sprinkler machine, which consisted solely of a man swishing water from side to side from hog-hide containers. Besides serving as street sprinklers, hog-hides are universally used as bellows by eastern blacksmiths.

While I was walking beneath the old city wall, near the cattle hide tanneries, a woman from a second-story window drenched me with a bucket of decidedly dirty dish water— unintentionally of course. I had to wash and dry my clothes in the country before continuing my wanderings under the old Arche de Triomphe to the magnificent Mosque Omayud (this historic old edifice was once a Christian cathedral), with its multitude of prayer towers, domes, and Corinthian-columned, rectangular arcade around the great inner courtyard.

The mosque doorkeeper recognized me on sight and with a typical display of Syrian hospitality, he refused my three-franc entrance fee, begged me to enter gratis, and enjoy myself. His only request was that I remember to tell the folks back home that he, "Abdullah Hassan Wahiddin Sabbagh, was a good man." I now take the liberty of issuing this proclamation.

Several stories of super-imposed arched columns were required to reach the lofty mosaic ceiling of this great mosque. Hundreds of fine rugs completely covered the floor, while fountains bubbled in the mosque, as at other places over the city. Many blind beggars slept on the soft cool carpets; others prayed at the little domed altars beneath the beautifully stained glass windows.

Outside the mosque walls, women street-workers were hauling and mixing sacks of sand and cement. In the near-by spacious restaurant garden, men of a higher social order entered the cinema section of the garden, or sat at tea tables, listening to Oriental music, playing dominoes

[172]

and smoking, while charcoal vendors carried glowing coals from table to table to place upon the tobacco resting on their water-vased pipes.

All the Oriental songs which I heard here sounded exactly like the one I had learned while among the Bedouins of northern Arabia. When singing this song before a potential American audience, I decided that I should call it the "Unfinished Symphony of the Arabian Desert," as I was confident that no American or European audience would hear its mournful wailing discords through to the finish of the piece!

Several times in my ramblings, I met a childish, talkative old Arab who had lived in America long enough to learn English. He proudly exhibited his knowledge before an admiring audience quickly encircling us as he spoke. Hemmed hopelessly in a corner, I had no alternative but to hear his story.

The old fellow told of the trip to the United States with three of his six brothers, when he was only fourteen years of age. Like his brothers, he had worked for a financial foundation in a factory before finally establishing a grocery business. So successful were the four brothers in their trade, that all made enough money to return to Damascus to see the homefolks again.

While in Syria, all four married and their intended brief visit to the homeland became a permanent one. They rejoined their three other brothers and eighty-year-old mother in cooperative farming at the old homestead, which nestled among the beautiful Lebanon cedars around the base of Mount Hermon. He stated that among themselves, his three Americanized brothers still spoke English, much to the bewilderment and vexation of the 100% Arab members of the family.

He was dressed exactly like all the other Moslem Arabs around us, and only by his American speech could I tell that my friend had really visited my own country. It

[173]

seemed almost unbelievable that forty years in America could leave him with so few characteristics of our modern civilization. After all those years abroad, he had come home to take up life at fifty-four where he had abruptly left off at fourteen. He answered my dubious look by saying that while he had lived on American soil, he had been able to retain his native Moslem atmosphere since all of his associates had belonged to Allah's flock of faithful children. He astounded me with his assurances that a large percentage of the people in America's cosmopolitan cities were even followers of Mahomet.

As I was a good listener and my friend an even better talker, we agreed that it would be fine if I could return home with him and spend a few weeks hunting quail, rabbit, fox, and other game on Mount Hermon. He assured me that I could have all the camel and goat milk, fruit and fried chicken that I could consume. It was a splendid opportunity for a real adventure in the Moslem home of a prosperous farmer, but I regretfully rejected the pressing invitation with the excuse that the monsoon would strike me in India if I did not set out immediately for the Land of the Rising Sun.

Anyway, my past experience had indicated that whatever road one travels, one may rest assured the way will be full of adventure.

END OF PART THREE

[174]

"If from society we learn to live,
Tis solitude should teach us how to die;
It hath no flatterers; vanity can give
No hollow aid; alone—man with his God must
strive."

Byron
Childe Harold

PART FOUR

HEJIRA TO HIGH ASIA

CHAPTER XXIX

Cycling Across the Great Syrian Desert

After a week of walking and cycling in circles around Damascus, I filled my bread kit with bars of chocolate, my water flasks with concentrated lime juice, and sallied forth on the sunrise trail across the Syrian Desert toward Bagdad.

Each of the hundreds of little patches of grain and fig groves on the outskirts of Damascus was enclosed by high mud and straw walls, shielding the vegetation from the hot sun. Just as the artistic absurdity of the Arabs was evident in the checkerboard figures on their camels and donkeys as a result of shaving them in spots, so likewise was their extreme love for exterior decoration manifest in the elaborate network of walls, in all sorts of geometric shapes, scattered across the desert plains.

My first attempt at crossing the desert ended in failure at the frontier post of Khan Abou Charnat, only a half hour's journey from Damascus. It seems that several years ago two American cyclists tried to cross this 800-kilometer stretch of hot, dry sand and were found mad from heat and thirst. After this incident, the Syrian government made it a criminal offense, punishable by imprisonment, for any one to cycle across the desert. The police warned me that even if I slipped past the Syrian Duane (Frontier Patrol) and succeeded in crossing the desert, I would perhaps be rewarded by being thrown into jail in Bagdad.

There was nothing for me to do but return to Damascus to wait for the next motorcade. As there was no road across this mighty ocean of sand, it was quite easy to wander from the little posts marking the "trail" every two kilometers along the way. Even autos are not allowed to make the trip alone. Only on Tuesdays and Fridays, the mail trucks, natives, and tourists make the journey in one long train of cars, which have been carefully tuned and tested.

It cost $35.00 to make the trip in the twenty-four-wheeled bus of the Nairn Transport Company. This locomotive palace was equipped with upper and lower berths and kitchenette where meals were cooked and served en route. However, as the Jewish owner of one of the smaller native busses insisted that I ride gratis in his vehicle, I accepted the invitation. He, as usual, thought I was one of the persecuted German Jews.

During my unforeseen extra day of waiting, I climbed to the top of Mahajorin mountain, towering above this little green oasis on the edge of the desert, and obtained my last view of the city. On the way down the mountain, I stopped for the night with the long-bearded old fathers of Saint Franciscan Cloister.

At dawn, just before my rattle-trap autobus of Occidentals and Orientals started eastward, the west-bound motorcade arrived from Bagdad, bringing a fuzzy-faced stranger who introduced himself as Osmyn Stout, American Exchange Student from San Pedro, California, to Canton, China. He had started westward from China on a globe-circling cycle trip, but had given up the idea before reaching India. He was now finishing his trip via train, lorry, bus, ship and other available means of locomotion.

We were headed in opposite directions for our common goal: America. Neither of us dreamed that I was destined to cross Asia and the Pacific to San Pedro even before Osmyn reached Europe.

I had not motored many miles into the desert before I regretted having done so. It would not have been difficult to cycle across these hard-surfaced, sparsely grassed

[177]

plains, dotted with occasional sand drifts through which I could have easily pushed my cycle. Yet, the autobus stuck so fast in each sand pile that we all piled out and pushed. Our ship of the desert rolled and rumbled along so slowly through the stifling heat waves that two small boys became sea-sick in the seat directly behind me. Their example was soon followed by their mother and the other passengers.

Our human cargo was composed chiefly of devout pilgrims on their way to Mecca. Thus, numerous stops were necessary for prayers to Allah. Each worshipper removed his shoes and placed a pair of valuable trinkets about six inches apart in the middle of his blanket, which he had spread across the sand; he then touched his hands twice from desert dust to forehead, looking at them and praying each time after removing the finger tips from his brows. All these were merely preliminary exercises to the real prayer in which he went from erect to bowed position, with hands, knees, and forehead touching the ground at least a dozen times.

Even after recovering to some extent from sea-sickness, the bevy of brawling brats in the back seats of the bus were in ill humor. Upon my making faces at them, the whole bunch soon overwhelmed me, much to my own distress and to the delighted relief of their parents.

To one youngster who persisted in crying, I gave a stick of Wrigley's chewing gum. The child's mother immediately sampled the gum herself, before passing it all the way round the bus until every passenger had sampled the strange American food. After watching this chunk of gum make the round of thirty different mouths before returning to its original proud possessor (the crying baby), the piece which I alone was chewing soon lost its savor and I threw it away.

Whenever we stopped to repair punctures, most of the occupants of the bus rushed out in all directions across the

[178]

desert and brought back bunches of sage brush to take home with them. In addition to the sage, several joyfully returned with little sand snakes squirming between their fingers.

This was the last straw. I patiently endured the snail's pace of our bus only so long as these snakes were not sharing the seats with us. When we arrived for a few hours' rest at Rudbah Wells, airplane re-fueling station, I pulled Bucephalus and my sleeping bag from the top of the bus and started up the pathway of the rising moon with the worst of the trail still ahead of me.

Late that night, as I lay alone in the middle of the desert, the long string of headlights approached, with my erstwhile bus rattling along in the rear. The great caravan moved on, and I was too tired to wonder whether or not I should be thankful that I was no longer a part of the noisy procession.

When I awoke next morning, the desert seemed more like a beautiful dream than a reality. From my cycle seat it did not seem so desolate as when viewed from the bus window. My silent steed neither drowned out the music of desert birds, nor frightened them from the trail. So tame were the many flocks of quail, peering up in curious wonder at me, that I could have easily captured some for dinner if necessary. However, I suffered no lack of food, as all along the way there were camel caravans from which I obtained rich milk and cheese.

Many books have been written on the terrors of the Great Syrian Desert, "the world's most inhospitable waste," but I found it delightful, though at times a trifle monotonous. I cycled hour after hour up from the center of this broad bronze bowl of the universe without ever seeming to get nearer the rim.

True, my sunblasted hide took on the shriveled appearance of an Egyptian mummy; my lips cracked so greatly that blood oozed from gashes which opened afresh every time I moved my mouth the slightest bit; my throat

[179]

became so parched and dry that when I tried to swallow, swollen tonsils and tongue scraped together with suffocating pain; the piercing heat waves parboiled my eyes and sizzled through my whole system with the burning effect of lightning or an electric current.

But what are these insignificant hardships compared to enjoyments of the natural beauty of the desert and its "peace that passeth all understanding!" "Life is a path of roses," but to appreciate the roses one must willingly accept the thorns too. Few experiences are worth while which do not involve risks and penalties. Had I been unwilling to pay the price demanded by the laws of nature and man, Bucephalus never would have become a 'round the world reality.

The greatest single charm of the desert is the sight of a great caravan of camels as they glide along the horizon in silhouette, like real ships, their great humped backs resembling sails and their necks and heads, the prows of the vessels, bobbing up and down across the heat waves rippling through the mirages. The camel legs being of the same rusty color as the desert, are invisible, so that on an unusually hot day the illusion of ship on a rolling sea is perfect.

I passed also several thousand wild white camels grazing in the thin grasslands of the desert. Multitudes of doves perched upon their backs, or sailed in sun-eclipsing flight overhead.

My Arabic stood me in good stead with the few Bedouins I met. I used to advantage such phrases as "A dash" (how much does it cost?) and "Marhaba" (How do you do?); and when the old Arabs bade me "Portrak" (goodbye), I knew to reply to this parting greeting with a "Ma salame" (go in peace). To omit such niceties was to incur the suspicion or hatred of a passer-by. In all of the forty-three countries through which I cycled, I made it a point to learn how to render greetings and thanks in understandable native fashion.

The calm surroundings of these desert nomads do not

develop in them the correspondingly gentle, peace-loving natures which should characterize camel shepherds of the desert. On the contrary, they are ferocious of temperament and inveterate cattle stealers, unscrupulously killing each other if necessary to accomplish their purpose.

Many times I stopped to exchange stories with them of wolves, hyenas, and snakes in their great Garden of Allah. In conversation, these mysterious men never drop the tone of voice at the end of a sentence. Instead, they slightly raise the pitch of the last syllable, so that the sentence, ending in a long-drawn-out wistful-like breath, sounds as if it is incomplete.

Near Bagdad, I passed the Ziggurat tower of a lost Kassite city, called Dur Kurajalzu. This great sphinx-like structure is a mass of brick inlaid with straw matting. Goats and camels nibble and chew these brick with seeming enjoyment. Though the mounds surrounding the Ziggurat have never been excavated, natives visit the place after heavy rains and pick up Roman coins and miscellaneous bits of tile, clay, and glass pottery exposed on the surface of the ground.

Crossing the Maude Bridge (pontoon bridge, built in 1915 by British troops) over the Tigris filled with its odd, circular-shaped, wicker basket boats, I suddenly found myself in the city of a Thousand and One Arabian Nights of mysterious mesmerism, romance, and adventure: the home of Sinbad the Sailor and the Forty Thieves.

My first impression of Bagdad was that it resembled one of those dirty, uninteresting little Western towns one sees in the Wild West movies. I wondered how such a hot, desolate, ugly country as Iraq could ever have been a paradise. Yet, this very same country of mud and straw huts and goat -hair tents scattered over the cracked mud plains, between the forks of the Tigris and Euphrates river, is said to be the site of the Garden of Eden, the incubator of the human race.

[181]

Damascus peep show

Two ships of the desert

BEFORE (the author)
and
AFTER (Osmyn Stout)
taking a dose of India
and the Far East

Bucephalus enjoys a few moments of "expiration" while two other flat-footed ships sail silently across the deeps of the great Syrian desert

Rubbing elbows with a Mecca-bound pilgrim

Persian peasants (Author's note: That's not I holding Bucephalus)

Teheran's Gateway to High Asia

Small Ford busses straddled the drain ditches in the middle of the streets while "kurds," rag-a-muffin men with belts bristling with knives, and hair glistening with grease, ran alongside with piano-size boxes and barrels balanced upon their rug-jacketed backs. Typical of the East, the females, whether infants or old grandmothers, dressed practically the same, from leather moccasined feet to shawl enshrouded heads.

An endless stream of pilgrims passed in and out the picturesquely arched gates leading to Kadimain with its glorious domes and minarets of gold. Being in one of the four most holy Moslem cities, this mosque area is visited by thousands of devout Shiite Moslems, who travel from the remotest parts of the Moslem world to witness the Passion Play of the East, which is held here. It struck me as strangely amusing that Christians should not be allowed to approach this Holy Shrine district; yet storks could nest unmolested on the golden and blue domes of Kadimain and Seraj mosques.

Slowly but surely, as I cycled through the streets of this old city, my first disappointed and disgusted impression faded and the Bagdad of my imagination loomed brighter.

While resting on the cushioned divans of one of the bazaar cafes, I played chess and dominoes with an old sheik from Mosul. I soon discovered that my companion was one of the 60,000 Yezidis, or "Devil Worshippers," of this old village. Though these queer folk worship God, they also render homage to Satan whom they reverently call "Melek Tans" (the Peacock King). Members of this world's strangest religious sect, they will never utter the word "Shartan," or any other word beginning with "sh" or rhyming with "an." If one pronounces such a syllable in their presence, they feel grossly insulted.

Along the river street I found little cave-like shops of Amarna silver workers who belong to the strange Sabean sect. These long-haired, unshaved creatures claim

[184]

relationship to John the Baptist whom they worship. They all wear red "kufeyah" headgear, and like the Yezidis, abhor the color blue. These Amarnas use the same secret process of engraving beaten silver and treating it with antimony as the smiths of Damascus.

At the river market, corn was being measured by the same crude methods employed a thousand years ago, by means of balance scales. Holding the center connecting piece by his left hand, the corn merchant with his right placed round rocks in soft, padded, steel scales suspended by a leather strap, from one side of the pole, while the buyer poured corn into the wicker basket container suspended in similar manner from the other end of the pole. When both persons agreed that proper balance had been established between the corn and the rocks, the basket was emptied into the customer's cloth sack, and the deal was closed over a cup of tea or eastern ice cream.

While in Iraq, I practically lived on ice cream, as it cost only ten fils (five cents U.S. money—one royal or two hundred fils are equivalent to one American dollar) per pint, whereas oranges, not in season, cost ten fils each.

As the moon rose across the palm fringed bank of the Tigris, and raced up the side of an arabesquely tiled minaret, I began my exploration of the tombs on the western shore, Zubeidah's tomb soared up from the shadows like a giant pineapple, its spire being a series of arches, inside which were rows of connected cells, capped with stalactites. Through the small round holes in each cell, the moonbeams passed in beautiful interlacing streams of blue light.

Several hundred meters farther down the Tigris, I pondered over the tomb of Sheik Janayad. Even today, childless women visit the tomb of this tenth century mystic, draw water from its courtyard well and empty the basin of water three times, saying, "Be fruitful; be fruitful."

If the spirit of Sheik Janayad sees fit to answer the

[185]

prayer of childless women, they make their new-born babies brave by carrying them over and under Abu Khazama, the famous old gun in the citadel courtyard of the King's residence on the river bank, beside blue-domed Maidan Mosque. On the great feast day of Wakt Aluan ("Time of Visiting," the only day in the year that Moslem women are given a "free rein" outside their husbands' harems) mothers, of all religious sects, visit the gun and place lighted candles in its barrel, one candle for each baby born during the three months preceding the feast.

In the tomb of Baklul, Jester to Haran el Rashid, there is a stone-paved courtyard on which natives build cairns and miniature houses of sticks to contain their heart's desire. As most of these people cannot write, they identify their individual houses with the impressions of their finger tips.

Had I been able to dispose of my heart's desire in such convenient manner, I would have gladly built my own little cairn and tarried at Bagdad; but like Maeterlink's bluebird of happiness, my heart's desire seemed always to lie in a land just over the horizon. At dawn, the rising sun lured Bucephalus onward across the plains of Persia, toward Khanagin, Kermanshah, Hamadan, Kosvin and Teheran.

CHAPTER XXX

Travels in a Harem

At break of day Bucephalus and I began our trip from Bagdad to Persia. The King of Iraq, also an early riser, almost ran over me as his French auto whizzed down New Street, preceded and followed by two pairs of screaming motorcycles. On the edge of town, the uniformed Iraqian cavalrymen, with sabres flashing in air, were dashing around the training grounds on their beautiful Arabian steeds. Airplanes buzzed overhead like swarms of angry bees.

[186]

Large herds of water buffalo were bathing in the muddy road-side streams. Great storks lazily stretched their wings and legs as they perched by dozens on the mud walls and roofs of the huts along the trail. The air was vibrating with the music of a million birds, whose sweetness of song was surpassed only by the beautiful blending of all colors of the rainbow in their feathers. There were blue and green parakeets with black-fringed wings spreading gracefully from their slender bodies; also, many "stream-lined" red-under-wing green birds with queer stingaree-like points extending beyond the ends of their fan tails. Nature had added a touch of color even to the old crows cawing by the road. Though head, tail, and wings were black, the rest of their bodies was almost snow white instead of the soft grey of Egyptian and Scandinavian crows, or the jet black of those of America.

All through the plains, peasants were planting grain in moisture-retaining holes, which they had dug for such agricultural purposes. Other workers were engaged in charcoal-making by placing chunks of wood in pits of slow-burning camel dung and covering the hole with a thin layer of sand.

At a tiny oasis ten miles out from Bagdad, I stopped to watch two sun-blackened girls shear sheep. With her legs locked around the sheep's neck in a wrestler's scissors hold, one girl rolled and tumbled on the ground with the sheep, but held fast, until the second girl had plied her shears. Everywhere, the wheels of animal and human industry were turning while the day was still young and cool. There would be time to sleep during the heat of midday when the thermometer would soar up to 120 degrees in the shade.

My chief form of entertainment as I cycled over the fifty-mile stretch of desolate, hard-baked plain outside Bagdad, was in seeing how many of the myriads of locusts (grasshoppers) I could run over and "sqush" as

[187]

they hopped across the road. In Palestine and other parts of the world, where there was more vegetation, there were huge flocks of starlings, which destroyed all such insects. One starling has been known to eat more than 500 locusts per day.

When an unexpected but welcome cloudburst overtook me near Diala, I asked a passing native if summer showers were not unusual for Persia. He replied, "Yes, the raindrops are tears of the Old Man."

As we stopped beneath the sheltering roof of a roadside cafe (native cafes consist solely of straw mat roofing, above a half-dozen huge pots of food cooking on stone fireplaces), my sharp-eyed comrade told me Proverbs and Fables of Persian mythology, which ante-dates even that of the ancient Greeks.

I wished to share my lunch with this clever old Arabian Knight; but almost insulted, he insisted that I share his own meat and bread. Like all the other natives, he termed me a "traveling man" and as such, it was his solemn duty to see me safely through his country. Though I met all sorts of characters, many with noses, ears, and eyes split, or torn out by the roots—thus indicating vicious cruelty on the part of some of them—all were alike in their hospitable respect for the "traveling man." That the peasants did not trust each other was quite evident by the iron bars completely and securely covering the fronts of the village bazaar shops.

My road ended suddenly at Diala, and I had to carry Bucephalus across the railroad river trestle to the tropical jungle oasis of Baqubah. A little toy-like train almost overtook me before I reached the bank. The unusual seating situation in this local train consisted of four parallel benches running the full length of the car, two benches facing outward on either side.

From a tangled mass of vine-covered palm, pear, and pomegranate trees which darkened the trail, I emerged

[188]

into the middle of town, where a group of young men were bathing in their "birthday suits" in the little river flowing alongside the main thoroughfare. The national peasant costume of Persia seemed to be rags, though a few boasted long, black, respectable-looking hooded capes.

As neither man nor beast in this part of Persia had ever seen a bicycle, both usually tumbled off the roadside at sight of my iron steed, unless the native used foresight (which he seldom did) and threw a cloak across his donkey's eyes so that he could not see Bucephalus approaching.

Had not the cooler hills called me onward, I would have stopped at Shaklabar for the night. Several hours later, while cycling across Table Mountain near a great World War monument to British, Turkish, and Indian forces, I was nearly shocked from my seat when an airplane swooped down on the plateau beside me. The pilot, Leslie Savage, a young English member of the Royal Air Force of Iraq, had sighted my cycle and dropped to investigate. We camped together far out in Persia's no man's land and listened over the airship's radio set to an N.B.C. network program from the United States!

At dawn I penetrated farther into the wild hill country. It was necessary to cross many bridgeless waterways, which were perilously swollen by the melting snows of the higher mountains to the northeast. The fragrant-flowered plains were dotted with herds of sheep, fields of grain, and cities of black tents.

Many of the villages in the vales were compact masses of mud with a common roof over all the houses. These roofs, covered in several feet of earth, grew grass, grain and flowers, and actually served as pastures for cattle, which I frequently saw grazing upon the house-tops! In time of war, these villages should certainly be safe from aerial bombardment because of their invisibility from above. I also noticed little boys playing ball on many of

[189]

the housetop meadows.

There was something indescribably strange about the landscape of long mountain ranges interspersed with plateaus and little conical hills like breakers on a stormy sea beach. There were also many jagged ranges resembling giant lizards or dinosaurs stretching across the countryside.

Not only were the fields full of birds, but clinging to the walls and rafters in every house, were at least a score of little mud and straw nests, each filled with six or eight chirping birdlets, which seemed to be all mouths as the forked-tailed mother birds flitted in the house windows with food for their babies.

At Khanaqin, the native schoolmaster showed me through the school rooms of straw mat roofs and floors, with lattice work of holes in the mud walls to serve as windows. After watching the first grade children read and write their Arabic "A B C's," we crossed the street to my first (and last—I hope!) real Turkish bath. All day it had been like roasting in a frying pan as I cycled across the burning plains; now, it was jumping from the frying pan into the fire itself.

In the East, nudity is more shameful among men than among women. Therefore, after leaving our clothes in an outer chamber we encircled our waists with bath rugs, entered the dark-domed furnace and seated ourselves beside hot basins of water bubbling through the sizzling hot stone floor, beneath which was a charcoal fire. As our oven was air-tight, we lost a couple of pounds in perspiration in a very few minutes; then, with silver cups of water from stone basins cleft in the arched walls, we drenched our sweating carcasses to complete the bath—except for a glass of Turkish-bath tea, the most deliciously flavored beverage I had ever tasted. Unlike the ordinary hot tea which natives drink every few minutes during the day, this special "after-bath" drink is spiked with cloves, cardamon,

[190]

and other spices.

Never can I forget that scene as I sat wrapped in towels, sipping tea on the great platform in the lounge room adjoining the baths, while a dozen similarly garbed swarthy patrons of the place followed up their tea with a smoke upon bubbling water pipes.

Wondering what was next on the evening's program for my entertainment, I hesitatingly accompanied my hospitable host to his home. The professor apologized for the long wait outside, even after clanging loudly upon the metal disk beside his brass-braided door. He explained that Moslem etiquette strictly forbade women to show themselves upon the arrival of men, and, although his harem consisted of only three wives, they probably all had been weaving in the courtyard just inside the door and it was taking them some time to gather up their work and retire to the penetralia of the house.

Finally a small boy tremblingly opened the door and we stepped into a beautiful but deserted garden courtyard, in the center of which several appetizing dishes were spread on a large Persian rug. Sitting down to our supper, my host and I dived into the mutton balls containing corn, beans and other vegetables. Even in this cultured house, we had between us a common bowl of clabber in which we "dunked" our flat bread and dates.

For once in my life I was having enough dates. Earlier that same day, when I asked for two fils worth (one cent) of this luscious fruit of the palm tree, the market vendor had poured nearly two gallons of them into my bread kit. Evidently, Mesopotamia, like Egypt, was an ideal country for dates.

The professor rounded off our repast with an analyzing discourse upon Iraqian government affairs as conducted by the king and houses of lords and commons, a parliamentary set-up fashioned after England's form of government. Being pro-war and anti-world peace, the country was now beginning a remilitarization program, which the professor earnestly assured me would ultimately result in the reunion politically as well as religiously of the Arabian peoples (Persia, Iraq, Egypt, Palestine, Syria, Afghanistan, et cetera) who had been broken up and divided after the World War.

Our discussion came to an embarrassing stand-still when the smothered laughter of a female voice reached our ears. The professor stopped in the middle of a sentence to apologize for this terrible rudeness on the part of one of his wives.

My disappointment at not meeting the other members of this Moslem family was so obvious that my host agreed to bestow this great honor upon his wives, if I felt that it would not insult my superior station in life for them to come before my presence.

A true Moslem, my host held his wives on the same level as his cows, camels, and "other cattle." The knowledge of reading and writing having been strictly forbidden these women, many of them really possessed little more mentality than cattle.

While the professor sent his small son to the harem with orders for his wives to dress for our reception, we inspected the other sections of the house. Like most village homes of the Near East, an outside staircase led to the summer sleeping quarters on the mud roof of the house, which was covered by a carpet of soft growing grass to furnish better foundation for sleeping.

Almost an hour elapsed before the little boy returned to say that all was in readiness for our visit. As we walked down a narrow tiled hallway, the professor whispered his regret that I must see his wives in their usual indoor dress plus the veiled street masks covering their noses and mouths. He said that even the walls of all houses possessed ears and eyes, and should an infidel (the term Moslems commonly use in referring to a Christian) be

[192]

allowed to gaze upon an unveiled Moslem woman, it would be considered a gross insult to Allah.

In the light of this apologetic explanation on the part of the professor, together with the long time taken for his wives to dress for the gala occasion, I naturally expected to find them almost drowned beneath the folds of gold and silver embroidered, silken robes and shawls totally concealing their persons from view.

As my host pushed aside a bead-embroidered purple velvet curtain and ushered me into the presence of his wives, all my pre-conceived mental pictures of the inside of a harem were "gone with the wind."

Instead of thin straw matting for floor covering, as in other rooms of the house, this spacious den was completely covered by a single beautiful Persian rug of a soft downy texture. Rugs of odd shapes and designs also decorated the creamy clay walls and ceilings. In one corner of the room exotic perfume emanated from a little incense container to harmonize perfectly with the hazy twilight atmosphere of the harem. It made me feel as if I were suddenly transported into a dreamy make-believe world.

Though the room contained no chairs—as was true of all the others I had seen—there were a dozen beautifully colored silk and velvet cushions and half as many equally exquisite lounges. Upon these, the three wives reclined like couchant goddesses in dreamy contemplation.

True to their Moslem faith, the women were masked, with only brown eyes peering mysteriously over the black veils. However, these mouth and nose veils seemed to emphasize the almost stark nudity of the rest of their bodies, which were bare of all clothing. Except for jewel-inlaid gold and silver earrings, bracelets, anklets, and a pendant necklace upon one of the women, and a beaded coin waist band loosely draped about the hips of another, they were dressed exactly like the young maiden in the picture "September Morn."

[193]

I looked anxiously toward the husband, expecting him to blow the harem and all its contents to pieces. The look of glowing pride upon his face shocked me even more than the sight of his immodestly dressed wives—he was actually gloating over the wonderful impression his wives had made, and was as proud to display their nude beauty as if they had been a trio of finely built camels or pure-bred Arabian horses!

I was further shocked at the obvious difference in the ages of husband and wives. My host was at least fifty years of age, while the oldest wife did not appear to be more than nineteen or twenty. The professor soon enlightened me by pronouncing nineteen, seventeen, and fourteen as he named and pointed to the damsels. He explained that Eastern men do not age as we Westerners, but that Eastern women suddenly change from extremely beautiful young maidens into extremely ugly old hags. Thus it is not uncommon for an old grandfatherly-looking Easterner to take unto himself a wife when she is still only a child.

The surprising scene had been slightly more than I could digest, so that I heartily approved of the professor's suggestion that we take a stroll toward the village streets.

As we wandered through town, stopping at each shop for a sociable cup of hot tea, the professor's pupils gathered about him. By the time we reached Bucephalus at the police barracks, almost the entire village had fallen in line to turn our leisurely ramblings into a royal progress.

As the night was still young and the moon fascinatingly beautiful as it hung like a halo around a snowy Persian peak, I bade my brethren adieu and mounted Bucephalus. We charged down the dark lane leading to the wild mountains of the Persian border.

CHAPTER XXXI

Kermanshah to Teheran

After cycling through hail and rain storms, and splashing through several sparkling rivers up the high mountain gorges of the western Persian border, I was ready for a rest when I dropped down to Kermanshah's 4,000-foot plateau lying like a beautiful emerald in an encircling silvery setting of 10,000-foot mountain ranges.

During my brief stay in Kermanshah, I met Yoush Peera, one of the 5,000 Assyrians wandering through Persia without home, family, or country. Although unfamiliar with "school learning," he was a "self-made" man and an interesting conversationalist.

In reply to my remark concerning the unusual Western appearance of the nomads I had seen in the Syrian Desert, Yoush related the weird history of these former "Arab slaves" who are really direct descendants of Romans, captured by Saladin during the Second Crusade, and who, even today, have a language of their own.

He then told the fascinating story of his own journey through life—of the years he lived with the "Arab slaves" in the desert; of his adventures in Russia; and of his escape three years earlier, in time to fight with 700 Assyrians against Kurds and Arabs in the Mosla Mountains 300 miles north of Bagdad. Since they were outnumbered by the thousands of Arabs, the war was carried on in guerilla fashion. While the men were thus fighting in the mountains, 600 Assyrian women and children were surprised and slain in the village below. The Assyrians counter-attacked to burn out the Arabs, and, in fierce fighting, killed 5,000 Sons of Allah without losing more than a few hundred of their own avenging men.

Like the Arab-Jewish conflict through which I had just

passed, it was the same old story of the conflict of religions.

Yoush was so happy that I sympathized with his unfortunate race of vanishing Assyrians, that he carried me to dine and drink tea with a dozen others of his Christian friends. Later, in a group, we rode through the village and surrounding country in the horse-drawn carriages called droshkies, which rumbled about the streets by the hundreds.

The streets were teeming also with long trains of donkeys heavily laden with six-foot-long blue jars hanging from each side, and great sheets of bread packed on top. Scores of beggars chanted their monotonous stories to all passers-by. Heavily armed, blue-uniformed (with orange stripes down the sides) soldiers smoked their thick-stemmed, "shotgun-barrelled" pipes as they swaggered down the street.

Street workers were using rug stretchers for dirt and gravel transportation. The same rug material adorned the walls, windows, and floors of shops. Over the doorways of most of the houses were awful paintings of dragons and serpents resembling pictures over circus side-shows.

Along the sidewalk were many cigarette stands. As Persians smoke their own individual length cigarettes, the slender cylinders of tobacco on display were five and six feet in length. The customer cuts these long cigarettes into whatever size suits his taste.

In the public pool in the middle of town, natives were washing everything, from their own feet and clothes to vegetables for dinner. On the corner diagonally across from the pool, we stopped at an attractive cafe to eat a few eggs roasted in charcoal, and to watch the industrious culinary artists make their exotic concoctions. One delicious dish called "kabob" consisted of meat cubes smothered in layers of onion, potatoes, saffron, cloves, cardamon seed, tomato juice, salt, pepper, and butter. Before steaming this motley mixture in a hollow metal utensil over a charcoal fire, the meat cubes are strung upon stripped fig twigs

[196]

which make them so tender that they melt in the mouth.

By watching the cook, I also got some ideas on how to make real barbecue, Persian style. He slit open a whole sheep, removed the insides, refilled it with raisins, plums, apricots, dates, pistachio nuts, and also many frying size chickens which were in like manner stuffed with fruits and nuts. He then sewed the sheep together again (hide, wool and all) and placed it in a great hole surrounded by embers. The whole was then covered with slowly burning camel dung, smouldering beneath a top layer of earth, to simmer and cook the sheep in the same fashion as charcoal is made. Of course the hide and outer layers of flesh would be burned, but the rest of the sheep would make the finest flavored, most tender dish imaginable.

A third favorite delicacy to which the cafe cook's customers seemed to be addicted was "cirk angebin," a mixture of pure cider vinegar boiled with sugar and cucumbers. The resulting fluid is used as sauce for lettuce, or diluted with water and snow and drunk as a beverage during the hot summer months.

The most surprising of all dishes was wisteria cooked in egg batter—the same delicious combination of egg and flower blossoms which I had enjoyed in Athens, Greece.

Passing through this disorderly Drama of Life along the black, windowless bazaar streets, we traveled into the open country, where the whistling trills of the birds and the bleating of the sheep in the green pastures reminded me that it was the first day of the month of May.

Yoush produced a snake charmer flute, and, for the next two hours, entertained our party with the maddening music which, by inhaling and exhaling simultaneously, he was able to make continuous and incessant. This seemingly impossible trick was accomplished by puffing his mouth full of the last breath in his lungs and releasing it of its own pressure into the flute reed at the same instant that he inhaled a new draft of air through his nose.

[197]

Along our winding road, peasant girls, engaged in milking goats or cutting cubes of clay brick for house-building material, stopped their work to listen to the rhythm of the music. Several times we piled out of our carriages and joined these merry maidens in Assyrian hop-skip-step folk dances.

At Toq-Boston, we viewed the famous old mountain-side carvings cut 1600 years ago by Emperor Cyrus to commemorate his victory over the Romans. One magnificent alabaster bas relief of figures, sculptured in an arched vault in the base of the rock cliff, portrays mounted Persian princes standing upon the heads of defeated Roman knights. On the walls of the open-fronted vault are beautifully carved and colored bronze figures of birds, animals, and human beings.

In addition to these memorials, there are beautiful swimming pools and baths hewn in the mountain side, from which a river of clear water bubbles. Here, the kings of 2,000 years ago enjoyed their summer vacations. A stairway hewn in the solid rock winds from these national monuments at the base of the cliff to the mountain top, which commands a view of the great plateau.

Our day of celebration culminated in a dinner party given by Yoush in the hotel garden on the sloping mountain side above Kermanshah. After the physical strain of steady bicycling up from Egypt, it was a welcome day of rest.

The richly spiced and sweetened foods of the East were not so healthful as the plain fare of Europe. After crossing the Syrian Desert, a small boil on the calf of my leg had required attention at the Royal Iraqian Hospital in Bagdad. As the constant strain on the muscles of my leg aggravated the sore, it gradually became serious. Luckily, I found an American Hospital in Kermanshah where the wound was lanced and a drainage tube inserted, so that I could continue my journey in safety the next day, through the region of old fire worshippers and over the 8,000-foot passes across Assabad and Ectaban mountains to Hamadan.

As I penetrated farther eastward, the gradual drop in the standard of living was alarmingly obvious. The filth, disease, and poverty is almost inconceivable to the average American. While lunching in Hamadan, I inadvertently dropped a few bits of bread. Immediately, the old rag bundles of beggars, stretched out in seeming slumber on the sidewalk, came to life and fought and scrambled after the treasured crumbs almost before they touched the ground.

These same beggars, without food, clothing, money, or chattels, perhaps possessed exquisite rugs which would do honor to any palatial American home. Everywhere, I saw poverty-stricken peasants sitting on their housetops weaving their beautifully designed and colored tapestries to serve as bed mats and table cloths in their homes.

The value of these rugs is determined by the number of knots in a space covered by a small cigarette paper. In such a limited space, there are often more than one hundred tied knots so small that a microscope is necessary to see them.

The true Persian rug invariably contains a design which some say is symbolic of the stamp of the side of the king's hand after it has been dipped in blood; others interpret the symbol as representing a cypress tree heavily bowed with snow; still others say that it is a representation of an almond nut in its shell; while a fifth group insists that it is a bird motif; this design is known in America under the title of "Palmy Leaf Pattern."

As I cycled singing up the road to Kosvin, wild pigeons cooed their disapproval, and donkeys "hee-hawed" in close harmony. The mountain slopes of this region were sparklingly green as if showers of emerald paint had fresh-ly fallen from the sky. The bare rock knobs of these grassy mountains looked like great warts protruding from giant noses. My ever-winding road cut through several serrated

[199]

rock cliffs extending down into a red canyon river, and finally made a bee-line shot across another fifty-mile-wide, windswept plateau.

My intended camp site was abandoned on the appearance of wolves. Having already enjoyed the novel experience of sitting up half the night and throwing rocks at such beasts while crossing Sinai, I was not in the mood for doing so again. Although dead tired from more than a hundred miles of cycling that day, I continued my journey until I reached a peasant hut on whose grassy roof I slumbered in peace until dawn sent me scurrying into Teheran.

The recent estrangement of American-Persian relations, growing out of an insult to the Persian minister by a New Jersey speed cop, was being "backfired" against the few Americans who happened to be in Persia at the time. My American passport meant very little to Persian officials save as incriminatory evidence of my status as an American citizen. This was even more disreputable in the eyes of the Persian government than if I had been a Russian Communist.

No Americans in the country were allowed to receive foreign newspapers or printed matter of any sort, and all personal letters were censored. If an American resident in Persia wished to invite a few friends to lunch or tea, he first had to get a permit from the government officials who, not satisfied with taking names and descriptions of all persons attending the party, also came to stand guard over the party to see that no plot was manufactured against the Persian government.

I was strictly warned, on penalty of imprisonment, not to take a single kodak picture in Persia. Thus, my hundreds of Persian snapshots were taken at great risk. Fortunately, the only time I was caught taking pictures, the official was broad-minded and turned me loose after I opened the camera and convinced him, by perforating the film with a pin, that it was no longer good. He did not know that the

Moslem saint in Paradise

Diseased father and...

Healthy sons in Meshed's great leper colony

ucephalus
uses midst
ud mansions
Meshed

*Traveling
salesman*

*Bucephalus meets the mayor (ri[g]
and councilman of Ish-a-Bosh*

*"Washed out" village
of West Afghan
border*

*Afghan Boy Scouts
discover Bucephalus
near Ish-a-Bosh*

*Ish-a-Bosh
(window in upper left
corner is where I slept
with the two old men
of the town)*

*Wild hills
of West Afghanistan*

scratched and destroyed portion of the film had never been exposed—the film he was seeking to have destroyed was safely stowed away inside the film cartridge!

As officials of each village delayed me several hours to grant permission of entry into their locality, and then another several hours to give me permission to leave, I "breezed" into Teheran nearly a week behind schedule time.

It had been a slow but inexpensive trip. Furnishing my own locomotive power, and sleeping in the out-of-doors, meant that my whole expense amounted to only a few cents for food. The entire trip from Cairo to Teheran had cost only $3.00.

The great capital of Persia is now one of the most up-to-date looking cities in the Near East. Since the king's recent orders that the Moslem women discard their veils and adopt modern dress, there is a bit of European atmosphere blending with that of the Orient.

The beautiful snowy-peaked Elburz Mountains rise to a height of 18,500 feet (Demovan, the highest peak) above the many exquisitely tiled gateways of Teheran. The buildings of the city—from Anglo-Iranian Oil Company to banking establishments—possess such wonderfully designed tiled domes and turreted spires that they resemble cathedrals.

While watching bricklayers erect a new building, I caught their words as they "sang to the bricks," as the Persians express it, "God bless you, brother; give me another brick." These sing-song words are effectively repeated by the bricklayers from the moment they start work until the job is finished. On the opposite corner was an old blind man singing another mournful tune.

It is noteworthy that the sad strain running through all Persian music dates back to the time of the Mogul invasion, when Persia's population was reduced to three million and threatened with total extinction.

[203]

Cycling over the shady, smooth-stoned streets beneath the tall, graceful chenarr (plane) trees lining the sidewalks, I went directly to the American Hospital and had Dr. Edward Blair give me a typhoid shot. Though I drank only water boiled in tea samovars, I was taking no chances of being one of the many foreigners who find their graves in this country where typhoid rages.

Holding the highest medical post in Persia, as the honored head of the anatomical department of the American University, Dr. Blair lacked no material assistance which the government could furnish him. He took me to his classrooms where I saw scores of human bodies in the process of dissection. The first year medical students were carving into arms and legs while the upper classmen were consigned to the other parts of the corpses. In the storage rooms downstairs, were a dozen great tanks, each containing forty pickled human bodies. In the hospital ward we visited some of the live patients who were waiting to die and be pickled (i.e., the unclaimed bodies would be pickled for experimental purposes).

The sick ward presented a motley scene of mournful men: here was a young nomad with the calf of his right leg nipped out by the bite of a camel; another with his arm amputated as a result of an infected bite of a sand fly; and still another cut hopelessly to pieces from a sword fight. The happiest patient was a young Jugoslav who had been left to die in the Persian wilds, after his leg had been mangled by dynamite. However, he had reached the hospital, and Dr. Blair was not only saving his life, but miraculously, his injured leg also.

I sat till midnight enjoying with Dr. and Mrs. Blair the victrola records of far away "Suwanee River," "Old Black Joe," and other spirituals. The gateman retired, and I had to climb over the high gate entrance into the hospital grounds, and then over a second twenty-foot-high, iron-spiked, "burglar-proof" one into the Presbyterian Mission

[204]

grounds, where I was the guest of Dr. William Miller, one of the most devout Christians I ever met.

Besides myself, there were three other guests in Dr. Miller's home: Mr. Hazegh (a recently retrieved opium eater), and Clarence and Henry Mueller, two American missionaries who had been forced to flee for their lives from Kurdistan. They had many harrowing experiences to tell of malaria, ruptured appendix, and other usually fatal ailments in the back hills of Kurdistan, hundreds of miles from the nearest doctor. Yet, they had pulled through, and even after being thrown from the train in the middle of the desert, had lived to tell the tale.

Still more thrilling was the story of another visitor who dropped into the Mission to tell his life story. He had been converted to Christianity fifty years before and had had to leave home to avoid being murdered by his Moslem brother. After studying medicine in London, he returned to practice in Teheran. This old Persian was none other than Dr. Saeed Khan, the "Beloved Physician of Teheran," whose remarkable life has been the inspiration for several biographical publications.

Another life story, sounding like a testimonial ceremony in a North Georgia Methodist camp meeting, was that related by Mr. Banam. This young Persian had come to Teheran three months earlier to kill three people, but was too overcome by opium to carry out his plans. Arrested for his attempted murders, he was so violent that he was removed to the insane asylum. Here he managed to secure his favorite drug (opium), which he twice imbibed in overdoses with intent to kill himself.

Upon surviving, he suddenly recalled his respectable boyhood schooldays, and decided to start anew in life. As he sat in his asylum cell, he began to study Comparative Religions. He thought, "Although Mohammed had quite a flock of wives and concubines, God's curse was evidently upon him as He allowed only one sickly son and daughter

[205]

to be born to him."

"Animals are monogamous, yet Mohammed was a proponent of polygamy. Are we to be even less than beasts?" shouted the excited Mr. Banam, as he portrayed to me the mental processes through which he had gone in finally deciding that Christianity was the only true religion. For a half-hour longer he carefully dissected Mohammed, showing his absolute unworthiness in all the realms and phases of human thought and activity (business ethics, music, art, et cetera), all of which virtues he found perfected in Christian faith.

In one final burst of oratory, Mr. Banam exclaimed: "Before I denounced Mohammed, I pointed with pride to the fact that I was directly descended from the daughter of this great prophet. A true Moslem, I was a successful merchant until I lost all faith in religion of any kind, and almost lost myself in a suicide's grave. Now that I am a Christian, my mercantile business has become bankrupt for lack of customers. But for the help of Dr. Miller, I would be starving. Nevertheless, I am happy. Before, I was unhappy."

When he had finished, I sat in stupefied amazement at the thought of this man, depraved lunatic only three months previously, now sitting before me and delivering a sermon which would grace the pulpit of some of our most eloquent preachers.

Truly, there is no lukewarmness about these zealous Christian sons of Mohammed, few though they be. Needless to say, Christians of the Orient must be strong if they are to survive the persecutions of the overwhelming Moslem crowd.

CHAPTER XXXII

The Peacock Throne

Among other interesting personalities I met while in Teheran was Dr. Jordan, a Pennsylvanian, then President of the American College in Persia. This tall, lanky, cowboy-hatted gentleman had the outward appearance of a ranch owner of the Old West, while his "human" and unassuming characteristics betrayed qualities strikingly similar to those of the late Will Rogers.

Dr. Jordan was the only "safe" American in Persia. Having educated most of the high government officials, he was their intimate and influential friend. Little did I dream that this influence could be so powerfully exercised as to secure for me an invitation to visit the king's royal palace of Gulistan, and inspect its gardens, treasure rooms, and even the world-renowned Peacock Throne, which was brought up from India to Teheran by Nadir Shah in 1739.

I had just finished reading a book describing the experiences of one of the few foreigners ever to view this thirty-million-dollar throne. The author told of the many weeks of unavailing effort to obtain a glimpse of this almost priceless treasure. At that time, the Shah was visiting in Paris. The author was about to journey back to that great French metropolis in one last attempt to prevail upon the Shah, when the Prime Minister of Persia finally consented to let him take a peek into the Throne Room for the supreme thrill of his lifetime.

Naturally, I could scarcely believe my own ears when Dr. Paine, the mediator of foreigners and Persian government officials, told me that he and Dr. Jordan had secured the coveted invitation; and that on the following morning I was to be the guest of the Prime Minister, and accompany him on an inspection tour of Gulistan Palace.

[207]

With a whole day of waiting still ahead, Dr. Jordan accompanied me to places of interest about the city. We visited everything from his own school to the strange ice plant where ice freezes naturally within the thick, shaded, mud walls in the high, dry atmosphere of the plateau. On the streets outside the same walls poor natives nearly die of sunstroke.

I was chagrined at having to come to Persia to see the most modern type of college building. The wonderfully constructed American College in Teheran is a living memorial to Dr. Jordan. The building of this magnificent edifice revolutionized Persian architecture, inspiring it to blossom forth anew in the many beautiful, cathedral-like buildings which I saw rising in all parts of this great city, whereas it had hitherto been on the downward grade. The mosaic tiles of most of the old structures are of such poor design and construction that they are anathema to Persian art.

A riot of richly colored, tile designs adorned the outer walls of this castle-like college, while the classrooms inside were equipped with up-to-date conveniences, useful as well as ornamental. Even the seating arrangement, instead of being in parallel rows, was slightly compact beside the windows and extended in divergent V-shaped rows across the room so that light obstructed by one desk would not cast a shadow upon the next. Thus, in the botanical department, all species of fungi and other specimens of plant life were potted and planted between the rows of classroom seats.

In the afternoon, we hailed a droshke and rode eight kilometers out to the partially excavated ruins of the semi-prehistoric city of Ray (frequently referred to as Rhe-Rhages), which dates back almost 6,000 years, and at one time boasted of more than two million inhabitants.

We found Pennsylvania University archaeologists excavating in this old city, the major part of which was

[208]

still underground. Slowly they were unearthing secrets of the much-discussed but little-known Parthian civilization. The already exposed 2,000-year-old mud brick walls of the last city of Ray draped across the mountainsides like the Great Wall of China.

In descending into a deep pit cut like a cross section through a half-dozen different cities of Ray, each of which had been built upon the crumbling ruins of a previous one, I gasped in awe at the human skeletons in graveyards on top of houses which were, in turn, on top of still more ancient graveyards!

Many Hittite gods and other strange figures were being brought to light by these archaeologists. At the bottom of the seventh city were great rubbish pits in which many valuable articles were being found. These great wells contained a world of pottery, rings, cylinder seals, pestles, which lay just as they had been thrown 6,000 years before.

A wonderful insight into life in action in ancient times was given by the multitude of designs on the 6,000-year-old pottery: scenes of tigers chasing ibexes, reindeers fighting, and groups of human figures holding hands as if in a ceremonial dance. Tons of pottery had been broken and discarded in huge piles near the excavations. If only I could convey several truckloads of these broken bits to America I might sell them for a small fortune to souvenir hunters!

When the zero hour approached for me to visit Gulistan Palace, I discarded my Bavarian buckskin shorts, and donned Dr. Miller's dress suit. Like legendary Ichabod Crane as he rode his noble steed to Sleepy Hollow, I mounted my iron horse, and sped away to the wonderful dreamland where everything was made of gold, silver, and precious stones.

I was so awed and dazzled by the splendor of the king's palace, that my bewildered mind could scarcely "take it all in." Though prosaic from the outside, the interior decorations of Gulistan represented an entirely different type of man-made beauty from anything I had previously seen. Just as in the junk yards, respectable business houses, and homes of rich and poor, the floors, window-sills, and doorways were carpeted with all sizes and shapes of exquisite rugs, varying from small triangular pieces only a few inches in circumference to gigantic rectangular rugs, one hundred feet in length. The arched walls and ceilings consisted of myriads of pure prismatic mirrors, which glistened like millions of diamonds.

The richly ornamented King's Study commanded a wonderful view of Gulistan Garden (the "Garden of Roses"), with its many pools and fountains of sparkling mountain water, and the great domed royal theater in the background, where the annual Mohammedan Passion Plays are held.

To retain its fresh greenness, the garden received constant irrigation from the crystal streams of water running down the cobbled conduits on both sides of the city streets. What a wonderful sight these gardens must be at coronation ceremonies when they are decorated with tens of thousands of colored electric lights!

The beautiful scene reminded me of the royal palace at Isfahan with its sparkling fountains bubbling forth, not only in its gardens, but even on the fourth and fifth floors. A strange feature of the music room on the top floor of this oriental skyscraper is the ceiling of hollow boxes, resembling trumpet ends, violins, and other musical instruments. (So perfect are the acoustics, that even after a concert has finished its performance in this room, the doors may be opened and the same music, pent up as it were in the imitation musical instrument boxes in the ceiling, can be heard ringing down through the corridors of the whole palace!)

When the grandfather of Sultan Ahmed Shah (king "ex officio") was seated on the Peacock Throne during his

[210]

coronation ceremonies, he was crowned by an ecclesiastic, who carelessly put the crown on crooked. As it is an historical fact that everything went "crooked" during that reign, Riza Shah Pahlavi, superstitious self-made sovereign of Persia, following the example of Napoleon the Great, personally placed the crown upon his own head, at his coronation ceremony in 1926. Napoleon's esteem for the earlier Shah is evidenced by his gift to Persia of the magnificent rugs now decorating the walls of the great reception room of Gulistan Palace.

Because of the outstanding fame and beauty attached to the Peacock Throne, I had never heard of a second great throne which also graced the halls of Gulistan. Thus, it was an unexpected pleasure to run into the Marble Throne, on the ground floor of the royal palace. As I looked beyond a bubbling fountain which had been removed from Shiraz and placed before this great marble structure with its columns of animal and human figures of tusked savages armed with crooked swords, I wondered if it were possible for the Peacock Throne to be so beautiful. On either side in front of the Marble Throne were towering columns, which supported one end of the place. These gracefully slender stems were unique in construction, with their spiralled surfaces culminating at the top in vertical, stream lines—like the pipes of a church organ— while at the base, the pillars were decorated with flower designs. Many other treasures from the ruins of Persepolis surrounded this great throne which is used by the king as military pageant processions pass in review before him.

Wonderful products of Oriental leisure were the many intricately carved ivory balls, containing large numbers of similarly designed smaller balls, each within a slightly larger ball, whose finely chased surface represented years of arduous, skilled labor.

There were also "back scratchers" consisting of long ivory sticks with miniature ivory hands at the end to do

[211]

the scratching; immense bowls of imported china; mirrors of all sizes and shapes; royal crowns of inestimable value; long, leather-handled, precious stone-studded, blunderbuss pistols; crescent knives; purple carved trumpets of elephant tusks; and in the treasure closets at one end of the palace, literally bushels of beautiful pearls, and other precious stones, some of which had never been cut and polished.

With this preliminary introduction into the wealth of the East, I was in some degree prepared for the final dazzling spectacle as I entered the largest room of the palace and beheld the famous Peacock Throne, mounted on a dais, in glorious splendor at the far end of the great hall. As I approached I saw that it was made of gold, which was almost entirely concealed from view by jewels studding its surface with all sorts of fantastic designs.

Under each arm of the throne were two golf ball-size rubies. Over the middle of the back of the throne a rising sun was carved in quite appropriate surroundings of glistening gold and diamonds, as if it were spreading its golden rays of light upon sparkling dew drops at dawn. Towering majestically on either side of the rising sun were two golden hoopoe birds, their rainbow of colored feathers being represented by settings of vari-colored jewels and precious stones.

The throne was of such great length that two extra legs were necessary to support it in the middle. This gigantic structure, resembling a bed more than it does a throne, is said to have really been used as the bed of the mysterious Peacock Lady.

Having seen this Pride of Persia, I was ready to explore Afghanistan and India. When the Afghan minister in Teheran informed me of the impossibility of granting a visa to enter his forbidden country, I was all the more anxious to obtain entree. My last hope lay in the Afghan Consulate in Meshed, 600 miles farther, in the northeastern corner of Persia, which penetrates like a wedge between Russia and Afghanistan. Should I fail to obtain my coveted visa in Meshed, it would be necessary to make a long, circuitous detour to the south through the hot Baluchistan Desert to India, instead of cycling across the wild tribal regions of central and northern Afghanistan.

As Persia was not a British Protectorate, like Iraq, Palestine and other countries, the natives understood only Arabic or Turkish tongues. There being practically no tourist traffic through the wild, desolate mountains and plains of northern Persia, road signs were written only in Arabic. Since my knowledge of this language was scant, I relied solely upon the map Dr. Miller drew for me, and a few words of the northern Persian dialect: "Meshed Kojast?" (where is Meshed?), "chard?" (how much?), "ab" (water), "nan" (bread), "most" (sour milk), "tokhen" (egg), "panir" (cheese), "sabzi" (vegetable), "keshmesh" (raisin), "bactam" (almond), and "pilau" (the national rice and mutton dish of Persia). I also changed my "rials" (silver six-cent piece) to small copper coins with which to purchase food along the way, always being careful to carry no more than two or three pennies about my person at any one time.

When my bicycle was repaired, re-tired and tubed, with bicycle equipment imported from Germany, and my bread kit and water flasks were well filled with almonds, raisins, cheese, bread, and lime juice, all my friends in Teheran gathered to see me off.

As the road ahead was full of danger and desolation, Dr. Miller asked the group to join in a short prayer service as they stood around my cycle. Each in turn prayed that I might have a safe journey through this wild country. Mr. Banam, who had personally supervised the cleaning, oiling, and repairing of Bucephalus, insisted that I let him tie a bouquet of flowers on the handlebars. Dr. Miller then walked the two kilometers out to the eastern city gate with me.

One of the world's most worthy Christians, Dr. Miller had spent his lifetime among these wild people of Persia. In his mission work, he had walked over most of the road I was now following. He knew the true value of a friend's kind words of encouragement in this lonely region of unfriendly beggars, cut-throats, and robbers.

We parted with a hearty handshake and I continued alone toward the orange-colored horizon. As I started over the hill, I looked back for a last view of the great Persian capital. Still standing immobile beside the old tiled gateway, Dr. Miller was watching my cycle sink from his eyes forever—perhaps.

CHAPTER XXXIII

On the Road to Meshed

Although practically barren of vegetation, nearly every one of the 600 milestones of my long trail was marked by some change in the appearance of the landscape, atmosphere, architecture, animal life, and people about me. From the very outset, I was confronted by towering peaks of the Elburz range, which looked as if whipped cream or tooth paste had been smeared on their tops, while silvery ribbons of cream adorned the indented sides. The lower ranges were bare of snow; but like the colors of rainbow ice cream, the strata of earth and rock varied from rosy red to emerald green.

Everywhere in the rolling plains and rugged mountains along the road, Persia's unique tunnel and well combination of conveying water was in evidence. This strange method of carrying water for drinking and irrigation purposes, from the mountains to distant cities, is called "ghanout." The old Romans used aqueducts elevated above the earth, but because of absorption by both sun and earth (water will not long remain on the gravel surface of northern Persia), Persians are compelled to adopt the underground method where no water is lost by absorption or evaporation.

Pathways of this great network of subterranean channels are marked by rows of great wells, dug in the ground to the water level. Every few feet along the water course from mountain stream to city reservoir, these wells are dug and are united by little connecting tunnels beneath each well. In the wilder mountainous regions, I noticed that most of these wells were covered with layers of straw matting and stone, to keep wild animals from falling into the canals and contaminating the water. In more populated places, where wells are left uncovered, great care must be exercised by the natives to keep themselves and their animals from falling into them.

Just after surmounting a high snowy pass at the village of Firuz Koh, my trail wound down through a river gorge so deep and narrow that the hot sun was replaced by a shadowy twilight between the towering overhanging mountains, which, with their colorful, cathedral-like, rocky spires, put even the Dolomites of Italy to shame.

Every single drop of the river water is utilized by the Persian peasants, who convert it into little irrigation canals, tunnelled along the mountains, to their tiny sheep pastures, or vegetable and grain patches.

At one little mountain mud hut I saw a man planting grain, flower and vegetable seed on the roof of his home, as nonchalantly as we Americans would apply a coat of paint to our house tops. In the East, sage brush roofing, covered with earth and manure, makes an ideal garden spot.

Though all houses were of mud, they were not all of the same box-like shape. Many were in the shape of tall mud cylinders, resembling light houses; others were like bee hives with little concentric circles of horizontal walkways extending from the cone tips to the pyramid bases; still

[215]

others were little domed cubes with duplex cave-like entrances on either side. Whenever a mud village has been washed or eroded so much that it needs repairing, the natives merely abandon it and build a new one nearby.

After nearly freezing while cycling over several snowy passes, I plunged so speedily downward to the little mud town of Seminar, that I almost had a sunstroke. Then a long, straight road led me once again from the purple plain to higher ground.

For the past 300 miles I had cycled safely through the swarms of beggars burrowed in little mud huts or even in the gullies of the roadside. I had even safely passed the almost endless stream of terrible-looking tramps who traveled in large groups like tin can armies, and who asked nothing more than that I share my canteens of water and lime juice with them. However, on my third day out from Teheran, while cycling up a dried river bed winding through a wild mountain gorge, a long expected, but unwelcome event befell me.

Leaning wearily against the shady side of the gorge, a seemingly old man was crying "ab! ab!" (water) in a faint, gasping voice, as though his tongue had already swollen from thirst and was suffocating him by cutting off his windpipe. As I extended the flask of coveted fluid toward the crouching figure, he suddenly elevated himself to his full height, and grabbed my collar in the steel-like fingers of his left hand, while his right hand drew a flashing knife from his waist belt.

I had been in the Egyptian riots and been chased through Palestine by Arabs, but this was the first time that one actually had me "on the spot." This grizzly bearded giant could and would have killed me instantly, but for an even more instantaneous and mechanical movement of my own free right hand, which connected with his chin and caused him to shrink in stature until his nose rested somewhat uncomfortably on the ground.

[216]

As I beat a hasty yet respectable retreat on my bicycle, I looked back to find the would-be thief and murderer sitting in a stupor where he had fallen on the ground. He was rubbing his jaw and appeared to be as surprised and awed at the unexpected result of our encounter as I.

In 40,000 miles of solo ramblings through the wildest regions around the world, this was destined to be the only hand-to-hand encounter wherein my eight years of boxing experience would be put to the test. My many years of training in the art of self-defense were worth the effort, if only for the good they did me in that brief moment while my adversary, with his knife poised in mid-air, prepared to send me on my last Great Adventure into the "Land from whence no man returneth."

With the wildest hill country still ahead, I stopped to play good Samaritan to no more tramps along the trail. The days of notorious bands of brigands sweeping down from these mountain gulches were passing because the government police could now track them down when they attacked. However, my own little experience showed that the blood-thirsty spirit of these wild folk could not be so easily quelled, and merely meant that a more clever artifice had to be employed.

Even more dangerous than the tramps were the forces of nature. So torrential are the cloud bursts among the Persian hills that a rainy day is a holiday for road traffic until the bridge-less swollen streams subside to a fordable state. So powerful is the current of these flooded rivers as they plunge down from the rains and melting snows of the higher mountains, that pedestrians and motor trucks are washed helplessly away if they attempt to cross the onrushing waters. A few hours before I crossed a dangerous waist-deep river near Sharud, by balancing the heavy cycle overhead to weight me down, three natives were killed at the same spot, when one lost his footing and pulled the other two down with him. Just as I arrived upon the scene, two were being rescued by horsemen who forced their steeds a short distance out into the powerful current, threw ropes to the poor wretches, and pulled them out alive and conscious. However, they were so beaten and exhausted by the swirling water and sharp stones, that both died a few minutes later. Not only are human lives lost in these overnight floods, but many sheep and goats are swept away also. At three different river crossings I found rice trucks overturned in mid-stream. Near Mianet another truck was standing on its nose in a deep gully, which had undermined and washed out a large portion of the road.

Shortly after sunset of the sixth day of steady cycling, I scaled the last mountain pass and coasted down into Meshed to beat even the mail truck from Teheran, by thirty minutes' time.

I found the city to be laid out like a miniature Washington, D.C., with the golden and blue domes of its holy mosques resting in the center circle of the city and main avenues extending outward from all sides.

Extending up the middle of each main avenue was a small rivulet, the center of varied activities: a small child letting nature take its course in the creek while a woman washed clothing just below; farther down, a woman washed vegetables for dinner in this same creek which her son was using as a bath tub; others, sitting on the creek bank, were spinning woolen thread by means of little wooden "tops" which, after attaching a few strands of unspun wool wrapped about their arms, they sent spinning from finger tips to the ground to remind me faintly of the "yo-yo" craze in America.

One look at the homes on both sides of these busy streets was little more inspiring. Evidently, Easterners are not concerned with outward appearances, but rather with cool, comfortable, beautiful interior decorations. Passing strangers viewing these cities from the outside think them to be drab, dirty, and the antithesis of attractiveness; yet, behind these ugly mud walls and dirty streets are hundreds of wonderful gardens filled with fountains, flowers, trees, and arcaded courtyards.

As I cycled through the avenues and narrow lanes of the city, hundreds of strange sights registered in my mind's eye: a circle of rich old turbaned merchants squatted on their haunches, their twelve-inch beards fluttering in the breeze; colorful bakery shops with their great newspaper-size sheets and circles of bread strung on display outside the arched tile shop doors, or else draped like shawls across the shoulders of the street baker boys; "old Santa Clauses" with their fine rugs spread for sale across the sidewalk, the choicest rug resting comically on top of the head of the vendor; women concealing their features behind purple-fringed white silk shawls, which served as good substitutes for the veils which the king had forbidden them to wear; small children with huge sticks of wild rhubarb in their mouths; swarthy savage-miened sheepherders, wrapped in raw wool cloaks; caravans of henna-haired donkeys laden with fowl, fruit, vegetables, and lumber; and even armies of grey-enshrouded Afghan women, with their monkey-like eyes peering through small, embroidered lace slits in the headgear of their robes.

In bazaar shops, blind camels ground corn into finely powdered meal by pulling, in circles, huge wooden beams attached to a central axis of grinding stone, nine feet in height and weighing several tons. The scene of this great ten-foot-in-diameter stone, resting on its smooth rock base elevated three feet from the ground, reminded me of the one I had seen in a picture of blind Samson in the grist mill.

The streets were dotted with many fanatics torturing themselves with all sorts of insane cruelties. I saw one man eternally walking with his head thrown back and eyes

[219]

Holy man "at home"

Afghan churn

Herat merchant

Herat beggar

Look at the little birdie

e bend in my trail in upper right? Well, Bucephalus didn't "bend" – he came head-over-heels aight down the mountain! (Note rug weaver in foreground, "cellars" and manure wall of these sy turvy houses in which live cattle and on which live humans)

Horse or camel!!?? (Note missing pedal – nearly 400 miles yet to go over the world's wildest, roughest region with a "one-legged" bicycle!)

glaring at the sun so that after a few months of simmering and sweating he would be totally blind. The face of another religious fanatic was set in a frozen grin while her withering hands were held outward to receive alms.

There are no barber shops in Meshed; hair cuts are obtained by stopping itinerant razor wielders in any shady spot along the street, squatting on the ground and letting him do the work. As such a multitude of Persians are nearly bald from scalp disease (favus), and the blood flows freely when the barber unavoidably cuts through a few sore scabs on his victim's head, to an unknowing passer-by, it seems that the barber is really committing murder by scalping. Razors are never washed between shaves or hair cuts, and scalp diseases quickly spread from one to another. Needless to say, I did not bother to get a hair cut while in Persia.

As the bones of Imam Rezeh, the great Moslem saint, rest inside the golden-domed mosque of the Holy City of Meshed, it is one of the twelve great Moslem shrines to which thousands of pilgrims come each year. Many of them give out of money en route and remain as starving beggars in Meshed.

Since the king is trying to make these folk adopt European dress, more colorful and comical-looking scenes parade the streets than ever before. With just enough European dress—a hat two sizes too small, or a pair of pants extending just below the knee cap—added to their sheep-skin robes, vari-colored woolen waist bands, socks and tire-rubber-soled sandals, to give them a motley, clownish appearance, Persian peasants stroll the streets as proudly as peacocks. Many of them now even allow their wives to appear with them at public functions.

However, such reforms in dress are opposed to Moslem teachings, and I found Meshed still in an uproar over a great massacre only a few weeks previous. Several hundred old-fashioned Moslems gathered in Imam Rezeh

Mosque with the king's chief minister and denounced dress reform, until troops with machine guns entered the mosque, locked the doors behind them, and riddled the bodies of all with bullets. Among others eighty-eight Indian and Afghan pilgrims were slain, and now their respective governments were brewing trouble for the Iranian king.

Dodging the deep refuse pits, which perforate the very city streets themselves, I started up a bazaar lane within the magic circle of the holy city. I was immediately threatened with mob murder. The holy mosque domes loomed ahead like a great spider in the center of its web, a network of labyrinthine lanes extending in concentric circles around the magic circle and the main avenues leading from the outskirts of the city, directly to the very mouth of the golden mosque. This beautiful golden spider beckoned me slowly into its parlor; but the fly flew out again in front of enraged pilgrims who assured me in cogent fashion that Christians were not allowed within the magic circle.

Bucephalus was always the fastest thing moving at such times, and he quickly carried me to safety in the American Hospital on the edge of town. There I settled down in safety as a new member of Dr. Rolla E. Hoffman's family until the acquisition of an Afghan visa would let me continue my journey.

CHAPTER XXXIV

The Holy City of Meshed

During my two weeks of waiting in Meshed, I accompanied Dr. Hoffman on many strange medical calls. As most of the winding lanes of the city were so narrow that droshkies were frequently unable to pass on them, Dr. Hoffman used his bicycle as the most efficient carriage for

Persia.

Thus we rode, between reeking opium dens of the city, to the Mission's huge leper colony, five miles out in the white poppy fields encircling the city. Miss Elizabeth Reynolds (American evangelist), and Miss Wilson, a native of northern India, rode donkeys out to the colony where they sang with the leper women and children, while Dr. Hoffman gave each of the helpless patients his monthly five crowns and administered injections in arms, legs, noses, or hips.

Unfortunately the sickening sights of that day can never be erased from my mind's eye: men with all the flesh eaten from their faces by the deadly leprosy, leaving ghastly blackened bits of flesh clinging to jaw bones and forehead, like that of corpses after several months of decomposition had set in; others with whole hands eaten off by suppurating sores, until only little nubs were left at the ends of the wrists; others with no feet or eyes, while the pus-filled eyes of those who had not yet lost sight, shone like red coals from their bloated, tallow-like, ulcerated faces. There were hundreds of pitiful little women and children who might otherwise have been beautiful, had this dreadful disease not eaten away their noses and mouths and turned their whole bodies into one great mass of infection. The foul stench of decomposing bodies of these living dead was almost unbearable.

Though somewhat hesitant about asking for permission to take pictures of these poor creatures, I was surprised when they literally fought to be in the middle of my snapshots!

The victims in this colony were about evenly divided into the two classes of leprosy: one deadens the nerves, swells the hands and bloats the face with great bubble-like sores, giving a distorted, lion-faced appearance; the other is a more deadly skin leprosy type in which the eyebrows fall out and the entire body becomes a decaying mass of

[224]

flesh. Leprosy seems neither contagious nor infectious, except to people with weakened, undernourished constitutions. I was shocked when Dr. Hoffman showed me a perfectly healthy woman, who, though born of leper parents and wedded to several leper husbands, was herself free from the disease and had given birth to several children who were also healthy and free from leprosy, even though living in this terrible colony!

As if leprosy were not enough, most of Dr. Hoffman's colonists were afflicted with favus, the horrible scalp disease whose infectious nature has left so many thousands of small boys and girls and older men and women hopelessly bald. The native cure for favus is too much like the primitive American Indian method of scalping. A type of tar is poured over the infected head, allowed to harden and then removed, taking with it not only the diseased hairs, but sometimes the scalp also.

Instead of resorting to this painful remedy, Dr. Hoffman administers thallium treatment internally, with the result that the patient becomes completely bald for a few weeks before a new growth of healthy hair appears. Although an overdose of thallium is occasionally fatal, it is worth the risk, as the cures are many and the deaths are few.

After a miserable but instructive morning at the leper colony, I spent a quiet but enjoyable afternoon playing Persian games with little ten-year-old Harriet Hoffman in the beautiful rose garden adjoining her home. Nearly all of the games which Harriet took delight in teaching me were different from any I had known as a child. Even "hide and seek" had its Oriental touch, the object of the game being for "hiders" to reach "home base," place the palms of their hands on the base and say, "I've washed my hands in henna." If any of the hiders failed to perform this ceremony before the "seeker" laid his hands upon their heads, they were "caught."

There was always an endless stream of patients pouring

[225]

into the Mission hospital, from savage Afghan tribesmen and idol-worshipping Tibetans, to Zoroastrian Indians. Many Russian refugees, a part of the vast human wastage spread out by the Communist "experiment," were there also.

One day an old Persian brought his son for an appendicitis operation. Dr. Hoffman unexpectedly sneezed once and the operation was immediately withheld until the old Moslem father had time to try the "Koran Test." As one must sneeze twice or not at all, the Doctor's singular sneeze was ill-omened and it was therefore necessary to open the Koran at random and read the first verse which met the reader's gaze. As the verse was of an optimistic tenor, the old father was convinced that the ill-begotten sneeze predicted danger to another than his son. Consequently, he permitted the performance of the operation.

On another occasion when I was visiting the hospital, a man entered with his unconscious wife slung across his back—the only type ambulance many natives have, even though the distance may be many miles from their homes. She had just given premature birth to a three-pound child, which was given a chance to live by being placed immediately with a Persian nurse in the hospital.

Dr. Hoffman learned that the mother had previously given birth to thirteen children, seven of whom had died before reaching adolescence. Such was the usual situation in Persia where venereal disease, the ignorance of immature and untrained mothers, lack of proper care at the time of childbirth, lack of protection against such diseases as measles, scarlet fever, whooping cough, smallpox, typhoid, dysentery, and other causes, result in a death rate far exceeding the percentage of children who live to maturity.

This same day, a big, burly Afghan dashed into the hospital, with knives in a sash around his waist, a tall gun strapped to his shoulder, and a half-dozen fellow tribesmen following at his heels as if on the war path. I tried to imagine the excitement such an entree would produce in a peaceful little hospital like the one in my old home town in Georgia!

Taking the unusual appearance as a matter of course, Dr. Hoffman calmly listened as the haughtily headdressed, feverish-faced fellow told his story in broken, rapid-fire Persian: "In my arm I have twelve days' old gun-shot wound and the Great God does not seem to hear my prayer; can you help me?" Naturally Dr. Hoffman could be of assistance, since the half-dozen tribesmen would be only too glad to kill the doctor should he refuse to do so.

The Afghan had scarcely been attended to, when a yoke of oxen drew a cart into the hospital yard with a pitiful mass of humanity huddled on the rough hewn boards. Before lapsing into a comatose state, the man barely had time to whisper that he had been bitten by a snake on the previous day and had traveled all night in order to reach the hospital. However, he had arrived too late, as his arm was badly gangrenous from the tight rope bandage he had twisted above the bite, and amputation of the arm failed to save him.

It was an unfortunate coincidence that at the time of this unavoidable death, the deceased had a niece who was recovering, in the same hospital, from a successful operation on a necrosed bone protruding from her arm. So frightened was the father of the girl when her uncle died in the adjoining ward, that he came without the knowledge of the hospital attendants and spirited his little girl away.

In the children's ward, little Harriet Hoffman was kept busy supplying the patients with hand-painted picture-books and American newspaper comics.

One child in the hospital belonged to a class of cases seen more frequently in winter: she had crawled too close to the "stove" (merely an open spherical hole in the clay

[227]

floor) and fallen in the dying embers, which badly burned her body before her little sister could come to the rescue.

Dr. Hoffman was continually embarrassed by convalescent patients who insisted that they be allowed to pay tribute to his services by kissing his feet. The only perplexing features of effective cures for sick patients was that after dismissal from the hospital, they invariably returned with all the invalids and ailing of their communities or tribes that they, too, might receive treatment from the great White Doctor.

Some of the most pathetic-looking patients were the obsequious Armenian women from Lilaban district of Armenia. In their own country, these poor creatures had been treated more like dogs than Moslem women of other countries, where the women are at least permitted to unveil in the privacy of their homes. Even this is not possible in Armenia, where the women must wear a kerchief over the lower part of their faces, both day and night. They never eat with the men of the family and can never speak aloud in the presence of their elders. Little wonder that such poor inmates of our hospital in Meshed had such hang-dog expressions on their faces.

I remained in Meshed long enough to see completely recovered a young Kurdish boy who was brought to the hospital several months after his thigh had been so seriously injured by a beating that a section of it had to be removed. He left with a shorter leg, but a longer vision of what love and friendship mean.

When the long-awaited Afghan visa arrived and I was ready to resume my journey, Dr. Hoffman, the other missionaries, and an ex-German count, in Meshed to select marble pillars for the Shah's palace in Teheran, gave me a farewell feast featured with geranium-flavored tea, rose-jam-jelly rolls, and other exotic delicacies.

For the past ten days little Harriet Hoffman had been looking forward to strawberry shortcake, and now at last she anticipated having her fill of this delicious dessert. Unfortunately she ate too much pilau and Persian cookie. The look on her face was the perfection of pathos as she placed a piece of cream-covered shortcake on her plate and suddenly realized that her constitution was already so replete with good things that she didn't even feel like tasting the dish. I felt sorry for her as she ran tearfully to her room, after handing me the huge cake to eat for her.

It had been worth it to go alone and half-starved, sometimes living many days with only a few crumbs of bread, and sleeping on the hard ground, if only to appreciate by contrast a good spring bed, fine food, and association with the delightful family and friends of Dr. Hoffman.

The desolate desert is fine enough for awhile for the foreigners, and fine forever for the nomad who has never seen anything else and can conceive of no sort of place different from his broad plains of sand and sage. To him, a loaf of bread, a jug of wine, and a companion beside him in the wilderness would make that wilderness paradise enough. Omar Khayyam would never have written lines as he did had he first laid eyes on that endless panorama of landscapes from Georgia's rock-ribbed hills of Habersham to its gold and green valleys of Hall.

Perhaps Tennyson was right when he said, "A sorrow's crown of sorrow is remembering happier days." Though enjoying my transient journeys over the deserts, I could hardly imagine being in paradise in one of them, so long as I retained memories of my little blue-eyed lass in the green mountains of Norway, moonlit nights on the Isle of Capri, ski trips to "dream castles," Christmas in "Thüringen Wald" in Germany, and hundreds of other beautiful spots in my garden of memories, to which I expected some day to return.

Not the least cherished was my memory of Sinai, where I had fought through the blinding, deafening, trail-blocking ocean of flying sand. As I looked back at the true perspective of this wonderful trip just East of the Suez, I could not restrain a smile of knowing satisfaction as I realized that my indelible mental pictures of this thrilling experience could never be crystallized into concrete form. It was just another of my experiences so unbelievably and indescribably terrible, weird, and beautiful, that even an attempt to put it into words would almost be a sacrilege.

And now, as Bucephalus turned his nose toward the wild tribe country of Afghanistan, he carried me steadily and speedily to other strange places and unusual experiences.

More than 2,000 years before, my bicycle's namesake, Bucephalus, the famous war horse of Alexander the Great, had carried his master to glory through the weird region I was now entering. Not only was my own proud iron horse to carry me through this country, but he was also to lead me into new worlds of conquest, for which Alexander wept in vain.

END OF PART FOUR

"I have believed the best of every man
And find that to believe it is enough
To make a bad man show him at his best,
Or even a good man swing his lantern higher."

Yeats
Deirdre

PART FIVE

BLAZING A NEW AFGHAN TRAIL WITH A BICYCLE

CHAPTER XXXV

First Adventures on a Virgin Trail

That the milk of human kindness is not confined to my own fair country was quite evident to me as I neared Afghanistan after cycling alone, unarmed yet unharmed, through Europe and Africa, up Moses' trail across Sinai Wilderness into the midst of the Arab-Jewish conflicts in Palestine, across the Great Syrian Desert from Damascus to Bagdad, the reputed Garden of Eden, and Persia.

The Koran teaches that the head of a Christian is worth an extra star in the heavenly crown of his Moslem murderer, but so hospitable are these Easterners that they cast aside all religious prejudices in their treatment of Christian guests. True, the Moslem host may smash the vessel of sour milk or mulberry cake just as soon as it is removed from the unclean lips of the infidel Christian, but he performs this ceremony gracefully and graciously, and is ready to serve his guest from as many more of his most beautiful vessels as the guest wishes to contaminate with his touch.

On Sunday, May 24, with a coveted, hard-won Afghan visa in my passport, a goodly supply of provisions in my bread basket, and no misgivings in my mind, I bade farewell to Meshed, Persia, jumped on my faithful Bucephalus, and started up the trail which was destined to lead me to the Land of the Rising Sun via the new, untrodden "motor road" up the Hari Rud valley and through the heart of hitherto unexplored tribal regions of central

[232]

Afghanistan. Previously all traffic across Afghanistan had been confined to the southern route via Kandahar. I was now to be the first foreigner to traverse the new highway up the Hari Rud through the very heart of the country to Kabul.

From a distance, Meshed resembled a giant octopus with one blue and one golden eye (the turquoise and golden domes of the mosque of Hazrat Iman Reza, Eighth Apostle of Mohammed) glistening in the early morning sunlight. Near the outskirts of the city I met a fuzzy old Persian with his army of twelve wives following on a string of donkeys. They were making a royal progress into the Holy City of Meshed. Many other donkey caravans were bound to market with desert sage to be sold as fuel, and rose petals as flavoring in ice cream, cakes, and soft drinks.

All day the trail carried me up the middle of a broad, green valley bordered on both sides by grass-covered mountain ranges. Women and girls supplied with huge iron tubs were milking the village herd of goats and sheep, while the men were either smoking opium or sleeping on the tops of their mud-brick houses. At Turbat-Sheikh-Jam, while women were splitting poppy ovaries in preparation for making opium, an old man amused himself by stuffing his little granddaughter's mouth with poppy seed. Many of these border folk were afflicted with leprosy, trachoma, favus, and other dreadful diseases. As the only other bicycle they had seen was that of a peripatetic doctor, they were convinced that I, too, was of that profession. So insistent were they in their demands for medical treatment that I gave them what satisfaction I could with my only two medicines: boric acid (for eye diseases) and quinine (for everything else), and suggested that they take their ailments to Dr. Hoffman back at Meshed, for further treatment.

The nearer I came to the Afghan border, the slower was

my progress, as police at each village thoroughly examined and took note of my passport and personal effects. When I unintentionally overlooked the police station at Aman Abad, a whole cavalry contingent dashed out on white horses and escorted me back to town for examination. The nearby soldiers drilling through the desert heat waves certainly presented an unromantic spectacle.

The last twelve forsakes (the unit of measure of Iran— one forsake equals three miles) to the border were over such wild, sandy wastes that the journey might have carried me far into the night had not four large, lion-faced sheep dogs loomed up out of the yellow twilight and inspired me to accelerate my speed until the sound of their vicious snaps at my heels came to my ears only as distant echoes reverberating among the undulating grey slopes.

Three miles from the border I found a stack of fresh, crisp, golden hay several hundred yards off the road and almost totally concealed from view by intervening earth-works of subterranean canals. Nestled snugly here in my goose-down sleeping bag, with a little pile of big rocks at my side on the haystack (ever since the band of wolves surprised me that night as I lay asleep in the wilderness near Mount Sinai I had kept a few rocks handy), it was thrilling to be alive and able to enjoy the beauty of this moment, to watch the stars come out and the mellow mountain ranges fade away into night, as a gentle breeze soothed the feverish throbbing of my sun-burned arms and face.

I was on my bike again at dawn and into Afghanistan before sunrise in spite of a half-dozen intervening ditches and high embankments put deliberately across the road to prevent traffic. Before twenty minutes had elapsed, I had cycled the four miles from Duguran, the last outpost on the Persian frontier, to Islam Kalah, the first Afghan station. The world's slowest postal service is between these two stations. If a letter is mailed from Islam Kalah to

[234]

Duguran, it must go via foot messenger to Herat; by truck to Kandahar, five hundred miles to the southeast; from here by auto to Chaman; thence by train six hundred miles to Karachi; thence thirteen hundred miles via steamship up the Persian Gulf to Bushire; thence via auto to Teheran, Meshed, Kariz, and finally to Duguran—four thousand miles and seven weeks of time from a town only four miles distant! No wonder many Easterners act as private mail-carriers here for their friends. In such cases, according to law, the carrier must have the letter stamped and cancelled by the postmaster who then returns it to the carrier.

At Islam Kalah I entered a new world. The women were weirdly dressed, with every inch of flesh covered in flowing black or white tunics thrown over their heads and long bloomers fastened below their ankles by elastic bands. All face coverings were of the same stereotyped cotton cloths with small latticed squares for eye-sight. Foot-gear of both men and women was highly gilt and embroidered, turned-up-toed slippers which could be easily removed whenever the wearer entered a carpeted mud-house. The long, loose-waisted white blouses and baggy breeches worn by the men are quite practical, as they catch the wind and keep the wearer cool. The great, foot-thick turbans counter-balancing the long, shaggy mous-taches of these virile men have many varied uses other than mere head-gear and protection against the onslaughts of sun, sand and snow. The ends of the turbans serve con-veniently as handkerchiefs, towels, or bed covering. In spite of horrible hygienic conditions, all too evident in their villages, it is remarkable how tall and athletically built are these tribesmen. In their red, purple, and gold-embroidered, sleeveless top-jackets they look like a bunch of American football players dressed as pirates at a costume ball.

I was immediately surrounded by the entire village of

[235]

curious natives who did not seem to understand the locomotion of my motorless, donkeyless vehicle. One swarthy giant grabbed my bicycle, another my knapsack, and all escorted me through old ruined octagonal courts beside sparkling pools of water, through fallen, arched corridors, and finally up a brick, ladder-like stairway into a beautifully carpeted little room in the penetralia of a house. Here I was deposited with my luggage while my hosts, three of them, brought in red-dyed, boiled eggs, whole wheat cakes, luscious new-born lamb, and several china kettles of hot tea ("chayeh"). My hosts were shocked and disappointed when I refused to drink opium with them. After bringing a half-dozen different types of tobacco, cigarettes, and pipes—all of which I refused— they were finally convinced that I was not a smoker, and thereupon, complacently sat, Oriental fashion, in a circle with me, and babbled through their great opium pipe. While water in the pipe gurgled, the smoke poured out of a little exhaust hole in thick puffs, as the smoker removed his finger-tips from the hole like the player of a strange wind instrument.

At last my hosts aroused themselves from the soporific stupor of their pipe, ordered extra pillows and carpets, and left me to meditate and sleep. The dazzling sunlight shining through the keyhole reflected their retreating forms on the darkened mud walls of my room exactly like an upside-down cinema. This tiny, topsy-turvy picture show is one of many such little things which I can never forget. They returned at frequent intervals for a social cup of tea with me. Like many Easterners they ate sugar cubes before drinking the tea instead of following our custom of dissolving the sugar in the tea.

At four p.m. my passport was returned and I was permit- ted to leave for Herat—twelve hours detention for a tiny rectangular stamp in my passport! However, I was too pleased with my royal reception in this reputedly blood-

[236]

thirsty country to be vexed by the unnecessary delay. In making up for lost time, I pedaled too vigorously through sandy stretches, broke the handlebars and right pedal completely off, and discovered a leak in the rear tire—all within the space of five minutes. Necessity is a wonderful teacher. I fixed the tire and, cycling without handlebars and with only the "stump" of my right pedal, I stopped to push only when going up hill or through sand.

At dusk, I reached the castle-like town of Ish-a-bosh, four forsakes west of Herat. The shadowy forms of natives were barely discernible, as they stood on their "mud-bubble" housetops (oval-shaped roofs are very practical in this country of deep winter snows) at prayer, or spread their long turbans over their bodies from back of head to heels as coverlet and protection against insects during the night's repose. I was royally received and given the privilege of sleeping with the two oldest men of the village in a little room high up over the city gate and built in the city wall itself. My arched, wooden-latticed windows commanded a wonderful view of the broad Hari Rud valley stretching eastward between wild, barren, storm-lashed hills. The pond at the base of the wall was filled with hundreds of croaking bullfrogs plainly visible in the moonlight. Bleating and baaing flocks of sheep, followed by a string of barefoot maidens balancing large water jugs upon their heads, wound slowly over the lea and up the winding stairway beneath my window. Next in the procession were the last of the men emerging from their prayers in the open court and colonnades of the rectangular mosque. Peasants on donkeys with bundles of wheat and crude shovels instead of guns were a pleasant sight. They were coming in from a hard day at the "threshing machine," a huge, frame wheel with eight straw mat blades which did the threshing.

My enjoyment of this moving picture of Afghan village life was interrupted by the entree of a dozen old "fuzzy

[237]

wuzzies" (I call them such because of their long beards and hair) who wished to entertain me with weird dancing. I helped furnish music by beating upon an iron bowl which had contained my supper of "most" (sour milk).

The next day, with my handlebars in "splints" of copper bands, the entire village escorted me to the highway for a good send-off to Herat.

Contrary to popular belief, there is plenty of good water in this part of the Afghanistan desert country. About eleven miles west of Herat I ran across an open well leading down to an ice cold subterranean stream (the same irrigation canal or "karez" system as employed in Iran) fresh from the mountains a few miles to the north. Closer observation revealed large schools of fish in the sparkling waters of the rocky tunnel.

Along the above-ground, irrigation canals, women were pounding wet clothes on wooden platters with baseball-bat-sized sticks, while the men were cooperatively tilling the soil, one man pushing the spade into the ground and another pulling up the shovel full of dirt by means of an attached rope.

I entered Herat from the northwest, my road weaving through seven of the original nine towering, tile and marble-encased minarets of one of the world's largest mosques, built by Hassan Messah Shah, ruler of Persia and Afghanistan in 1263 A.D. These seven great pillars are all that remain of the Mosalla since its destruction in 1885.

For several days, I explored Herat, from the old prison in the citadel to the eternal twilight along the winding catacombs of the bazaars. Frequently, in these rambles, my trail led suddenly into dark holes in the walls, where I stepped down through low, damp cellars, and as quickly emerged into another bustling bazaar street, or to a cool underground lake of drinking water. Everywhere the air was vibrating with the orchestral music of birds which had

In the heart of central Afghan hills. (This is the most valuable of my 5000 round-the-world photos as it is not only the only picture of me in Central Afghanistan, but is the only picture of any foreigner ever to go through this region and come out alive!)

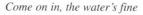
Come on in, the water's fine

*The men rushed out
like a mad army
to greet me
(Note tribal tower
in upper left
corner)*

*Sunrise somewhere in
Central Afghanistan
(My bed was always
where night overtook me)*

*"Heap big chief"
at Chack-cha-ran poses
before the only camera
to ever visit his region*

*Afghan
hospitality:
no eat;
no go*

been captured from their desert nests and were now being peddled on the streets of the city. Afghanees are very fond of birds and always keep several cages of them in their homes and shops.

My last supper in Herat was a memorable occasion. My host, Dr. Sherif (Indian physician for both civil and military hospitals in Herat), had invited as a special guest an old Afghanee who had just completed on horseback the long trip from Kabul through central Afghanistan to Herat. As we sat cross-legged in true Oriental fashion sipping our "shir" (hot goat milk flavored with cardamon seed, a few tea leaves, and spices), over the embroidered rug table-cloth stretched across the floor, the weary traveler helped map my route of the following day up the Hari Rud to Obe and Kajachist; southward over the top of the Kasamurgh range and back to Chackcharan, Doulat Yar, and the head-waters of the Hari Rud to Deksangi; then northward to Bamian, eastward to Charikar, and southward to Kabul—a distance of nearly 750 miles via the zigzag trail, though only 290 miles airline!

Next day as I started up the Hari Rud, my friends bade me goodbye forever. They assumed that should I escape from injury at the hands of wild tribesmen, wolves, bears, or snakes, I would die from sheer physical exhaustion in trying to push over the hundred high passes of this rugged roof of the world, or else drown while fording one of the mountain streams dangerously swollen by melting snows.

On the way out of the city I passed several young Afghanees on horseback singing and playing on little two-string guitars. Farther on, I stopped to listen to the dashing marching song of soldiers. Never can I forget this thrilling melody briskly sung by the Afghan goosesteppers who threw up their hands at each step with a mechanical motion as if they were so many automatons or little tin soldiers. The words to this charming tune sounded like "Hei la" and the notes were even with a snappy, staccato

[241]

tempo:

He la   hei la   hei la   hei.   Hei la   hei la   hei la   hei

Sing this verse over a dozen times and see if you don't like it!

All morning it was great fun carrying my bicycle over irrigation ditches cut across the road alongside the beautiful Hari Rud. This broad, green valley, dotted with "bubble-house" mud villages, is very thickly settled. An endless stream of Afghans was dashing down the dusty trail on their fine mares, each followed by a young colt. The most beautiful structures in the villages of this region are latticed, mud-brick temples inhabited by pigeons and other birds. Thousands of various species of birds nest in holes perforating the cliffs overhanging the trail (I noticed owls, doves, sparrows, parakeets).

Roadside graveyards look like miniature Stonehenges with their collections of huge, granite headstones. Colored flags and metal "hands" stretch out from the tops of long poles over the graves of tribal chieftains and holy men. Ram's heads and horns, around the rims of such graves, are symbolic of the highest degree of sanctity. I counted sixty-five such horns and heads on one grave.

Just east of Chashma Obe, the healthful hot springs resort of ailing Afghans, the trail winds up over mountain tops overhanging the river gorge, and down again into emerald-green oases. I cycled past Kajachist by moonlight as the natives slept on the mud roofs of their houses, and the trees hung lazily over the rippling waters of Hari Rud, the beautiful river of mystery which dashes courageously through the whole of western Afghan wild lands only to lose itself in the desert along the Persian border.

After crossing over the new steel bridge (the only one on the whole route) to the southern bank of the Hari Rud above Kajachist, I began running into sportsmen's

[242]

paradise on the high Kasamurgh Ranges. Myriads of ugly dragon lizards, beautiful pheasants and partridges darted across the road as it wound steeply up one rocky gorge and down another. Every few feet along the trail I caught glimpses of orange-colored woodchucks standing in suspended animation on their hind legs like fat young bears for a few undecided moments before emitting sharp, whistling sounds of surprise through their lips and making a dive for their dens. Once, as I knelt to drink from a small brook, whom should I see through the dense foliage on the opposite bank but mother brown bear and her baby! Evidently they were as surprised as I because we both turned in opposite directions and sought safety in flight. One night as I lay in my sleeping bag on a soft, mountain-top snowbank, watching stars shoot like rockets across the heavens, two wolves crept stealthily within a hundred feet of my resting place, stood motionless for a few minutes, and then as silently stole away.

Somehow, it never occurred to me that I should fear these creeping and crawling creatures of night. As I lay on wild, rugged heights and watched the golden sea of the sunset sky sweep westward over the horizon, the winds seemed to sing me to sleep with the soft, soothing strains:

> "Day is dying in the west
> Heaven is touching earth with rest."

Then, from the stillness of the twilight shadows I seemed to hear the comforting whisperings of one last sweet song:

> "Day is done,
> Gone the sun
> From the lakes,
> From the hills,
>   From the sky.

[243]

> All is well,
> Safely rest,
>   God is nigh."

It was the end of one of those perfect days when "Earth's crammed with heaven and every common bush afire with God."

Most true Afghanees are nomads, wandering across the country, camping in their black tents beside a stream at night, and moving with their large herds of sheep, goats, camels, horses, donkeys, and bullocks to greener slopes beneath a melting snowbank the next week. The progress of a great tribal caravan is one of the most fascinating sights imaginable, with its well-ordered procession of animals segregated according to age and species. The baby lambs, kids, camels, human infants, chickens and ducks ride on the backs of the older camels, while henna-haired, jewel-bedecked men and women plod alongside the train, maintaining order. The women wear red and purple blouses, and big, baggy, green bloomers. Their headdress of glittering gold and silver coins is tied to the ends of their scores of tiny braids of hair. They are further weighted down with huge silver-plate neck collars, anklets, bracelets, earrings, coin-embroidered jackets, and even a little gold nose button plastered like a bug on the left nostril. The eyelids of both sexes, especially the men, are daubed with antimony, partially to sharpen the eyesight and protect the eyes from glare of sun and snow, but primarily for the beautifying effect. In like manner, henna is attributed with remarkable curative powers of ailments ranging from hoof and mouth disease to headaches. But the real reason for splashing henna on human heads, bodies of horses and cattle, is for aesthetic decoration. As the prophet Mahomet was red-headed, that color is naturally greatly admired in Moslem countries.

Most of the route from Deksangi to Kabul was one

grand, colorful, circus parade of these caravans. More than once, I enjoyed the warm hospitality of their fireside, and did justice to the lambs stuffed with apricots, raisins, and curry, and buried whole (wool, hide, and all) in the midst of a charcoal fire in a hole in the ground. Everywhere, I was invited to join in the men's tribal circle; and, with fingers, sop "charack" (eggs fried in sheep blubber), and "most" from a huge common bowl. While the men ate, little girls brought pistachio and sage to the campfire, or helped their mothers weaving at the loom or tanning sheep-hides with pumice. Nearly always the little boys sat on the mountain-tops where they could keep a good view of their flocks. Many times I shepherded their sheep while the boys ran down to their tents in the vales below to bring me good sour milk.

The only time I gave an Afghan cause to commit murder was on just such an occasion. It had required nearly a whole day to climb to the top of a wild and rugged range where I found a young lad standing statue-like in the middle of a huge flock of black sheep. Having gone since dawn with nothing to eat or drink, I had no trouble at all in making known my wants. I was so weak from hunger and thirst after an unusually hard grind of cycling up and down mountains, with the added handicap of an ill-functioning pedal making the possibility of the venture seen more hopeless than ever, that I didn't feel like doing my duty and guarding the flock while the boy raced with his shaggy sheep dog down to the black dots of tents some miles below and returned with my elixir of life. No sooner had the boy disappeared in a cloud of dust over the crest of the hill than the sheep became restless. I checked them as they raced madly after the young shepherd but in my effort to drive them back to the mountain top, I overdid the matter and instead of stopping, they rushed headlong over the hill in the opposite direction and left me wearily wondering if they could ever be rounded up again. My

[245]

speculations were soon interrupted by the arrival of a muscular middle-aged man with a wounded lamb draped across the pommel of his horse's saddle and a dark-eyed damsel riding astraddle the rump of his snowy white steed. Already the flock of sheep was at least two miles away down the mountain side and when this swarthy giant pointed angrily toward their retreating forms, a murderous glare blazed from his eyes. He fingered nervously with first the hilt of one of his waist knives and then the trigger of his long gun. I was about to say my prayers when the boy appeared on the scene of tense inaction with my flask of "most."

The man raised his sword to strike the lad; he dropped the thermos flask, and pointed accusingly toward me. Thank God I had no weapons, as I might have committed instant murder in "self-defense."

This fierce old tribesman had just threatened to slash his son's throat for letting his flock run amuck—what would he not do to a helpless stranger who was really the one at fault! Such neglect of duty would be enough to excite murderous passions in a civilized Texas ranchowner, but having crossed one of these untamed mountain nomads of central Afghanistan who are supposed to kill all foreigners coming their way, whether "crossing" them (as I had just done) or not, I could not conceive of a punishment fittingly severe enough for me. But I was not in Texas—I was in Afghanistan where "men are men."

"Yecki musselman?" queried my adversary.

Sooner or later I knew this inevitable question would be popped. All other Afghanees had made this same inquiry; yet under the present circumstances it struck me like a thunderbolt to shatter my last hope of appeasing this tempestuous fellow. A lump in my throat choked back all speech and I replied in very broken Arabic: "Yes, I am traveling alone, but as a Christian infidel and not as a true Moslem like yourself." His countenance clouded and I

[246]

waited an eternal ten minutes for the approaching storm. Why should it take so long for him to make up his mind to act when he now had every reason for disposing of me as quickly as possible? Was I not a hated Christian dog and alone and unarmed besides?

But even above religious prejudice the Afghanee admires and respects what he calls the highest degree of courage and what we in America appropriately (perhaps) relegate to the realms of insanity. Mine was the perfect example of what this wild creature designated as supreme courage. It took fully ten minutes for him to digest this fact, before he came out of the fog and the storm finally broke. Instead of showering his wrathful vengeance down upon me, a broad grin transfigured his face as he leaped from the horse and gave me the affectionate Afghan salute.

During all this time the young maiden had remained as immobile and astonished as the older man; now her smile was so suddenly radiant that I could not keep from noticing her.

Praised be Allah for not requiring the fairest flowers of the East to hide their beauty behind ugly shrouds and veils. The loveliest landscapes throughout Afghanistan are those framed around the wild beauty of her nomad women of the tribal regions. In the cities where there is danger of exposure to the gaze of an occasional stranger, veils must be worn at all times, but out here on the hillsides, they don't even know what veils are. But as many of them don't know what strangers are either, their beauty is safe.

The voluptuous young valkyr who sat poised above me, as if in anticipation of carrying my battle-scarred body on her winged horse to the pleasures and palaces of Valhalla, bore a slight resemblance to the girls of colonial America. The red and green frills of her pantalets showed conspicuously below the broad brim of the purple silk skirt, and a graceful, athletic form of perfect mould stood out darkly but distinctly beneath this flimsy summer apparel. However, one look into the soft velvety depths of her jet black eyes and I forgot all about colonial girls and everything else—even my hunger, thirst, exhaustion, and recent close call with a hot-tempered tribesman.

She was really a jewel. Her smile revealed two perfect rows of pearly teeth which contrasted strikingly with the tantalizing curves of her rich, red lips, sun-tanned cheeks, and raven black hair and eyes. She wore no headgear except a plain gold pendant suspended from the left ear lobe, and a tiny silver crescent, containing a single emerald, which ornamented the end of her nose in true tribal fashion. She was a pure, unadulterated daughter of nature such as no traveler had ever seen before—and lived to tell the tale!

"My daughter, Chakra Khan, you like take her." My erstwhile antagonist spoke as nonchalantly as if he were merely offering me a smoke from his mud pipe.

I had heard of Eastern hospitality but didn't know it was carried to such extremes. However, there were lots of things I didn't know. I looked at the girl to see how she reacted to her father's shocking speech in broken Arabic dialect; she not only didn't bat an eye, but even elevated one eyebrow and laughed playfully at me. Why, the little flirt! And I had thought Mother Nature reared her children in innocent freedom from the wiles of worldly women.

The nomad is at home wherever he happens to be. Here was as good a spot as any for building a fire and roasting the wounded lamb for dinner. The tribesman gave his daughter orders to that effect.

"Chakra Khan good cook," he chuckled. "Stay with us and she help you plenty. You like her much." "Yes, perhaps too much," I thought, as I rose to my feet and prepared to continue my journey, after chasing a whole leg of lamb down my throat with a half-gallon of "most."

"You no take her with you?" he exclaimed in wide-eyed

[248]

wonder. "No, Abdul Khan, if I were to remain here the rest of my life it might be all right. But I am going back to my people in a strange world many, many forsakes from your beloved hills. In my country, your daughter would be unhappy."

"You not even leave her with a son!" he cried, obviously hurt and insulted that I should refuse this request of his daughter. "Then, her son would be brave like you," he stubbornly insisted, with the same serious composure as if he were bargaining for a stud horse to keep his white mare company.

"No, no, nothing like that," I hurriedly replied. "Besides I could never tear myself from Afghanistan if anything like that happened; and even if I should do so, imagine spending the rest of my life in America wondering if it was a boy or a girl (or both!), and if it looked like its father!"

As Bucephalus and I wound down the other side of the Pass, I wondered what new, strange revelation should unfold itself just around the next bend in the road. Old Eastern customs were becoming more and more interesting, to say the least.

Had I known what hardships lay ahead, I might have been tempted to turn nomad and linger with the wandering tribe of Abdul Khan—but Abdul Khan was not the only Afghan chieftain who had a beautiful daughter!

CHAPTER XXXVI

Among the Wild Tribesmen

Deep in the Kasamurgh Range I plunged down a beautiful red Grand Canyon with cathedral-spired cliffs towering one thousand feet on either side. So absorbed was I in the beauty of this landscape that I did not notice a large boulder in the middle of the road until after it had stopped poor old Bucephalus and sent me catapulting through space. I was unhurt, but the right pedal, which had been repaired at Herat, was irreparably severed and the front tire cut in several places. With all my patching glue evaporated in this high, dry atmosphere, I desperately but successfully slowed down the leaks by vulcanizing pieces of an old tire to the perforations. However, the physical handicap of cycling the remaining three hundred and fifty miles to Kabul is indescribable. Long before reaching a decent highway and "civilization" at Bamian, the iron stub of the severed pedal had worn completely through my inch-thick alpine shoes and my right leg was almost paralyzed from strain.

Before I could cycle from the scene of my untimely accident several caravans of city merchants and their hordes of wives and children passed. The husband and two heavily armed soldiers led each procession while two more soldiers brought up the rear, in case of a surprise attack by bandits from that quarter. The women and children were crowded into the middle of the group in silk-curtained, double-barrelled howdahs fastened onto the backs of horses. Everyone asked if I were "yecki" (a lone traveler). They could scarcely believe it possible for one to travel alone, even if he were Afghanee, to say nothing of a foreigner and "infidel" at that!

Although Afghan nomads are extremely orthodox Moslems in most respects, when it came to veiling their women, I found them, without a single exception, departing from this religious practice. Only in the larger cities, such as Kabul and Herat, are the women veiled. The children (both boys and girls) of Kasamurgh region wear strange coiffures like the monks of ancient Rome, with heads closely shaved except for a thin crown of hair around the middle of the head.

For some time, I was amazed by discovery of the tread of real auto and bicycle tires in this rugged region. Then I noticed that the marks were made by shoes imported from Iran, where soles cut from old rubber tires are universally worn. (Several months later I was to see similar shoes worn by ricksha coolies in far away Saigon, French Indo-China.) However, most of these Afghan nomads wear crude shoes of inverted, raw sheep hide bound to feet and legs with goat-hair rope.

Although the tribesmen of central Afghanistan love their long tobacco pipes, they seldom bother to carry them with them on horseback journeys from their camp or mud village. Instead, they improvise pipes from Mother Earth whenever and wherever the spirit moves them to smoke. One of the most convenient and common types is the "mud egg" pipe, made by simply molding an oval chunk of mud between the palms of the hands; then, with the thumb, press a shallow tobacco basin in the top of the "mud egg"; finally, make a hollow stem by inserting and then withdrawing a straw or stick from one end of the "pipe" into the hollow basin; light the tobacco, apply lips to the stem of the pipe, and enjoy your smoke. As such pipes can be made in less time than it takes an American to roll a cigarette, they are very popular among Afghan tribesmen.

It was five miles west of Doulat Yar that I ran across the most weird and original pipe that I ever expect to see. Just as I started over the top of a high pass into a green vale in which large herds of camels and goats were grazing, I espied two swarthy old men near the roadside. One was resting in a perfectly normal manner on a large rock, but the other had his nose to the ground about three feet from a point where smoke came out of the earth in large puffs. Suddenly, the two swapped positions, and the smoking continued. Curiosity overcame my better judgment that I should mind my own business. Upon inquiry, the old tribesmen kindly initiated me into the intricate ingenuities of their novel pipe. A piece of goat hair rope was stretched

[251]

across the ground and covered with a thin layer of mud; the rope was then removed, leaving a hollow mud stem; a shallow basin was dug at one end of the stem and filled with tobacco; at the other end of the stem a straw was placed in vertical position, surrounded by mud, and then withdrawn, leaving a hollow mouthpiece. After applying a piece of burning charcoal to the tobacco basin, the old man got down upon all-fours, placed his lips against the mouthpiece, and enjoyed a long smoke.

After six days of circuitous travel over the top of the Kasamurgh Range, I reached the fortified village of Chackcharan, situated on the upper Hari Rud about halfway between Herat and Kabul. Being the first "European" most of the natives had ever seen (many of them had never even heard of America), I was received as a sort of god on a mysterious animal which seemed to come to life and move at my bidding, or drop dead at my desire.

Mohammed Sherif Khan, commander of the fortress, escorted me, through files of bearded, long-haired, wild-eyed men squatting along the sides of the gate, into an open rectangular court surrounded by mud pueblo rooms built against the inner walls of the fortress. The scores of rifle slits perforating the thick battle-scarred walls were grim reminders of bloody, tribal warfare. A small stream of water had been diverted through the courtyard for drinking, washing, and irrigation purposes. In one corner, an odoriferous lamb stew was cooking in a great copper pot on the stove (the "stove" consisted of two large stone slabs placed in parallel, vertical position).

After a tent was erected and several soldiers placed on guard at the entrance, I was ushered inside to enjoy true Afghan hospitality. Five varieties of tea were brought in for my inspection; and, as I indicated no preference, all five were prepared to insure satisfaction. Sheets of white and whole wheat bread, mulberry and pistachio meal cakes, were brought in beautiful "rug" napkins, and unfolded before my eyes, followed by a half-dozen beautifully chased silver platters containing a concoction of lamb cubes, rice, nuts, fruits, and curry, very similar to the Persian pilau.

After a hearty meal, during which a pair of six-foot giants waved straw mat fans over my head as if it were that of an Oriental potentate, I invited several of the soldiers and villagers to go with me for their first—and no doubt their last—swim in the nearby river. Though only two were bold enough to take the plunge, the entire group of men joined me in skimming flat stones across the surface of the water, tried to imitate my handstands, acted and enjoyed themselves in general like a bunch of school-boys on a holiday. Even here, I found that "one touch of nature which makes the whole world kin." The old men laughed, shouted, and danced, as I rode my bicycle around for their pleasure. By striking an answering chord in the human part of their hearts, I had won the undying friend-ship of these untamed people who entertain no scruples against killing a human being if they feel so inclined.

Next morning, Mohammed Sherif Khan insisted that I be accompanied by armed escorts for the remainder of the journey. I was rather amused that my first companion should be one of the fiercest type of hawk-faced gunmen, sent to protect me against men far less savage than he. Mounted on a beautiful white Arabian steed, he sported a long, fork-pronged bayonet on the end of his five-foot gun; and a number of knives and cartridge belts were draped about his waist. A tangled mass of raven black, unshorn locks flowing down to his wiry, well-knit shoulders completed the wild picture.

As my bodyguards took advantage of their important position, by displaying me publicly on the mud platforms, where the men smoked, just inside the gates of each vil-lage or caravansary, the novelty of having companions

[253]

after many months of solo-cycling throughout Europe, northern Africa, and the Near East was very shortlived. Too, since my escort would not consider passing a village without stopping until the next day, even though we had arrived in the village in the early morning, it is little wonder that I put Bucephalus in "high gear" and left my guards, long before reaching Deksangi.

Throughout this region the natives live in summer on the tops of their mud-houses piled high with walls of sun-baked pancakes of goat and camel dung, while the cattle occupy the inside of these crude dwellings. Near Doulat Yar were many modern cave-dwellers living in man-made caves along the river gorge. Though more than a hundred miles of my trail lay over a beautiful velvety carpet of grass, winding up camel and goat-dotted coves and vales, more often the trail climbed steeply over one rugged, barren mountain-top to another. Many tribal watchtowers decorated the hilltops along the way, where in olden days sentinels stood constant watch in these round, grey stone edifices and sounded the alarm of the approach of a warring tribe.

As I approached the villages of these regions, women and children, wearing metal-embroidered garments, peered down like monkeys from their mud roofs, while the men rushed out like a mad army to greet me. Paradoxical though it may seem, the wilder the natives, the more royal and glamorous was my reception. Usually they showed their goodwill by inviting me to take a dip of snuff or a puff from the village pipe. Each village boasts a large pipe in the charge of one man whose whole business is devoted to carrying this highly cherished "peace pipe" from one mouth to another and blowing out the "exhaust" smoke between each draw.

The natives enjoy their wrestling matches, bird fights, and horse races. They also indulge in a sport strikingly similar to modern polo, displaying uncanny skill in

[254]

knocking round stones back and forth across the meadows as they gallop at full speed, wielding wooden mallets in their right hands. On one occasion I was pleasantly surprised when a handsome old patriarch produced a chequered-board with figures which were unmistakably chess-men, and with a twinkle in his eye, challenged me to a duel of Eastern chess. The chief difference between Eastern and European chess is in the substitution of a Prime Minister for the Queen.

However, the primary pastime of the people is quarreling. The term Afghan, meaning "noisy," "turbulent," or " quarrelsome," is well chosen. The chief delight of the natives is to sit on the public platform within the inner walls of the village gate and, as the "peace pipe" makes its round, listen to two of their number begin an argument. At the zero hour when one of the contestants, usually the one who is on the losing end, decides to express himself more forcefully and cogently with a knife instead of mere gesticulation and thunderous speech, his opponent grabs him by the beard. The effect is instantaneously miraculous. The would-be knifer grabs his erstwhile enemy's beard and for several minutes they stroke each other's beards and talk soothingly like the purring of two contented old tom-cats, their faces aglow with pride at the effect they have produced upon their awed audience by such a dazzling display of self-control. After a cup of tea, two fresh debaters are ready to start another such scene. Such occurrences are not rare exceptions, for from Jela la Bad (a weird little town ten miles north of Doulat Yar and not to be confused with the historic village by the same name near Khyber Pass) to Bamian they are the general rule.

Upon reaching Kizil fortress, I was escorted into a temple-like enclosure dimly lighted, in the usual Afghan fashion, by means of a small rectangular hole in the roof. The shaft of light revealed a group of Afghan government workers nearly drowned in a huge pile of documents, on the carpeted floor, beside a pool of water in the center of the building. I drank tea with the tribal chief and his son on the seat of honor, an elevated rug-covered platform in one corner of the room. When I was ready to resume my journey, this swarthy savage led me by the hand in true Afghan fashion to Bucephalus, and with a parting blessing sent me down the trail with the invariable gift of cookies and sweetmeats tied neatly in red and purple silk cloths.

The Afghan character is one of strange contradictions. Almost effeminate in their love for beautiful silks and other dress materials, the roughest, toughest man among them may be seen publicly painting or admiring his physiognomy in a little mirror which is as much one of his prized possessions as his little arm-belt containing pages from the Koran. Like a child he will walk hand-in-hand with equally savage fellow-tribesmen or visitors, and send his guests away bountifully laden with gifts. He may often be seen holding a rosebud in one hand and a gun in the other. Withal, these are most likeable fellows. No people on earth have more "camaraderie" among themselves than the Afghan tribesmen. They draw no class distinctions which are so evident in other countries. They eat from a common bowl, smoke a common pipe, and associate with each other, from poorest beggar to richest chieftain, as if all were members of the same happy family.

Upon the entrance of a newcomer to their village teahouse or "smoker," all the men rise, shake both hands of the visitor, recite a five-minute greeting, and then embrace the guest before resuming their seats. Because the people are so curious and asked hundreds of questions at every village, I always pretended to know absolutely nothing of the Afghan language. Everywhere I was greeted with: "Are you musselman? Why are you an infidel? Are you married? Why, or why not? How many wives have you? Why are you here? How old are you? How old are your parents? etc."

[256]

The most beautiful and interesting portion of my trail lay between Deksangi and Bamian. I had scaled many high peaks, but never until I started over the high passes of Koh-i-baba's 18,000-foot ranges had my nose bled because of altitude. Up in this land of eternal snow, the blood oozing from my nose and the odd sensation of roaring in my ears like the sound of a distant waterfall, was too novel an experience to be enjoyable. At times the path was only a small white ribbon of dirt winding up green lawns between mountain peaks of pure limestone, iron ore, copper and other rich, "undiscovered" mineral deposits, topped with picturesque natural bridges and arches through which the blue sky shone—a formation I have seen in no other country. Again, the trail vanished entirely beneath an avalanche of melting snow and dis-lodged boulders. After several nasty spills in which I received a number of cuts and bruises about my legs, face, and arms, I was delighted to plunge suddenly into a beautiful green gorge (strikingly similar to Yosemite Valley in the western U.S.A.) and upon Band-i-Amir, the great chain of mineral lakes northwest of Bamian. So crystal clear are these lakes that I could see large fish swimming about in the deeps of the water.

The last but one in the chain of lakes was situated on a towering cliff between two still higher cliffs, and was yellow and thick with sediment from the sulphur and other rich minerals in the water. Here I camped and bathed my infected injuries in the healthful waters before proceeding down the caravan route to Bamian, famous for its great Buddha, one hundred and seventy-five feet high, carved into the cliffs by Buddha worshippers, who came up from India eighteen hundred years ago. I spent several days wandering through the network of caves and shrines which decorate the sides of the Bamian cliff, and resemble a cross-section of an ant-hill. Since the invasion of the Moslems, both the Great and Small Buddhas, the latter

[257]

so-called because it is sixty feet shorter than the Great Buddha, have been shorn of their faces from lips to forehead and relieved of their gilded outer surfaces.

Afghans are extremely orthodox Moslems following strictly the second commandment: "Thou shalt make unto thee no graven images." Consequently, no animate entity, as the Lion and Unicorn in English symbolism, may be pictured. The Afghan national symbol is a mosque shown by the four columns and dome. Inside the mosque is the "mambar" or pulpit, as indicated by a step-ladder on the right side. The whole is surcharged on the six-pointed star made of superimposed triangles referring to the popular tradition that the Afghans are the lost tribe of Israel. Often the seal is encircled by a wreath of two stalks of wheat. It is noteworthy that more varieties of wheat are found in Afghanistan than in any other country, thus leading botanists and horticulturists to believe this country to be the homeland of that most essential food.

Shortly after leaving the beautiful green valley of Bamian and striking the main highway near Bulola I saw the first vehicle since leaving Herat. A rattle-trap truck literally bursting with its load of Afghans, many of whom were hanging on the outside, or sitting playfully on top as if they were riding a horse, came thundering down the road with its wild crew, bound for Bulola. Several miles farther on, I passed a second car, which was being pulled by a team of horses up the steep grade over Shibar Pass.

At Charikar, I plunged through a dust storm followed by a devastating rain storm, which felled dozens of roadside mulberry and chinaberry trees across my highway, almost transforming my triumphal entry into a Waterloo. As if it were not difficult enough to reach Kabul and civilization without bucking through or evading the forces of man and nature! This was only one link in a chain of obstacles which unforeseen and unavoidable circumstances had strewn along my trail from Herat to Kabul.

[258]

Note howdah-chaired horse in merchant parade – (the Afghan traveling man carries his harem inside this double-barrel contraption)

Good Samaritan, Afghan fashion

Central Afghan circus parade

Fresh fuel for my power house

BEFORE
(Author's passport picture taken the day he started around the world)

AND
(snapshot at Afghan Consolate in Meshed – this photo gained admittance into Afghanistan territory after passport picture had failed to favorably impress the King)

AFTER
(Author in Kabul immediately after emerging from wild tribal region – note right pedal missing!)

But after all, was not Percy R. Hayward right when he said:

> "It is easy to foot the trodden path
>   Where thousands walked before.
> It is simple to push my fragile bark
>   Past reefs of a charted shore.
> I find it good to ride the road
>   Where others laid the trail.
> It is well to test the ocean's strength
>   Where others also sail.
>
> "But when a dream enslaves a man,
>   A dream of the vast untrod,
> A dream that says, 'Strike out with me,
>   Strike out or part with God'—
> A dream that leads to an untried path
>   Where unknown tempests blow;
> And the only chart a man can boast
>   Is his will that bids him go;
> Oh, then, my soul, bethink yourself,
>   For God has spread this scroll
> To test the stuff of your rough-hewn faith
>   And the fibre of your soul."

When I had slipped and fallen in the melting snows on the mountain-top trail far back in the Koh-i-baba Range, my injuries had proved more serious than I first thought. In addition to a few mere cuts and bruises, two ribs over my heart had been fractured (so I was to learn nearly a week later from the Irish doctor at the English Embassy in Kabul) by the impact of my camera against my chest in one of these swift and unexpected falls. My ribs were cracked, but the camera remained intact!

Pushing up the high passes required plenty of "steam" and consequently, lots of deep breathing. Yet every draft

[261]

of air entered my lungs like a two-edged knife slicing through my body. Instead of getting better, the pain was gradually becoming more unbearable. I was giving out about as rapidly as were my chewing-gum-patched bike tires. It was now a race against time to reach Kabul and a doctor before I should completely cave-in. With nearly two hundred miles of surging seas of mountain barriers still before me, I clung to the one chance in a million of "making the grade." But cruel fate is often anything but kind and considerate to those who seem down and almost out. She will try to snatch the last straw of hope from the clutch of a drowning man.

Deep down in that vague thing we call the subconscious mind, I felt the power to attain my goal, provided I should meet with no further detaining forces of an external nature. How close the margin between success and failure—between life and death! One more little slip, one more tiny puncture, or broken chain link—any one of a hundred little things might mark my epitaph.

I just couldn't afford to fall—even if I had already done a "slide, Kelly, slide" act over a dozen craggy cliffs. I couldn't afford to have another puncture—even if my tires had been exploding as regularly as the backfires of the first model-T Ford; nor could I afford another break in my chain—though only the fragile wire of a safety pin held it together now where one link was irretrievably missing.

To me, the most remarkable and inexplicable fact of my final two hundred miles to Kabul was not that I went through the wildest tribal regions without being torn asunder by man or beast, but that Bucephalus and I both maintained our equilibrium and held together till the very end.

However, that end threatened to come altogether too soon! Shortly after my escape from the royal Afghan soldier escort, swift horsemen had relayed this information back to Herat with the speed of the pony express. From Herat the intelligence was wired to Kabul where the king immediately sent a small detachment of cavalrymen to meet me from that end of the line.

Long before he reached Bamian, the royal riders found their wayward charge. Had they brought along a howdah-chaired horse so that Bucephalus and I might ride in restful repose, their presence would have been welcome. But to have a bunch of uniformed clowns along merely to slow down my speed and put me on display in each and every village was more than I could endure.

As for treatment of broken ribs, they knew no more about it than the man in the moon! When I complained that I was dying from pains in my chest, they merely replied: "Then Allah be with you. May you rest in peace!"

What comfort! Why if die I must, then let it be alone, and in peace, out of sight of these grinning "guardian angels!" I refused to budge—told the Afghan officer that I would die in my tracks before I would accompany him to Kabul.

"Bali, Sahib, that is bad. (In Afghan Arabic, "bali" means yes, and "bad" really means bad!) Die if you will, but Abdullah Shah will stand by you. Here are my orders to find and bring you to Kabul dead or alive," and with a look of supreme confidence in himself, he thrust before my eyes the convincing scroll stamped with the seal of royalty and signed by the king himself.

Seeing that my sit-down strike would not help matters in the least, I changed tactics:

"See here, Abdullah Shah, I am injured." By way of explanation I pointed to my chest to make sure that he understood. "It is necessary that I reach a doctor as quickly as possible. It is noble of the king to send you to protect me. It is noble of you to want to protect me and stop at each village and let the people honor me with feasting, dancing, and offering of the most beautiful of their daughters to me, but I must hurry to Kabul. My iron horse is faster than yours. If you will not let me go my

[263]

way in peace, I shall do so anyhow. If you harm me, the king will make you answer with your own life. And if you restrain me here, I will still get away from you when we come to the first long downhill grade. I escaped once from your noble horsemen; I can do so again."

This long and triumphal tirade was prematurely short-lived. So concentrated had been my thoughts upon the helplessness of this fierce warrior, heavily armed though he was, I failed to heed to take note of the cunning smile which crept over his face as he centered his gaze upon my shirt pocket. No sooner had the last syllable of speech left my lips than he tore my passport from the khaki shirt collar and smilingly placed it within the folds of his own garment.

"Looks like you're a better man than I, Abdullah Shah." I tried to force a smile in the face of defeat. "You know that without a passport I'm a man without a country, and as long as that precious document is in your possession, I have more sense than to run off and leave you."

But Abdullah Shah is not a better man than I, after all, Gunga Din! He sleeps too soundly. In the wee small hours of the morning after our first encampment, I retrieved my passport and stole away without waking Abdullah Shah and his brothers.

However, Abdullah Shah was not to be so easily outdone. The bird had flown from its cage but not for long. Abdullah Shah and his brothers knew a direct route from Deksangi to Kabul which was nearly a hundred kilo-meters shorter than my long, circuitous trail via Bamian.

My trail was difficult enough and the short cut straight over the mountains to Kabul was a foolish trip except for an experienced horseman. But Abdullah Shah and his brothers were experienced horsemen. They knew that a telephone line extended all the way from Kabul to Bamian. They could take this short cut and reach Kabul nearly as quickly as I could go to Bamian. Then the king

[264]

would telephone all the way up and down the line to have the "iron-horse-mounted" American stopped until the arrival of his guardians.

However, my journey was uninterrupted again until after I had passed the first little station several miles south of Bamian. Then the telephone wires over my trail began to "sing," and things began to happen.

As I approached the next village and saw a dozen natives lined across the road in front of me, I looked up at the buzzing telephone wires and knew at once what was in the air.

Fortunately, the road winds down a long river gorge nearly all the way from Bamian to Kabul. Instead of putting on the brakes I ducked my head and pedaled for all I was worth. Like a bunch of players sprawling out before a powerful buck over center in a football game, the amazed human wall parted before my onrushing steed. In every one of the remaining little villages along the route I met with the same sort of reception committee and faded away in flying colors, leaving them wondering whether that was really the American cyclist who had just visited them or the Indian monsoon.

Only once did a reception committee succeed in stopping the "iron-horse mounted" American, and that was when the village chanced to be on such a steep upgrade that Bucephalus was unable to muster the speed necessary to carry us over the top to the goal post. We bucked over center, but our legs were weak and wobbly. The human wall refused to budge. The "referee" (a tough-looking government official wearing royal riding boots as the " earmarks" of his authority), called time out for a rest. With the aid of a half-dozen Afghans, he "gently" placed Bucephalus and me on a straw mat in the front of the village tea house. "Here, Sahib, you remain two days as the guest of Messah Mohammed until the royal horsemen of his majesty the king arrive and escort your iron-horse-mounted-highness to Kabul." The official spoke in solemn, measured tones of finality.

"Why, in two more days I might be dead," I thought. Then, as another idea entered my head, "or perhaps I might be in Kabul."

"Messah Mohammed"—in the casual, lazy tones of one settled in one spot for life I addressed myself to the official host—"I fear that in stopping me a few moments ago you have injured the wheels of my iron horse so that they will no longer turn. May I see if they are still in order?"

"Bali, Sahib," was the innocent, unsuspecting reply. Once an Afghanee is stirred to action, he is quick as lightning and almost unstoppable, but luckily for me they are not always quickly stirred. In testing the rollability of my bicycle, I had cleared the line of defense and was doing some broken field running before it occurred to Messah Mohammed that the iron-horse-mounted American was about to make another getaway.

After all, one has four downs in a football game. Bucephalus and I had been downed three times, making fairly good gains on the first two plays, but being thrown for such a loss on the third trial that we had to have time called on us. Nevertheless, we still had one more chance to push over for the touchdown and were intent upon doing our dead level best to make a go of it.

Already we were shaking off the last back guardsmen. Their only chance of victory lay in knifing or shooting us, but the rules of the game as laid down by his majesty the king forbade any such foul play. We kicked the last stubborn guard in the shins while the referee wasn't looking and bolted off toward our goal like a bat out of Hades.

The field was slightly muddy and dangerous on the forty-kilometer home stretch from Charikar to Kabul, but what are a few measly mulberry trees across the rain-drenched road compared to punctures, broken chains, smashed ribs, semi-paralyzed right leg, infected cuts and bruises, wolves, bears, wild tribesmen, "guardian angel" soldiers, unbridged rivers, red gulches, mountains, and still more mountains!

Early in our Eastern travels we had learned from thieves, wise old soothsayers, border officials, and other such people (may God pardon them for existing!) that whatever cannot be overcome must be endured. By following this rule as closely as did Confucius, its originator, we had gone far in our desperate dash. The secret of the saying is not in seeing how much can be endured, but how much can be overcome to keep from having to endure anything! Bucephalus and I had overcome wherever possible and had endured in many instances what even seemed impossible.

Among these seeming impossibilities was the possibility of ever reaching Kabul alive. When Bucephalus and I finally came tearing into the city on the tail end of a storm, we must have presented a ghastly appearance to the alarmed inhabitants. Our entree is perhaps best described in the diary of Felix Howland, eccentric young American teacher, resident in Kabul at the time:

"Rex, Vivian and I had just sat down for a game of bridge when we heard a knock at the door. We called 'come in' and who should appear but a most weird creature. Short and light, wearing Bavarian leather shorts, topee and torn shirt, sockless but adorned with heavy Swiss Alpine boots, in strode a blazing blue-eyed, long-haired, bearded, blonde lad with an engaging Georgia drawl. He was groggy with fatigue, and could scarcely speak intelligibly. The tension was soon relieved when he presented me a letter of introduction from my old friend R. E. Hoffman in Meshed. Without going into details, suffice it to say that the spectral guest was Fred A. Birchmore, American International Exchange Student to Germany, who is now bicycling around the world. That he should be the first and only foreigner to complete the trip

[267]

across central Afghanistan—alone and on a bicycle, of all things!—seemed absurdly impossible to Rex and me until he produced a knapsack full of notes and photos—unmistakable proof of the most heroic and remarkable achievement of which I have ever heard. I first got him to pose for a photo and then supplied him with hot water to wash and shave after which I may add he looked much more human, and then we had dinner. Later I had to go to Schneiders on government business and left Rex in charge. When I got home both Rex and Birchmore were asleep, the latter snoring so stentoriously I had to drag my bed out in the hall and close the door. Even then, I had trouble sleeping."

From the above quotation, the reader may truly imagine that my first three days in Kabul were spent in restful repose at the insomniac expense of my friend Felix Howland. Vivian, the other American guest in Felix' home, was fast losing his mind after a few weeks of civil engineering for the king in Kabul. But Felix, the only real American resident in Afghanistan, could feel at home and maintain his equilibrium on Venus or Jupiter should circumstances place him on such far-away planets. Though thirty-nine years old he didn't look a day over twenty-five, but his had already been a full lifetime of experiences. In portraying to me the character of this strange prodigal son of Uncle Sam, Dr. Hoffman had said: "He's as much of a wanderer and adventurer in his way as you, Birchmore!" I had looked forward to meeting Felix and discovering what winds of Fate had blown him so far from home.

Shortly after my arrival and upon learning of my love for poetry, Felix showed me several volumes of his own composition. As he had the appearance of one who could write only satires and parodies of a superficial nature instead of sober, sincere, deeply moving philosophical poems, I was taken aback at the beauty of his soul-reaching

[268]

religious and amorous poetry. However, a pessimistic touch permeated the whole breadth and depth of his wide range of verse.

I suspected and soon discovered that the only girl he had ever loved married another suitor. Since this thwarted love affair, he had been quite a restless fellow, wandering around the world, accepting jobs for a few months in each country before moving on to the next.

Since graduating from Annapolis Naval Academy he had attended twelve foreign universities (Paris, London, Madrid, Heidelberg, et cetera), taught in French and Italian universities, the American College in Teheran, Persia, and now, had finally landed in Kabul, Afghanistan—the last outpost of civilization—to teach the king's royal warriors a little English.

Though Felix topped the list of interesting Europeans who helped make my sojourn in Kabul a pleasant one, I met several others of my homefolks—out in this wild and wooly country I considered anyone coming within a radius of three or four thousand miles of my Georgia home as "homefolks."

With never more than three or four American visitors each year, Kabul has no American Consulate. But there were the large family of Schneiders at the German Consulate—a little bit of old Rhineland hospitality out here to compete with the wild but willing favor of the Central Asiatics.

Then there was Felix's English friend Boome, a middle-aged son of old Cambridge who had wasted (?) the flower of his youth in muleteering over the Andes in search of South American gold, and was at present trying to rig up a new wireless station for his majesty the king. But I fear the king will have to wait awhile for his new wireless station, as Boome is not the sort of fellow to put business before pleasure—at least, not when the pleasure involves adventure.

[269]

Upon hearing of my trip through a region which even he in the wildest wanderings of his imaginative faculties had never dreamed of taking, Boome set out at once to buy a horse and cover my virgin route in reverse fashion. The king and his wireless could go hang! We live here only once, and here was the thrill of a lifetime within his grasp. After all, only one foreigner had ever come through alive. Even if he could not boast of being the first to blaze this new trail through the heart of wild Afghanistan, there would be glory enough to be second!

"Why, if this pusillanimous, blue-eyed blonde midget of a man could open up that trail on a bicycle, surely he could follow in his footsteps on a horse." I could almost see and hear Boome thinking out loud as these thoughts raced through his mind. As I left to finish my sight-seeing in the city, we drank a toast to the success of his proposed venture.

"Here's to you, Boome," I said; "may you rub those wild tribesmen the right way or Rupert Brooke won't be the only English soldier of fortune to find a grave in a foreign field. Yours may not be so pleasant either, because Afghans are anything but a consistently cool, calm, and collected people. They go to extremes of hospitality and cruelty. May you, like me, meet with only the hospitable portion of their nature."

While sight-seeing, I gave Bucephalus and my half-par-alyzed leg a rest, and used one of the native carriages called "tonga" or "guardi" (latter means "throne") to view the city and surrounding country. I visited the old royal palace of Bala Hissar on an imposing mountainside towering above the city, and walked along its great walls, extending in picturesque feudal fashion, to the top of the mountain range. Forty years ago, Amir Abdur Rahmen blew up the inside of the castle, and its massive stone walls now house an arsenal instead of the king.

The king's new palace is in the center of Kabul itself. A

red flag flying over the royal palace signifies that his majesty is at home.

Near the palace is a marble shaft commemorating Afghan Independence Day (1747 A.D.). Here during the month of August of each year, the King, Prime Minister, and other high officials, in full dress, gather with all the natives to spend the day (from dawn until dusk) speech-making and witnessing military displays.

On the outskirts of Kabul is a white mosque marking the spot where the head of Shah Do Shamshirah is believed to have fallen, as this famed two-sword king fought his way into the city during a great battle. The natives will calmly and in all sincerity and faith tell the visitor to Kabul today that, while fighting toward the city, with a sword in each hand, this mighty king's head was severed from his body at this point; nevertheless, in spite of such "handicap," the headless corpse continued fighting into the city for nearly two more miles before falling. Thus, the head of Shah Do Shamshirah is buried in one shrine and his body in another.

While in Kabul, I visited many curious shrines of local saints. The doorway to one such shrine is covered with hundreds of nails and bits of cloth placed there by faithful donors who made vows or wishes at the same time. Another shrine is decorated with myriads of locks. Should the vow or wish of a donor materialize, he will return to the shrine and remove the nail, rag, or lock, as the case may be.

Near Kabul is Cucumber Village. The inhabitants of this strangely named locality are quite appropriately referred to as "Sons of the Cucumber" because they are wholly occupied with the production of that healthful fruit of the vine.

Not the least interesting of Kabul's motley array of working class people are the highly efficient bakers in action. One youth makes the dough; another weighs the chunks (everything is weighed in the balance scales in

[271]

preference to volume measurement); a third flattens the dough pancake style; a fourth puts the design upon the bread with his finger tips; a fifth plasters the bread on the inside walls of the oven, and a sixth, by means of a "fish-hook" iron rod, pulls the sheets of baked bread from the oven walls.

In Kabul, stereotyped white cheese vendors have become an established class of workers, running about the streets like athletes of old Greece, scantily clad and carrying silk balloon sacks of cheese in each hand. Along the sidewalks are large iron cauldrons for dyeing material. Like makers of taffy candy, the dye workers wring out their colorful material and twist the strands upon cross sticks.

In this great capital of Afghanistan, I was disappointed at not finding beautifully designed, embroidered, and colored "chopins" (outer robes) or "ponteens," with their heavy, raw wool lining, such as those worn by the nomad shepherds on the cold, windswept mountain slopes between the upper Hari and Kabul rivers.

Part of my last day in Kabul was spent in an attempt to post a letter homeward according to Afghan regulations. The postmaster insisted that the stamps be placed on the back of the envelope, and that the address also be put in reverse (i.e., country, locality, street and number, and lastly, name of addressee).

As the cool shadows of evening crept across the sky, I headed down the same trail traversed more than eighty years ago by fifteen thousand British soldiers and camp followers (one thousand white men, four thousand Indians, and approximately ten thousand camp followers). Of that heavily armed army, only one person reached Peshawar alive. Had I entered Afghanistan heavily armed, suspicious, and distrustful of the people, this story would probably have never been written.

Two days later, with redoubled faith in humanity, I cycled over one of Khyber's four paved highways and headed down the Grand Trunk road through India to the Far East.

END OF PART FIVE

[272]

"In men whom men condemn as ill
I find so much of goodness still,
In men whom men pronounce divine
I find so much of sin and blot,
I do not dare to draw a line
Between the two, where God has not."

Byron

PART SIX

CHAPTER XXXVII

Khyber to Calcutta via the Grand Trunk Road

Upon starting over Khyber Pass for the Grand Trunk road of India, I was stopped by two Afghan warriors, heavily armed as usual. After we had conversed—in a fashion—for an hour or so about the weather, guns, horses and women—all important subjects with the Afghans—they pointed proudly to dark splotches in the road where the blood of three British soldiers had been spilled the previous day. Shooting foreign soldiers is considered great sport in Afghanistan.

However, I was not a soldier, but only a lone traveler—their guest—a guest of their country. As a token of esteem, one of the warriors presented me with a few lumps of brown-sugar candy tied in a purple silk sack, while the other insisted that I accept his huge curved knife as a parting gift.

I said to myself that having gone unarmed through the wilds of Afghanistan, weapons were certainly needless in a peaceful country like India. To them I said: "My bicycle is not strong like the horses of your beautiful land and it is already over-burdened. Too, would it not be more fitting to leave your hospitable country unarmed, for otherwise the savage people of India might think that I was forced to carry a weapon to protect myself and my poor possessions?"

With misgivings as to my safety among the blood-thirsty foreigners, the Afghans finally let me go after many blessings and hopes that Allah would protect me and again guide my strange iron horse to Afghanistan.

[274]

It was a matter of only a few minutes coasting from the fortressed top of Khyber down to Peshawar where Captain Geoffrey Taylor of the Indian Medical Service anxiously awaited my arrival.

At a banquet given in honor of the occasion the Indian Minister of Agriculture and other celebrities in the vicinity gathered to enjoy my voracious as well as loquacious propensities. However, I slightly disappointed my hosts by stopping with the mango ice cream, with several courses of the dinner still ahead.

For three days Bucephalus and I sauntered around Peshawar—through the English colony which smacked somewhat of old England—through parks adorned by beautiful trees of yellow wisteria—through exotic bridle paths. As soon as we entered the gates of old Peshawar, England vanished and India of the Indians surrounded us. Brown men in loin cloths sat cross-legged smoking their strange pipes, consisting of a clay water pot, topped with a tiny tobacco receptacle with a long reed stem inserted in the clay, or perhaps a little two-inch, cone shaped, waterless pipe closely resembling the mud egg pipes of Afghanistan.

On Monday, June 15, in the dead heat of summer, Bucephalus left Peshawar and started down the 1600 miles of Grand Trunk road, following the Ganges all the way down to its mouth at Calcutta.

In spite of 125-degree temperature, the going was much easier than in Afghanistan and other countries where I had found it not only hot but hilly, rough, desolate, and almost impassable. Like a broad, black ribbon, India's Grand Trunk asphalt road stretches down the fertile valley between endless rows of overhanging trees in striking similarity to the road up the Nile.

There are even the same old water-buffaloes turning irrigation wheels along the river here as in the Nile Delta. As Indians believe that turn about is fair play, one often sees them turning the irrigation wheel while the buffaloes rest and drink water.

Haystacks of India are giant , oblong masses resembling zeppelin hangars. After the hay is neatly packed in the huge piles, cane brushes and thin layers of wet mud are packed over the outer surface of the haystack to preserve it.

Wheat grains are separated from the stalk by teams of oxen and buffalo which drag heavy bundles of hay over the masses of unseparated wheat. Not only is the grain threshed but the straw is pulverized and thus prepared as animal food. The mass is then thrown into the wind which blows the chaff away and separates the grain from the straw.

Along the Indian road one seldom sees a woman walking to the community well with only one jug resting upon her head. Like a circus juggler, she invariably balances two or three big jugs at the same time.

Indians respect the topee hat regardless of what is under it. Every Indian along the road gave me the native salute "Salome, Sahib" as soon as he saw my topee.

Near Noschera, I saw for the first time one of India's thousands of Sadhus, a Mahatma Ghandi looking fellow with a silver aureole around the crown of his head, another around his neck, and a huge silver-chased ceremonial sword tied to his loin cloth.

At the Government military dairy in Noschera, I drank my fill of good fresh milk. It was something I had not found in many months. Only sour milk was available and that I always boiled to destroy germs, which process also destroyed vitamins.

After passing over the Attock bridge, I shied off the main highway ninety-five miles from Peshawar and cycled up the shady lane to the American Mission in Taxila.

Dr. Gregory Martin was well known for his fine classical collection of victrola records, which he was in the habit of playing at every meal, and I was intent upon hearing some real music, for a change from the wailing songs of Asia.

Though Dr. Martin was in America on leave of absence, his nurse, Miss Porter, was in Taxila. Like all Indian homes of the better type (both of natives and foreigners), the mission was equipped with "punkahs"—great rug fans suspended from the ceiling in every room and made to sweep all the way across the upper half of the room by means of rope attachment. As I entered the mission grounds, Miss Porter was enjoying a noonday nap in her room while one of the servants was seated on the porch outside manipulating the fan by pulling back and forth on a rope connected with the fan through a hole in the wall. The pendulum-like movement of the "punkah" sounded like wings of a million bats brushing out the sides of a cave.

Miss Porter was almost as glad to hear a familiar voice (she too was a Southerner) and see a familiar type face as I. Together, we walked through the famous old archaeological excavations of Taxila with its three Buddhist monasteries and ancient Grecian city.

The giant Buddha shrines, lapis lazuli floors, and grain-grinding basins carved out of the solid rock walls of the old bakeries, still reflect some of the beauty and industry of these two-thousand-year-old monasteries. In my mind's eye, I could see the old Buddhist monks as they walked round and round the circular promenade circumnavigating the globular rock temples in the center of the monasteries. Each trip around the temple represented a prayer, just as does each twirl of the prayer box or each telling of the Moslem beads.

In the days of their flowering glory, these Taxila temples were filled with priceless gifts and treasures to Buddha which have long since been rifled by thieves.

At Rawal Pindi, I enjoyed another day of rest in the typical Indian home of P. C. Bhasin, managing director of

Sitting bulls
on the marble floor
of Calcutta's
post office

Man's
most beautiful tribute
to woman

Haystacks,
Indian style

Wheels of India

Bucephalus and Vociferous –
the other two of "We Three"

More
Wheels of India

the United Printers Ltd., and editor of The Weekly Munsiff.

Like most Indian homes there was a huge rug-covered ceiling, with windows near the tops of the walls. As the living room was a sacred place of purity, our shoes, dirty from the filth of the street, were left in the usual manner outside the door. Since Indians eat only two meals a day (10 a.m. and again at 8:30 p.m.), my host insisted that both my meals be satisfying. He ordered a splendid Hindu dinner of pickled mango and mint ground, pounded and mixed with salt, pepper, and cardamon seed; potatoes in chili; creamy green pulse peas, six paper-thin whole wheat pancakes; and two fresh mangoes which I sucked, Indian fashion, like an orange after removing the navel.

The sum-total cost of this Indian dinner was only a couple of pies (one pie is equivalent to one-fourth cent U.S. currency), whereas the same meal would have cost not less than two rupees in a British restaurant. My host used this meal as an example of the low standard of living forced upon Indians by the British.

"Why don't the English lower their standard of living nearer to that of the Indians and turn their surplus salaries into more useful channels such as native educational purposes?" exclaimed my excited Indian host.

"But," I protested, "are there not Indian colleges and universities in nearly every city of any consequence in India? Do not all the hundreds of Indian doctors, lawyers, and other professional men boast of three or four degrees, whereas most European students are glad of an opportunity to receive their bachelor's degree?"

"That makes the situation even more unbearable," persisted the obstinate Mr. Bhasin. "Through education, the English inspire us with the yearning for freedom, yet hold us in servitude; they implant within us the seeds of culture and refinement, yet continue to treat us like dogs. Though living is cheap, the English in India are the

[280]

highest paid men on the globe. They live like Oriental potentates, on an even higher standard than in England, and never think of associating with the most cultured and intelligent of Indians except in master-servant relationship."

As the cool evening shadows crept over the city, I left the hospitable home of Mr. Bhasin to renew my journey by moonlight. All night I passed over a great network of canyons. The Punjab region is the most eroded country in the world to be so flat. The English should level off and reclaim the land again with gully-filling tractors.

At dawn Bucephalus and I started over one of the ghostly hills dotting the broad, flat plains of the southern Punjab. (Punjab means five waters.) So soft and silvery was the sun as it peeped over the dusty eastern monsoon horizon that it looked more like the moon than its own usually dazzling self.

At Jhelum, I stopped at the Good Samaritan Hospital to pay my respects to Miss Hartig, another one of the many missionaries who have literally lost themselves among the Indians. My visit was very brief, as Miss Hartig was helping her cook plan a wedding feast for the cook's five sons who were to be married next day, even though the youngest was only eleven years old.

This was a measure of economy since an old Indian custom demands that hundreds of rupees be spent, even by the poorest families, in wedding presents given to all relatives and friends by the parents of the marrying children. Thus one big, quintuple wedding costs one-fifth as much as five weddings at different times.

Miss Hartig voiced disapproval of the universal Indian custom of raising large families. "Two or three hundred rupees worth of fruit, flowers, clothing and jewelry are given by the proud parents at the celebration of the arrival of their newborn son," she said, "yet, they don't wish to pay even a pie to the hospital for its cost and trouble of bringing the child into the world."

[281]

Punjab India is the paradise for the peculiar type foreigner whose greatest pleasure is in watching the crash of pottery and glass bowls and vases. All of this entertainment in the street shops is free of charge, too, as all the foreigner must do is contaminate the vessel with his touch and the Hindu shopkeeper, even more fanatical than the Afghan Moslem, will instantly break the impure pot to bits. I soon learned to save the shopkeepers unnecessary embarrassment by breaking the vessels with my own hands just as soon as I had eaten or drunk from them. My consideration for the purity of their hands immediately won their favor and they always insisted that I accept gratis all that they had in store.

On the outskirts of Jhelum I cycled through several miles of elaborately dressed natives parading with drums and red flags. Some walked; others rode cycles, donkeys, and camels; or family groups sat from front singletree to rear axle of their great water buffalo carts.

I finally reached the cynosure of this pilgrimage of thousands, a huge rectangular building—the Old Home for Sacred Cows and Bulls! It was the annual reception to raise funds for the upkeep of these bovines by selling cider, sugar water, melon, et cetera, at booths around the building.

I was glad to find one place in India where these poor old dumb creatures were cared for. Usually they are turned loose on the streets to starve or eke out an existence as best they can. Being sacred and therefore untouchable, the Brahma bulls can enter a native grocery shop and help themselves unmolested. They walk about the streets of India and park their carcasses on palatial porches as if they owned the place. However, as they are not prevented from breaking up vegetable stands, so too are they not prevented from starving in case they fail to find food for themselves. Thus the streets are filled with these pitifully starving sacred creatures.

[282]

As there is no sacredness attached to Tonga ponies and water buffalo, these beasts of burden are brutally overworked by the natives.

Many of the men looked like American Indians on the warpath with red, yellow, and white splotches of paint over their faces, and heads shaved except for a little tuft of hair on top. Others, whose religious tenets forbade them to shave or cut hair, wore long unshorn locks and whiskers. Everyone held a certain type walking stick, staff, sword, or dagger, to denote his particular caste or sect.

Most of the men wore little golden earrings, while the women beautified themselves with bracelet-size nose rings exquisitely bejewelled, with pendants hanging from the center. Not only were lace patterns of pearls and rubies embroidered in the little wooden-soled clogs, or sandals of the women, but also in the purple and golden shawls enshrouding their symmetric figures.

The streets were crowded and congested with all sorts of creeping and crawling creatures, both human and otherwise.

Blind beggars paraded with drum and cymbal as I sat beneath a shady tree and sampled some of India's motley array of fruit. At each little fruit stand were walnut, almond, dry date, cashew nut, cardamon, litchi, loquat, jack fruit, shaddock, jaman, the "elephant" or wood apple, custard apple, mango, emblic, myrobolan, berjajubes, and other exotic fruits whose names I had never before heard. It was amusing to watch half-starved sacred bulls stop to sample the delicacies of the fruit vendors and then stalk leisurely down the streets as if fully conscious of their impregnable position.

The sidewalks were teeming with deadly cobras swaying to the rhythm of the snake-charmer flutes or "bins," which are made from a fruit called tiemba. The snuff gourds and boxes, which are equally popular with Indians and Afghans, are made in Peshawar from the shell of the "ball" fruit.

[283]

At one unusually chaotic street corner I stopped to ask what was the trouble. Between peals of laughter, an English-speaking Indian told me that while a lawyer sat smoking in front of the nearby cafe, a hungry cow had just disposed of his brief case.

Things were happening so fast before my eyes that I would probably have never reached the city's museum had it not been for my desire to see Kim's cannon, the old mortar made famous in one of Kipling's immortal poems. This historic gun rested directly in front of the museum, but I entered the building to delve into other treasures of the past.

Forty miles south of Jhelum I met the ominous forerunner of the monsoon destined to haunt my trail from Delhi to the Philippines. I ran through a storm of golf-ball-size hail-stones which would have knocked me out but for my cork-lined topee.

Huge grey, black, and white vultures dropped in the wayside trees seemingly unmindful of the onslaughts of the elements. The grey-bodied, black-faced Indian crows were cawing disapproval of Mother Nature's actions, while myriads of stingaree-tailed, emerald-green parrots raced through the air in real fright. Black and white striped chipmunks chirped shrilly as they clung to the sheltering branches of the trees.

Passing as quickly as it came, the storm left me high and dry on a little green elevation several miles north of Lahore, the capital of the Punjab. At this ideal resting place I lay down to sleep with only a mosquito net between me and the open sky, and a sleeping bag between me and the rain-drenched ground.

Next day, as I cycled southward into the clutches of the terrible, wet monsoon, the dry, blistering heat of the Punjab gradually gave way to stifling, sticky humidity. Except for the beautiful valley of Kashmir which I had already left behind, India is the hottest, most

[284]

uncomfortable place to visit during the month of June.

In Lahore I found thousands of Indians of all ages bathing at all hours of the day in little water conduits running through the city parks. The river on the edge of the city seemed to be the favorite washing place for clothes. Miles and miles of men were beating clothes on its rocky banks while great herds of water buffalo lay snorting in the middle of the stream. With only their noses visible above the water these animals resembled herds of hippopotami in the upper Blue Nile.

In tiny truck gardens around the city many natives were engaged in agricultural pursuits. Working in pairs, one man pushed the wooden prongs of a rake into the loamy ground while his partner, by means of a rope wrapped around his waist and tied to each end of the rake, tilled the soil Afghan farmer fashion, by dragging the rake through the ground. Oxen teams then pulled heavy wooden planks crosswise over the plowed ground preparatory to planting vegetable and grain seed.

It was barely light when I reached Amritsar and cycled through this old city to the Golden Temple, famous center of the Sikh religion.

Some say, "See the Taj Mahal by moonlight for the thrill of a lifetime." With equal fervor and assurance I say, "See the Golden Temple at sunrise."

I had many misgivings upon entering this shrine, as it was compulsory that I deposit my shoes at a booth outside and wash my feet in a special pool for the purpose before being allowed to enter the holy grounds.

Once inside the portals of the walled enclosure I stood awed at the beauty of this temple of pure, beaten, and molten gold glistening in manifold splendor, as the rising sun threw another shower of gold upon its polished domes. Like a priceless gem, this beautiful edifice rests in the midst of a crystal clear pool or moat of water, covering several square acres of territory. Broad promenades of black, white, and pink polished marble slabs surround the pool while a narrow marble causeway extends beneath an emerald-studded, golden arch to the temple itself. The arch is guarded on each side by solemn, old longbeards elaborately bedecked with jewels and silks, and with a mace of authority in each hand. Golden-grilled lamp-posts containing green stained glass, adorn both sides of the causeway. Great cypress trees line the water's edge.

As each one in the endless train of pilgrims to the shrine starts across the threshold of the golden-arched entrance to the causeway, he stops for a few moments to kneel in prayer before proceeding farther.

I would have joined the motley crowd picnicking beside the holy waters surrounding the temple, but memory of the hundreds of cholera victims I had seen being borne up the highway by mourning relatives did not inspire me to tarry in any one place long.

It was not until Bucephalus had carried me far down the Delhi road, beyond the noisy throng, that I again breathed peacefully. Not a sound broke the silence of the landscape. The platinum-colored monsoon sky hung overhead like transparent, greyish-purple glass. It was just a little lull in the storm.

On Sunday, June 21, I passed under Lal Darwaga (the old northern red gate of Sher Shah's capital) into Delhi, the great seat of seven historic empires.

It was Shivarati day, the birth anniversary of Shiva, goddess of the Hindu religion. The town was in a crowded chaotic uproar. Every woman was dressed in her finest gold-trimmed embroidered veil and gold-fringed pleated skirt of green, red, purple, yellow, orange, or blue. In true Indian style, all women wore nothing from waist up save tiny pastel-shaded brassieres. Many wore chain-lace shoes while even the poorest among them boasted dozens of gold, silver, copper and ivory bracelets, anklets, nose rings and buttons, and toe rings on the middle toes of both feet.

The only extraordinary features to the women's dress were the real and artificial bouquets, wreaths, and chains of rose petals and lilies of the valley which they pinned to their hair or twined like strings of beads about their necks. Though exquisitely beautiful, Indian girls, like those of other foreign lands, seemed more alike than our heterogeneous American girls. Their chief delight was to sit on the balconies and housetops overhanging the street and watch the passing show below.

As the heavy downpour of monsoon rain had made it a fine, cool day for picnicking and parading, everyone was out celebrating and visiting one astrologer and Islamic wishing-well after another. Had it been a clear summer day, all would have stayed indoors and slept.

Stationed at every corner were little boys who were kept busy pouring drinking water from huge copper pots into the palms of the hands of thirsty Hindus. Other little boys squatted beside their miscellaneous merchandise of dolls, trick mice, paper snakes, and rainbow-colored handkerchiefs, and sang their wares to passersby. Glass tumbler vendors rat-tat-tatted tumblers against the tiled pavement to show their unbreakability. An old goat assiduously followed in the footsteps of a workman and ate posters as soon as the man had pasted them on sign posts. Kites added further variety to the colorful scene by swooping down in the dirty Delhi streets and carrying filth away in their claws. Great fruit-eating, flying foxes dropped from all the street-side trees.

Here in these back alleys of old Delhi one sees horrible sights which guide-books for tourists carefully omit: a miserable wretch with both hands completely eaten away by leprosy; another, with a great sore foot five or six times the size of the other, swollen from leprosy and aggravated by walking upon it till the pain is unbearable; farther down the street is a haggard, naked woman sitting in the gutter and screaming at the top of her hoarse voice; still a

[287]

few paces farther is another idiot whose insanity is, luckily for her, of a more pleasant type: also seated in the gutter and covered only with shreds of loin cloth, this poor creature amuses herself by picking up grains of sand and dropping them one by one into the sewer conduit. From all shops and houses along the street emanated the incense of sandal dust or "Hoona," which is burned every evening by Hindus as a powerful antiseptic.

I passed a beggar shaking thousands of little bugs from his sleeping mat. He did not dare destroy the bugs, and they would immediately return to the mat. The beggar was just one of the millions of Indian fanatics of Jainism, a monastic Hindu sect, who wear gauze pads over their mouths to keep from swallowing a gnat or some other insect which contains the transmigrated soul of some person of the past or the future. Of course, the beggar could not kill a bug as it might be his own beloved grandpa or unborn child in disguise!

The sidewalks were lined with popular, painted medicine men, their three-pronged red tridents (like the Devil's pitchfork) sticking up in the ground beside their secret mixtures, of vari-colored powders and liquids in little bottles and other vessels, spread out on cloths before admiring audiences of ignorant Hindus. After examining their medicines I could easily understand why they were advertised as "panacea talismen to cure all sickness, frighten away all devils and evil spirits" They were thick black juices of pickled snakes, lizards, cockroaches, rats, and other delicious delicacies.

Holiday merrymakers were seated in pairs on the sidewalks playing on their bellows organs; one musician fingered the keys while his companion supplied the wind by pumping the accordion-like bellows attached to the back of the piano box.

At a clothing store, I was about to replace my khaki shirt with a new purchase when the storekeeper suddenly began his noonday prayers. After waiting nearly fifteen minutes for prayers to close, I grew restless and left without a shirt.

Between Delhi and Agra I began to run into large colonies of monkeys who raced across the road in front of me or sat grinning in the forks of wayside mango trees. As it was early summer, every mother monkey was nursing a tiny baby which clung tenaciously to her furry waist as she jumped from limb to limb.

After many months of solo cycling I was determined to adopt a baby monkey as a traveling companion. However, it was easier said than done. Every time I went up one side of a tree, the screaming mother monkey escaped down the other, or else jumped to a tiny limb of another tree. Once, I succeeded in cornering an unfortunate pair; but as the old monkey showed signs of battle before I could descend to Bucephalus with her kidnapped child, I gave up the chase as hopeless.

My chance finally came near Agra when an old mother monkey left her precious charge perched only about five feet above the road in the forks of a tree while she scampered across the trail to get some mangos and papayas for dinner. Without even dismounting from my iron steed I leaned against the tree trunk, grabbed the helpless infant, and cycled down the highway with the whole monkey colony in close pursuit.

My new companion I christened "Vociferous." Though it would be necessary to treat him as a baby for a few days and let him drink goat and buffalo milk from a nippled bottle inside our bread satchel, he would soon be strong enough to sit on my shoulder and eat bananas and other fruit which he himself should gather from the wayside trees.

Monkeys were not the only denizens of the Grand Trunk lane. I passed whole droves of grey foxes, feasting with vultures on the carcass of a dead water buffalo as

[289]

nonchalantly as if in the depths of the forest primeval instead of beside the greatest highway in India. Too, I was constantly dodging large red dragon lizards which lay across the road.

Flocks of ostrich-size birds squawked along the roadside. I began to see many pigs, pheasants, peacocks, parrots, and red-headed, golden-breasted woodpeckers. The wild peacocks were uncannily beautiful as they walked gracefully through the green fields and wild mango groves, or stood sedately on temple and mosque domes as if sculptured there. Several times I was sure these peacock statues were artificial until suddenly they spread wings and sailed down to earth.

Indians can truly boast of homes where the "buffalo roam, where the deer and the antelope play." In addition to the multitudes of wild and domestic water buffalo wandering at large over the plains of India, I frequently ran into large herds of antelope and red deer nibbling berries near my trail.

At Muttra, I chanced to meet Stanley Jones, who was just back from a vacation trip up in the hills where he had "sung the Doxology" to his new book, Victorious Living. We had both planned to spend the night with Mr. Temple, local Methodist preacher; but as Mr. Temple was not at home, we had to resort to our sleeping bags.

In comparing experiences, Mr. Jones corroborated my story of strange "mother earth" pipes of Afghanistan, by saying that he had seen similar pipes among the natives of northwestern Tibet. At dawn the following day we parted with mutual expressions of Godspeed, Stanley Jones bound via train and airplane to South Africa, and I by bicycle to the China Sea.

Passing along the broad, stone-slabbed streets ahead of me, were red and blue-spangled native troops and bag-pipers on parade. Once outside the city gates of Muttra, I galloped Bucephalus at breakneck speed down the thirty-five kilometers to Agra and the Taj Mahal.

Long before reaching this sacred shrine, I saw its white polished marble dome soaring ethereally upward into the black monsoon sky. It was the crystallization of the most beautiful of dreams. It was not of pure white marble as I had supposed, but was ornately decorated with designs of tulips, lilies, and other flowers in natural color, every stem, leaf and petal being a separate piece of marble. Finely latticed marble windows adorned every side and beautifully carved and arched sandalwood doorways (the original silver ones were stolen by Jats in 1764) led to the tombs beneath the central dome of the Taj.

Climbing up the winding stair on the top of one of the four marble minarets gracing the corners of the Taj court, I sat down to drink in the beauty of landscape (it was all the lunch I had). An old Indian Sadhu sat beside me and refreshed my memory with his story of the origin of this most beautiful of all man-made works of art.

The Taj Mahal, as everyone knows, contains the remains of Emperor Shah Jahan (1627-58) and his favorite wife Arjumand Bano Begam, better known as Mumtaz-uz-zamani or Mumtaz Mahal, "the ornament of the palace." She was the daughter of Asaf Khan, the richest and most powerful noble in the empire, and niece of Nur Jahan, wife of the Emperor Jahangir. She was born in 1592, married to Shah Jahan in 1612, and died in 1631 after giving birth to her fourteenth child.

The exact cost of the Taj with its complementary buildings is nowhere recorded, and the valuations hitherto made range from fifty lakks to six crores of rupees, but whatever its value, the Taj is unquestionably the most beautiful tribute any husband ever paid to his wife.

Having feasted my eyes for four hours on this richest gem of India, and bathed my feet in the limpid waters of the reflection pools (I would have taken a swim in the water but it was only a few inches deep—barely enough in which to wet my feet), I ventured to the ivory-towered red fortress and other architectural wonders of Agra.

However, I suddenly realized that whatever else India had to offer would be a sort of anti-climax to my vision of the Taj Mahal. As I looked at that beautiful gem in stone, the first tinge of homesickness touched me because there was no one save little Vociferous with whom to share the joy and beauty of those moments.

With redoubled speed and determination to reach Calcutta and embark for home "ere the silver sycle became her golden shield," Bucephalus breasted the onslaughts of monsoon wind and rain, plunged through rubber plantations, banana, date, and coconut groves, across endless stretches of rice fields and cow pastures, through thatch-roofed jungle villages, and finally emerged at the end of the trail. In thirteen days I had cycled the 1600 miles from Khyber Pass to Calcutta. Thousands of people I had passed during the thirteen days perhaps had already lived five times as long as I, yet had never seen beyond their own native province!

No wonder Indians who escape cholera and tuberculosis live so long. They eat sparingly only twice a day and average fifteen hours sleep a day so that 100-year-olds are not uncommon sights along the India road. Americans, on the other hand, eat too much, sleep too little, work too hard, and travel too fast to live to a ripe old age. Perhaps it is far better to live a short, useful life in the conscious pursuit of a worthy purpose than to sit for 110 years telling beads or reciting psalms in the shade of a palm tree.

CHAPTER XXXVIII

Criss-Crossing Through Calcutta and Rough Riding to Rangoon

Cycling through a crowded city of civilization is far more dangerous than bucking across wild tribal regions, through dark jungles, or over the burning sands of the desert.

I found Calcutta to be the worst of all places for locomotion. Not only was the traffic principally on the reverse side of the street from that in my native land, but the motley array of vehicles was allowed to zigzag across to either side of the street, cut corners, and wander at random like a bunch of wild steers. The speeding chaos required my undivided attention. Down the Grand Trunk road travel had been comparatively safe as there were seldom more than one or two interesting incidents simultaneously diverting my mind from the heavy traffic, whereas here in Calcutta things were happening on all sides at once.

During my first hour of sightseeing in the city, I had six minor accidents in collision with parked cars, wagons, sedan chairs, or rickshas. Fortunately, the only policeman who hailed me for careless cycling was unable to speak a word of English. Unable to understand each other, we mutually agreed to let the matter drop.

Cycling past "Lord and Christ, Attorneys at Law," I finally reached Kali Ghat Temple near the end of Chow Ringhee road. Just inside the temple courtyard of Kali, stood a little cactus bush to which barren women had tied stones, and prayed that the gods bless them with children. Even as I observed this charming little bush, three young Hindu women seated themselves around its base and began their mournful prayer.

Seated inside the temple door was the ghastly, gory fig-

[293]

ure of the goddess Kali, with her four arms and hands arranged about her three-eyed head (extra eye in center of forehead) like a fireworks whirl wheel. She was anything but lovely with her enormous golden tongue lolling out over her breast, encircled with a long chain of human-headed beads (heads of her enemies), and with her husband Siva reclining across her feet. In addition to Kali, there were the goddess of music, goddess of the Burning Heart, and about thirty lesser goddesses.

Next to Kali the most important god within the portals of the green-tiled temple is Siva. He is worshipped by the war-painted devils one sees running about Indian streets, proudly wearing bald heads except for a little tuft of hair called the "ticky." These strange people believe that upon dying it is by the "ticky" that they are lifted up to heaven.

As it was Sunday, the temple courtyard was in an unusual state of confusion, the squeals of sacrificed goats mingling weirdly and harmoniously with the wailing prayers and incantations of pilgrims to this holy Hindu shrine, the only place of animal sacrifice in India.

In addition to the twelve goats sacrificed between ten and twelve o'clock on Friday mornings, the Sunday offering to Kali was to feature the added attraction of a water buffalo. It was with curious wonder that I watched six white-robed women first sprinkle holy water and flower petals on the sacrificial altar and then drape the altar posts in chains of hollyhock and lily-of-the-valley blossoms. Flower vendors gave all pilgrims flower neck-laces also, and the insane and infirm among them were led to the altar where the mercy of goddess Kali was invoked for them.

After these preliminary ceremonies, the sacrifice fol-lowed. The priest held the heads of the animals between the "tuning fork" bars of the altar while a boy chopped off the heads with a hooked sword. The heads were then presented to the fire priest for offering to Kali while the bodies of the animals were donated to the poor pilgrims.

After witnessing this impressive ceremony, I was escorted by the old fat, naked Kali priest to the Burning Ghat, beside a picturesque little boat-filled canal. Here I saw nineteen great funeral pyres with greasy, thick spirals of flesh-smelling smoke oozing out of the charring embers. Upon closer inspection I discovered to my horror that human corpses lay horizontally in the midst of each pyre. One was just beginning to sizzle beneath newly lighted fire brands; another was fully barbecued; others were already reduced to ashes except the skulls which had fallen away from the flames and were being thrust back into the middle of the pyres; several others lay entirely naked (except for henna sprinkled over their bodies from head to foot, a few flower wreaths around the neck, and rose petals stuffed in the mouth) awaiting their turn to be cremated, the ashes put in a red pot, and then sent down the canal to be sprinkled on the holy waters of the Ganges.

The scene was distasteful enough, but it could have been much worse. The old woman who stood nearby and tear-fully watched her husband's body being reduced to ashes might have thrown herself upon the fire to be consumed with her beloved. Such things, though not uncommon, were occurring more infrequently since the British authorities even favored second marriages of Hindu widows, and rigidly enforced laws prohibiting punishments inflicted by Hindu religious fanatics as a result of such marriages.

The sickening sight of the animal sacrifices to Kali had been enough to turn my stomach, but even they were not nearly so terrible as those in which poor human victims are cruelly stuck through the back with a hook and swung seven times around the sacrificial pole to appease the gods. What crimes are committed in the name of religion!

Having viewed Calcutta from the outside, I hitched Bucephalus to the doorstep of the Indian Museum for a first and last glimpse into less familiar realms of native

[295]

society. Not since leaving the British Museum in London nearly a year before had I seen such a varied collection in one building.

The funniest of all the statues was the little God of Happiness. My beloved Chinese friend, Mr. Fan Hou, presented a facsimile of this jovial-featured figure to President Franklin D. Roosevelt, when these two representatives of two great countries met recently in my home town of Athens, Georgia.

The most interesting discovery in the museum was a real live person, a young widow who had just arrived after a six-weeks voyage from England.

On Sunday, June 28, I stood at the crossroads. In Calcutta docks there lay Atlanta City, a trim little freighter bound direct for Savannah, Georgia! Captain Walters had invited me to accompany him back to Athens, the fairest city of the Southland, but I had been foolish enough to refuse his hospitable offer.

I had cycled across Europe and Asia and was certainly not going to give up now that I was almost at the end of the trail. The monsoon floods had covered the swamp regions between Calcutta and Rangoon so that further progress in that direction had to be made by swimming or boating.

After obtaining special permit to sail deck passage "Indian fashion" for eleven rupees, instead of 150 rupees European style, Bucephalus, Vociferous and I boarded the Talamba just before she tooted her whistle and chugged away for Rangoon.

Everyone was tense with excitement as we sailed down the 120 perilous miles to open seas. The Hoogla is the most dangerous river in world navigation; and now that the monsoon floods were at their height, sand bars of the constantly shifting river course had to be resurveyed every day.

As we passed Old Glory flying atop the newly painted

Atlanta City, I experienced a sinking sensation as if letting a great opportunity slip through my fingers. Though this was the only American vessel in port, hundreds from other countries lined both sides of the river for miles. I recognized Trenenfels from Belgiium, Chan San and Hung Hi of China, Rinda of Norway, and the Royal Mail Clipper from England.

Lower down the river were dry docks and ship grave-yards, jungle jute gardens, colonial-columned mansions of millionaires, straw-covered Chinese barges propelled in the heavy, intermittent downpours of rain by well-trained crews of naked oarsmen, tiny dugouts filled with native fishermen spreading their nets—large crescents which extended almost across the river—and paddle-wheel river boats like those plying the Mississippi in antebellum days.

No sooner did my little freighter strike the river mouth than it began to do tail spins across mountainous waves of the monsoon sea. I had gone through rough water from Bergen to Hell, Norway, when I watched several hundred Norwegian scouts feed the fishes. But with 799 natives of India and Burma in a storm-tossed junk it was slightly more difficult to retain my digestive equilibrium! After two wild days at sea, with still another ahead before reaching Rangoon, I was almost ready to jump overboard and take my chances at swimming.

I wished I were home, in Timbuctoo, Podunk, Benares, or anywhere—so there was terra firma. Yes, Benares was the place! I felt like dying; and Benares should certainly be an ideal spot in which to pass away, as anyone dying there is sure of safe transportation directly to Heaven. I remembered the thirty-six miles of pilgrim road encircling this holy city of the upper Ganges—the six pilgrim rests where pilgrims spend the nights in their six-day procession around the circuit—the half-dozen parties of priest-led pilgrims I had seen wending their way around the holy route, in motley array like the pictured procession in

Canterbury Tales. How beautiful and firm that hard-surfaced road had felt as I trod it with the gaudily beaded and painted Hindu fanatics.

Still farther up the Ganges at one night's resting place at the site of the deserted city of Fatepur Sikri near Agra, almost a thousand miles from the nearest ocean, I had felt the security of Mother Earth beneath me as I revelled in the romantic history of old Akbar's queens (who lived at Fatepur Sikri), some Christian, others Hindu and Moslem, each possessing her own luxurious little palace within a palace in which she lived, surrounded by her own people. Akbar had been shrewd enough to arrange these quarters so that he could visit any one of his queens without the knowledge of the others.

Though a tenth centurian, Akbar manufactured what we would term ultra modern ideas. Typical of his creative genius was the great Pachin court on which games of chess were played, with slave girls acting as chessmen moving from square to square at the player's command.

In the reverie of such mental memories, I was able to endure the nauseating sights aboard my ship. Vociferous also helped distract my mind from the peculiar smells and noises emanating from the storm-tossed natives. My monkey's favorite pastime seemed to be scratching for imaginary fleas. This he did more as a calisthenic exercise for his artistic soul than for any other reason. In performing this task he applied his little human-like fingertips to the troublesome area, not in the regular scratch manner of human beings, but by rotating his entire arm in a series of graceful circles, the fingertips lightly touching the desired spot for one fleeting second at the completion of each   circle.

When hungry for a banana or his bottle of milk, Vociferous had a million-dollar look of pathetic pleading which permeated his whole personality to perfection. If human beggars could acquire such soulful eyes, longing

[298]

lips, distended nose, heartbroken voice, they would be rich overnight.

Toward evening of the third day at sea, our bruised and battered boat crossed the bay and started up the forty miles of river to Rangoon, scattering the flying fishes as we ploughed through the smooth, limpid waters.

From a distance I sighted the electrically lighted Shwe Dagan Pagoda, largest and most sacred pagoda in the world. Though situated several miles from the river bank, this towering shaft of gold was plainly visible from its imposing position atop an elevated terrace. Two giant leogryphs stood guard at the foot of a long flight of steps leading up to the pagoda. Curiously carved teakwood covered these steps to form an arcade in which were numerous vendors of artificial flowers, gold leaf, gongs and other articles which might be bought by pilgrims and placed as offerings upon the holy altar. The pagoda occupied the center of the terrace and soared three hundred and seventy feet into the air from a base thirteen hundred and fifty-five feet in circumference (so I learned from the Burmese boat captain). The richly gilt structure was capped by a solid gold, jewel-studded umbrella from which gold and silver bells tinkled, like the bewitching chimes of Dunkirk.

When the ship finally tied up at the dock, it was great sport passing through the customs examination with the "other" seven hundred and ninety-nine naked Indians, each of whom had to strip off his scant clothing and pile his belongings on his head as he passed in review before scores of bug-inspecting officials. No meticulous examination was made of Bucephalus or me. As for Vociferous, he played his part well, lying quietly concealed in my bread satchel and passing the customs unnoticed. Now that it is all over, I tremble to think what would have happened had the authorities known that I was smuggling a forbidden sacred monkey out of India!

[299]

Bamian Bhudda

Have water, will travel

Wives are to be protected

Tanks, tusks and turbans
on the Grand Trunk Road

Stalking Bigfoot with a camera

Cattle crossing at the old water buffalo hole

I met Stanley Jones at Muttra

British Army of India

As I mounted Bucephalus and rode out into the Strand—main thoroughfare of Rangoon—a gay cosmos of Eastern color greeted me.

Thousands of crows and parrots were going to roost in the beautiful royal poinciana and other flowering trees and jungle-like masses of vegetation; little bullet-shaped red street cars and ricksha runners screamed through the streets; pawn brokers and auctioneers advertised their wares with mellow-toned drums and gongs, incessantly beaten, along the sidewalks. Dainty, demure Burmese debutantes promenaded beneath Chinese umbrellas which were of course held high enough for passersby to see the roses and ivory combs adorning their masses of glossy silk hair. Younger girls wore bangs around the crown of their heads with the rest of their hair tied in a neat bundle on top.

I was surprised to see that the Burmese, both men and women, were powerfully and beautifully built specimens of humanity so strikingly different from the small-boned, fragile-framed Indians. However, I noticed quite a number whose bodies bore evidence of great wounds, so similar in several different natives that I ventured to ask a policeman if there was any significance attached to these strange scars.

"Yes, Sahib." he replied, "these people are Hindus who took part in the March festival to appease the wrath of the smallpox goddess. You see from their not-yet-healed wounds that they have run through coals of fire, stuck pins and nails through their bodies, and carried enormous loads supported by nails stuck in their naked flesh. Many brave Hindus died during these terrible tests of faith, but these strong men that you now see have survived."

Scarcely able to digest these grim realities of life, I cycled up the street to the American Consulate. That same night I donned Consul Himmel's tuxedo and attended a theater party given by the American delegation in my honor. After the show a midnight reception and dinner were held on the cool veranda of the Consul's home. My

[302]

brief stay in Rangoon was but a short interlude between the savage existence of the past few months and the far more unbelievably miserable yet fascinating experience hidden in the dark jungle just ahead of me.

Since leaving home more than a year before, I had been vacillating between extremes of deepest misery and profoundest joy. I had found the enjoyment of life to be quite a relative experience. To appreciate living and behaving like other human beings one must go to the other extreme and "go native" for a while. After he has endured real hardships in his rugged life among savages, the adventurer is then able (maybe) to appreciate the secure existence of ordinary life. At least it is worth a trial. Most Americans live concerned with business and home troubles and other little miscellaneous routine affairs of everyday life, and don't ever stop to realize how happy they really are.

END OF PART SIX

"There's a race of men that don't fit in,
    A race that can't stay still;
So they break the hearts of kith and kin,
    And they roam the world at will.

They range the field and they rove the flood,
    And they climb the mountain's crest.
Theirs is the curse of the gypsy blood
    And they don't know how to rest."

                    Robert W. Service

PART SEVEN

BICYCLING THROUGH BURMA

CHAPTER XXXIX

On the Road to Mandalay

At the crack of dawn, July 4, Bucephalus, Vociferous and I bade farewell to the Y.M.C.A. in Rangoon, and set out upon the road to Mandalay in a heavy downpour of rain.

Exactly one year earlier, I had landed at Rotterdam, Holland, and started a cycling trip which would ultimately carry me around the world. Now, it seemed that my only trail home lay in the direction of Indo-China.

It was going to be a long, circuitous trip through the flat rice fields to upper Burma, across the beautiful, but dangerous, jungle mountains of the Shan States, down to Bangkok, and finally across Cambodia and Cochin China to the China Sea—many thousands of miles of trail to reach the Pacific only a few hundred miles away! The wet monsoon season was at its peak, and the road would be teeming with snakes, seeking safety from drowning in the flooded fields and slimy jungles, with tarantulas, malarial mosquitoes, and all sorts of wild animals.

It would be all right as long as the road was good and I could keep to my saddle. But what would happen when the fine British-built road came to an end in upper Burma and I had to set out through the wildest jungle region in Asia? Dr. Grey (the Y.M.C.A. secretary at Rangoon) and Mr. Scott (American Consul) both insisted that no one had ever made the trip during the monsoon season except by airplane. There was little consolation in the fact that should I fail to come through, I would not be the first to

[305]

fall by the wayside. Nor was there any thrill at the thought of doing the "impossible." I had already received an overdose of "impossible" thrills by bicycling over Norwegian glaciers, Swiss alpine by-paths, great Syrian and "Garden of Eden" deserts, Himalayan highlands, and midsummer India. I was literally "fed up" and ready to go home the quickest, easiest way possible. I little dreamed that more nerve and energy would be required for this last little "home stretch" than I had used at any time during my previous twenty-three thousand miles of cycling.

I had negotiated in vain for deck passage to Singapore and China. The only Chinese boat in Rangoon dock, the Hai Shang, was bound for Calcutta. On all other boats, English shipping regulations confined deck passage to Indians. Indians could travel for $14.00, whereas the minimum for white people going around the Malay Peninsula to upper China was $150.00. That settled it.

I bought twelve pies worth of pineapple and bananas. Before reaching the big plantations near Mandalay where pineapples were free, a "pice apiece" was the customary price for a pineapple—a dozen pineapples for a penny! (A "pice" is an Indian copper coin one-third the value of a "pie" which in turn is only one-fourth the value of an American penny.) I tied the masses of fruit to the handle-bars of my bicycle, slung Vociferous around my neck where he was sheltered by my "umbrella hat" from the rain, and rode Bucephalus on the wings of the dawn. The earth trembled as blasts of thunder rumbled across the sky in the wake of dazzling sheets of lightning. I wondered if the eyes of the jungle tigers were half so brilliant or their roars so powerful and thrilling.

On the outskirts of Rangoon, we passed early morning golf enthusiasts wading through mud and rain, with caddies holding umbrellas over them as they trudged around the course. I was not the only one who did not have sense enough to get out of a shower of rain!

[306]

There was a touch of irony in the fact that I had crossed so many desert countries where the only things resembling water were the mirages; and now, as far as eye could see, there was nothing but water. Most of the region along the Mandalay road between the great Irrawaddy and Salween rivers is a vast ocean of rice fields—the scene of many varied activities. Children swim in the flooded fields as their mothers and fathers follow the paddle-wheel plows and furrow-makers drawn by the water buffalo. Many queer types of implements are used by the natives in preparing mud for rice cultivation. One need not go to Hawaii for aquaplaning. One can enjoy this sport in the fields of Burma where the rice planter, standing upon an oblong surface-board weighted down at the rear, is drawn across the drowned flats by buffalo instead of by motor-boat. At times, the water is so deep that both buffalo and driver are compelled to swim—fancy a farmer swimming behind a plow in one of my old red hills of Georgia! Little wonder that Burmese, walking all day long up to their waists or necks in mud and water, have such powerful legs. The aquaplane plows of the rice fields are also used as vehicles of conveyance, sliding across muddy stretches where wagon wheels would make no headway at all.

The rice fields are also favorite fishing grounds. All along the road I saw women and children fishing with pole and hook, or else seining for shrimp and crab in the wake of the plow by means of a little wicker fish-net contrivance resembling a lacrosse stick. Dipping this triangular-shaped "shovel" into the mud, they scooped up a half-gallon of shrimp each time and deposited them in a wicker basket tied to the waist.

Kipling was right when he said, "I seed her first a smokin' of a whackin' white cheroot." Smoking is universally indulged in, not only by Burmese women, but even by their babies scarcely old enough to hold the huge banana leaf or newspaper-wrapped pones of tobacco

[307]

which look more like "whackin' white smoke stacks" than cigars.

Here, as elsewhere in the East, women carry the burden of the work. In intellect, the Burmese women are far superior to the men and conduct business affairs, which in other countries are confined strictly to men.

At Intagaw, forty miles north of Rangoon, I stopped for a cup of native tea (fifty per cent rich goat milk and fifty per cent tea, sweetened with golden brown sugar) and enjoyed watching the local snake charmer "play the fool."

Squatting just within striking distance of his cobra, the man spread his knees apart each time the cobra struck at them. The snake always fell short of his mark by a few inches. The agile old charmer then squatted sideways within striking distance. In this new position, spreading legs apart would be of no avail when the snake struck. Instead, he merely gave the snake's neck a glancing blow with his forearm, thus deflecting the slimy viper aside. One fatal slip of the hand would mean death. The charmer was an elderly Indian past the prime of life. Since child-hood, he had played with snakes. I marvelled that he could pursue his profession for a lifetime without once making a mistake. Just as I turned to leave the weird scene, one of the thousands of yellow and black cur dogs rambling over Burma, dashed within the magic circle. The cobra struck and there was one fewer live dog in Intagaw. I left Intagaw without feeling a bit more comfortable for having stopped at the tea house.

Clad only in bathing trunks, I cycled up the sloppy trail through warm rain showers. Vociferous amused himself by climbing back and forth from the pack on the rear of the cycle, up over my head, down my arms to the handlebars, and into the bread satchel tied above the front wheel. He performed this "daily dozen" while the cycle was in motion, too!

The wooden cow-bells with six or more mellow-toned

gongs inside each bell reminded me of the triple-toned camel-bells I had enjoyed along the caravan routes of far-away Afghanistan. Still more unusual, but equally popular in Burma, are cowbells with gongs clapping like "jumping jack." or spider legs, against the outside of the bell instead of inside.

Houses in this region are built upon bamboo stilts beyond reach of both water and wild animals. In villages, though bamboo bridges connect each individual house to the road, there are no bridges nor sidewalks forming connecting links between the houses. The sides and roofs of the houses are matted with bamboo and banana leaves; the floors are made of springy strips of split bamboo which form an ideal resting place; water buckets, kitchen utensils, and other household appliances are made of bamboo; bamboo sprouts are the staple food of the natives—in fact, the Burmese native, without his bamboo, would be as helpless as the Afghan nomad without his flock of goat and camel. Even breastworks along the river banks to prevent erosion, bridges, boats, and rafts plying the thousands of little canals and rivers along the Mandalay road—all are made of bamboo.

(Kipling was again right when he said, "Can't you 'ear their paddles chunkin' from Rangoon to Mandalay?")

Unlike Egyptians, Persians, Indians and other Easterners, who beautify themselves with henna and antimony, the Burmese literally "white wash" their faces with powder and paint. Both men and women cover their bodies with red and purple tattoo designs. A tattoed "belt" of sacred monkeys around the waist is one of the most popular designs worn by the "well-dressed" native. There are many wayside, sacred monkey shrines reflecting the image of my own little Vociferous carved in the clay walls of the shrines, the long tail of the pictured monkey wrapped like a half-moon around his head. Everyone marvelled that the Hindus had not killed me when I

[309]

captured Vociferous. Being a member of the sacred stock of India, he proved to be a valuable asset: the natives continually showered us with gifts of fruit and vegetables.

Throughout Burma are many gigantic Buddhas and thousands of whitened and gilded pagodas with their little golden bells tinkling merrily in the gentle breeze. Kyngbun Pagoda, three miles south of Pegu, is particularly striking with its four great forty-five-foot high Buddhas seated with backs together. Nearby rests the world-famous "Reclining Buddha" with its head upon a pile of beautifully colored glass mosaic boxes.

At the village of Kyanksagaw, seventy-seven miles north of Rangoon, I rode into the full fury of the monsoon. Encompassing clouds were so thick and heavy that mid-day brightness suddenly changed to purple twilight. Thunder and lightning shook the earth. Vociferous clung to my neck for dear life as powerful gusts of wind threatened to fling us from the roads. In the distance, a great wall of water, extending from cloud to earth, was plainly visible as it advanced across jungle and rice field, wiping completely out of my line of vision everything in its wake.

Following the first terrific onslaught of water, myriads of motley snakes crawled upon my elevated roadway. At first I tried to avoid them altogether, but in cycling around a young boa stretched across the road I turned too suddenly and almost slipped and fell upon the snake. After that, I decided that safety lay in pursuing a straight course, raising my legs whenever crossing the body of a long snake which might make a counter or reflex action blow at me in passing.

It also seemed to "rain bullfrogs" here. Immediately after each heavy shower, the road was alive with teeming masses of tiny frogs which "squshed" much more agreeably beneath the big balloon tires on my wheel than did the snakes. It was as much fun running over these frogs as sticking my toes in hot tar bubbles oozing out of pavement cracks back home—a favorite summer pastime of my very early boyhood.

Burma is one country wherein weather conditions are not chief topics of conversation. During the monsoon season there is no need to speculate about rainfall—it is certain to rain every day, especially in the afternoon.

Beside the door of every jungle home are huge earthenware jugs of rainwater for drinking purposes. To a European, it is quite amusing to watch Burmese as they reach their homes across the road by swimming while at the same time holding open umbrellas above their heads to keep their long black hair dry.

Instead of building stables or fenced enclosures, Burmese peasants resort to a unique method of tying their cows to long fishing poles which are fastened upon an upright post and weighted down at one end by rocks so that the cows will not become entangled in the rope. Leeches are so prevalent in Burma that they cause serious loss of blood in both human beings and animals whom they attack unobserved.

Bucephalus, Vociferous and I broke up schoolroom classes along the road, as all schoolhouses were open-air structures with roofs and floors, but no walls. I was surprised to find the Burma children playing marbles and other games common in America. Their "hop-scotch" game is more complicated than our American type. The "scotch bag" is kicked into the proper square instead of thrown. Aside from games, both children and adults enjoy playing ragtime tunes with drum, cymbal, and guitar.

So novel and numerous were the spectacles along the Mandalay road that I ofttimes regretted nightfall when my cycling should cease.

At Nyaunglebin, 105 miles from Rangoon, a young, long-haired lad offered to escort me to the Baptist Mission. In pitch-black darkness, I carried my cycle over

[311]

two walls and through several pigpens before we finally emerged before candle-lit figures of the baby Jesus and Mary, carved in a granite boulder in the churchyard. Continuing our journey for another hundred laborious yards, we ended, not at the Mission, but at the home of the Burmese headmaster of the Roman Catholic School. In true Burmese style, my host brought forth dishes, in the form of large jungle leaves, and filled them with delicious shrimp and okra fried in egg batter and rice spiked with onions and hot pepper. Placing the food before me, he slowly, and almost solemnly, said, "Eat, drink and be merry, for tomorrow you may die."

CHAPTER XL

"We Three"

I did not die on the road to Mandalay though I bucked Bucephalus against the Burma monsoon, through heat, wind and rain.

After two days of strenuous cycling I sauntered silently into the beautiful little jungle village, Pyinmana, 250 miles from Rangoon, and stopped for the night, though it was not yet high noon. The village restaurants were in the form of ready-set-and-served tables on the streets, with chairs placed for customers who sat down as nonchalantly to their public meal as if taking supper at home. Large platters of rice were deposited upon poles at frequent intervals along the street to appease the appetites of the multitudes of crows which are thicker in Burma than in a Georgia cornfield. Brilliantly plumaged peacocks roamed the village streets and a huge army of red ants crossed the road like a muddy stream of water. A ricksha runner raced madly up the street in spite of the fact that one of his legs was swelled up like a balloon and all the blood vessels in it had burst. Long files of native boys trotted down the main street with gigantic bunches of plantains and pineapple balanced at each end of poles across theirs houlders, or else swung in the middle of a pole carried by two people. Every Burman is fond of betel nut mixed with lime to bring out the acidity of the nut. This red paste mixture oozing from their mouths imparts a strawberry-colored tinge to the lips.

Burma is a land of large, beautiful trees. Red-blossomed, royal poinciana and fragrant yellow mimosa thrive in the wild depths of the jungle. Large flocks of white heron, alighting in the towering banyan trees, look like showers of white paint falling upon the green foliage. In order to climb the slick trunks of coconut palm to fetch eggs or young birds from the strange, pear-shaped nests attached to the ends of palm leaves, the natives build bamboo ladders along the tree trunks.

There is very little twilight in Burma. At seven o'clock the sun set, as I sat at supper with Mr. Cummings of the Agricultural School in Pyinmana. Thirty minutes later it was pitch dark. Still two hours later, at 9:30 p.m., I witnessed one of the natives' rarest and most beautiful phenomena. Just before I started to bed, the evening rain shower ceased and the skies began clearing a gorgeous, silvery pathway for the full moon, which was already one hour high. My gaze was suddenly diverted from that beautiful orb to the opposite horizon and the pathway of the retreating monsoon.

There to my utter amazement, I beheld a beautiful moonlight rainbow extending in one magnificent unbroken arc of colors all the way across the sky. It was exactly like an ordinary rainbow of the sun except that the colors were of softer pastel shades. Mr. and Mrs. Cummings and I stood in silent awe until the wonderful vision vanished into the shadows of the night. Judging the future by the past, none of us would ever witness such a sight again.

[313]

Next morning while cycling through a dense thicket of banyan trees, whose roots dangled down to the ground and even across the road in several places, I was lost in thought of the beautiful lunar rainbow of the previous night. Suddenly, I was brought face to face with the realities of life, for an unusually large root curled up into a corkscrew shape directly in my path. Little Vociferous pointed, jumped up and down and talked excitedly, "Look out, Uncle Fred!"

Though I do not claim to be a coward, when I see a root or log, lying across the road, begin to move in a snaky manner, I am slightly weak in the knees. I stopped petrified, like Stonewall Jackson, except that Jackson stood from courage and not from terrified, involuntary paralysis. My unwanted companion soon relieved the tenseness of the situation by unwinding his masses of concentric circles and sliding gracefully, but slowly, off the road in a very dignified retreat, so much as to say, "I'm not afraid of you; I was just going off the road anyhow, of my own free will and accord."

Soon after leaving Pyinmana, I struck a dry spot in upper Burma. Sheltered from the monsoon by mountain ranges, the region around Meiktila suffers less from wholesale cloudbursts than any other part of the country. Evidently Vociferous had never seen the sun before. All day he sat upon my shoulder and stared directly at the dazzling disk until his face was as red as a beet.

Vociferous was always at his best when mad and "pouting." If I pretended to cycle off and leave him as he foraged in roadside fruit trees, his eyes puffed outward about two inches and he gritted his teeth and grunted like one so angry that he was speechless. I obtained many interesting, character-study camera shots of the natives by telling them to "look at the monkey on my head and smile."

Vociferous was in his full glory when we passed a group

[314]

of monkeys. Sitting on top of my cork helmet he would wink at the little monkey debutantes, and wave at the baby monkeys. Pride of his exalted position radiated through him. He reminded me very much of a young college student back home in Athens riding in a friend's Packard and greeting bystanders, "Hello there, sugar! Hey, buddy!" The wild monkeys would follow us for miles, carrying on lengthy conversations with my companion. "Look, Fred— see that monkey over there? He's so slow he could never catch me! Look out, Fred, that fool is trying to throw a mango at us. Let me at him. Let me at him. I'll slap him down. Hey you! If Fred would just stop this machine I would twist your tail. What's the matter, Fred—don't stop this bike. Get up, Bucephalus, get up! Fred, look! That gorilla is attacking! That's it. Throw at him again. Whew! We sure did mow 'em down! Hi there cutie! What are you doing tonight? How about a date? Look, Fred—ain't she a honey! Hello ugly; that your gal?"

The conveyances universally employed by Burmese are the two-wheeled, wicker, mat-covered bullock carts. The bodies of most of these carts were fashioned like boats and can be removed and pulled through mud or water when the wheels refuse to function.

The method of ploughing in upper Burma is unique. Here the farmer stands upon a horizontal ploughshare and grips the arched bamboo handlebars which fit in each end. Wooden pegs in the bottom of the ploughshare do the ploughing.

The fields of this region are thick with the large purple-headed dragon lizards (as distinguished from the ghastly orange-headed ones of India), which attain a length of six, seven and eight feet. The chief delight of youngsters is to shoot these alligator specimens with cross-bow arrows.

Upon entering the village of Pyawbwe, I was shocked to see most of the inhabitants perched in trees. Investigation led to the discovery of a Burmese hockey game in

[315]

progress on the opposite of a tall bamboo fence with most of the spectators on the outside looking in.

This sounds as if I were describing a scene common to any little American town, but the following excerpt from a Rangoon news-clipping indicates that Pyawbwe people have diversions other than ball games:

"The skin of a tiger was brought to the Deputy Commissioner, Yamethin, who was camping at Pyawbwe, the other day.

"A report was made by Maung Po Kywe, headman of Kan-U village, Pyawbwe Township, that on May 19, two cows were killed by the tiger. The tiger was tracked to a spot near the village. Banding themselves together, the villagers surrounded the tiger's lair with thorns and branches of trees, and made a fire which killed the animal.

"The tiger had destroyed five horses, over two hundred cows and pigs and attacked five men, of whom one died."

While cycling past two cowtenders, each with a pair of cows at the end of a rope in each hand, I learned something of the queer sense of Burmese humor: All of the frightened cows stampeded, throwing one of the tenders to the ground. His comrade smiled slightly, but the unfortunate victim of the cows' panic evidently enjoyed the joke upon himself, since he laughed loudly.

My last night on the road to Mandalay was spent on a grassy bluff, towering above the beautiful lake separating me from the village of Meiktila and its electrically lighted golden pagoda which shone wonderfully across the rippling waters.

Early the following morning, as I struck the first range of Shan mountains at Payangazu, my eyeballs nearly popped out when two young twelve-foot pythons slid sideways across the road directly in front of me. It was a mating scene, each revolving rapidly around the other like spirals of an automatic barber-shop pole, their heads towering three or four feet in the air like the King Cobra.

[316]

Big game hunting on a bicycle

Wild Animists

Monglin

(Note) Dark waist line is
Tattooed "belt" of purple monkeys

Transportation in the
Federated Shan States

(Note) "Road to 'Kataw'
absolutely impassable"

On the jungle road to Kalaw, five thousand feet higher up in the mountains, I began to see so many snakes every time I looked off the side of the road that I stopped looking for any except those lying in the trail itself. This latter precaution was absolutely necessary, as the region is famous for the deadly Russell vipers, one of the most poisonous and also most dangerous snakes in the world. Being stone deaf, the Russell viper never slides out of the trail from an approaching victim. When stepped upon, the viper quite naturally retaliates with his strike of death.

While I was sipping a cup of chocolate with two half-caste American boys (mother, Burmese; father, American), living in the last village on the edge of the jungle, a funeral procession passed by. The boys informed me that it was a double funeral of two natives killed by a bear the week before, just two miles up the road from where I now sat.

Out in this far-away country, mutual nationality in itself is enough to warrant a royal reception on behalf of an American resident, who considers it a rare privilege and pleasure to see one of his own race. The brothers insisted that I spend a few weeks with them as the jungle was full of tigers and other wild animals, making traveling too dangerous. It was for this very reason that I wished to get through the jungles and be done with it. My departure was so delayed by police who solicited the usual information required of travelers and then apologized for troubling me, that it was almost sundown when I started up the forty-mile climb to Kalaw. The last four hours of cycling through the inky darkness seemed like an eternity. The thousands of black-faced "day monkeys" and marmosets, which had screamed and made faces at Vociferous until nightfall, had now gone to sleep, and another tribe of "night monkeys" and baboons followed our progress noisily from the roadside trees.

Of all times for my headlight generator to cease

[319]

functioning! But I was running over so many masses of moving jelly which I knew to be snakes that I did not relish the idea of getting off my cycle to fix the light and perhaps step upon one of these vipers. Several times I heard beasts crashing through the jungle into the clearing behind me. Even had it been light enough to see what sort of brutes they were, I do not think I would have bothered to look around. I merely took for granted that they were following, ready to pounce upon me at any moment, and I, therefore, accelerated my speed accordingly. Once, a great black mass loomed up out of the shadowy trail directly in front of me. I wanted to stop but my legs would not let me. They had pedalled at such a constantly vigorous speed for the past six hours that the movement had become almost mechanical action, independent of and apart from my mind. As the cycle rushed toward the immobile green eyes in the middle of the trail, I rang my cycle bell and evoked a yell which would put even the roar of Tarzan of the Apes to shame.

The green-eyed shadow passed slowly off the trail as I whizzed by at full speed. Later that same night as we slept in the cold mountain-top village of Kalaw, Vociferous froze to death. I buried him beside an old pagoda sacred to his memory, and plunged alone into the dark, dismal depths of the jungle.

CHAPTER XLI

Across the Heho Plain

Emerging from the jungle above the clouds at Kalaw, my road wound gradually over the top of a high, rolling plateau, like the downs and dales of Devonshire, England. The long strings of Buddhist "tongis" (priests) were unusually colorful as they walked along the trail, clad in new orange-colored robes. Nearly every male in

[320]

Buddhism is a tongi at some time during life. This accounts for the multitude of orange-robed boys and men one sees throughout southeastern Asia. Tongis are supposed to possess nothing, save these orange robes and the bags of rice given to them at the beginning of Buddhist Lent season. On my last day in Rangoon, at Sehwe Dagan, I had witnessed this great Lent festival in which the tongis received their new robes. While visiting in the different pagodas, I learned that many tongis possessed little tin boxes containing all sorts of forbidden treasures.

The Burmese Buddhists, unlike the animal-sacrificing Hindus, forbid the killing or harming of any living thing, whether insect, animal, or human being. The offerings to Buddha are paper flowers, flags, candy, food, and live poultry, which are set free before Buddha's shrine. The courtyards of many pagodas are literally filled with Buddha's chickens, ducks, and pigeons.

The little fleas on one's head, the cur dogs on the street, not only possess souls of human beings of later date, but perhaps even the souls of future Buddhas. This accounts for the vast number of dogs here, as they are protected and propagate rapidly. In regard to insects and animals, the Buddhist adheres strictly to his religious creed; but no scruples seem to be entertained regarding man's welfare, as more murders occur in Burma than in any other part of the British Empire.

The Burmese Buddhist's idea of heaven really amounts to a state of extinction since they aspire to a gradual expulsion of desire as their souls transmigrate from one state to another until the supreme state is reached wherein desire is wholly absent.

As is true in other lands, the higher one penetrates into the wilder mountain fastnesses of the Shan States the more interesting and colorful are its people. Near Heho I got my first glimpse of the strange animist tribesmen, who

[321]

worship the "nats," or evil spirits dwelling on the mountain tops, in the jungle trees, in the sun, moon, evening star, et cetera.

These people are never seen alone. So great is their fear of evil spirits that they always go in groups to protect each other. They all wear bolo knives and "dahs" (sword with wooden scabbard, bound together with bamboo fibre), using them for all purposes from chopping wood and rice to killing tigers and evil spirits. The groups that I now met took a very friendly interest in my welfare. They marvelled that I should travel alone and the leader of the group refused to leave me until I accepted his dah as a gift.

Although not less than twenty were in the group, these weird people walked single file in true tribal fashion. Each was heavily weighted down with jewelry consisting of huge silver betel-nut lockets, necklaces, bracelets, anklets, and jewel-studded nose and earrings of crescent-moon shape. The women in the procession wore six-inch metal and beaded bands just below the naked knees, with tight-fitting "pants legs" extending down from these garter-like bands to the ankles. The exposed parts of the bodies of both sexes revealed myriads of fantastic dragons and other figures in a red and blue tattoo. The tribe was evidently making an overnight trip into the jungle, as each person carried upon his back the typical Shan bed, consisting simply of a tiny roll of straw matting.

Naturally, there are no "hotels" among tribesmen; but many travelers take great care to build small bamboo shelters along the trail and leave them for use by future pilgrims. This act of generosity is sure to result in an additional star in the heavenly crown of the builder of the platform or "zayat." Many a time was I to sleep in these zayats in the depths of the jungle before finally emerging upon the shores of the Pacific Ocean.

For the pilgrim's better progress, there are also bamboo water jug stands every few miles along the trails of the

Shan States, just as in Burma. Native travelers usually stop in out of the rain at these shelters to eat (tea at 6 a.m., breakfast at 11 a.m., and dinner at 8:30 p.m.)

Near Taunggyi, I entered a country of strange animals, beautiful vari-colored jungle fowl, orange-tailed heron, and wild, rugged natural scenery different from any I had yet seen. The deep gorges and towering cliffs were entirely covered with giant trees and green shrubbery whose roots grew into the very rocks themselves.

Crossing the broad Heho plain, I made a seven-mile detour to Yawnghwe and Inle lake, famous not only for the Intha oarsmen rowing with their legs, but also for the myriads of floating islands in the huge lake. So thick with vegetation and flotsam are many of these islands that native homes are built upon them.

It was fascinating to watch the rowers balance upon their little pilot boat platforms and, with uncanny skill and speed, ply the oars with similar backward movement of the feet that I used in cycling, and at the same time drag along behind them the long, narrow "razor-back" boats containing goods and passengers.

The local Shan State Sabwa (chieftain) lives on the bank of Inle lake. His home is not so regal in appearance as the wealthy Rajahs of India; but on the other hand, it is quite handsome in view of the poverty-stricken nature of the Shan States.

Taunggyi, the capital of the Shan States, is four hundred feet higher up in the clouds than Kalaw. Jerusalem would not seem so high in the Himalayas of Central Asia, but coming up from Jericho, twelve hundred feet below sea level, Jerusalem seems to be on top of the world. Nor would Taunggyi and other mountain-top Shan villages rest very high in the Himalayas; but when approached from the deep river valleys several thousand feet below, they certainly seem high enough.

On the way down through the ceiling of clouds to

Hopong, I passed fifty or more Shan horsemen giving their mounts a little morning exercise along the hazardous mountain-top steeplechase near Taunggyi. Long lines of "human donkeys" were bringing large baskets of betel nuts to market. Only a few meters below the gorgeous road near Htamsang, I explored a group of beautiful stalactite-stalagmite caves. To an adventurer, nothing is more fascinating than a winding road through practically unknown country. He is always wondering what new revelation of nature will unfold itself just around the next bend in the road.

After months of lonely wanderings among strange people, it was pleasant for a change to find a little American home atmosphere with missionaries. Of course, one of the most "un-American" features of all Eastern homes (American Consulate at Rangoon no exception) are the chirping lizards and giant, harmless tarantulas adorning the walls. In native homes, I was shocked to find wall paper designs quite readable—they were newspapers obtained from missionaries.

Although the bazaar is the most interesting part of all Eastern cities from Cairo to Shanghai, only in the Shan States are little bamboo bazaars built on the edges of towns or in the jungles as institutions complete within themselves and entirely segregated from nearby villages. Once every five days, these little bazaar cities come to life; tribesmen of the region ride into the hitherto deserted streets and pile out their goods, varying from jack fruit to jungle leaves used as dishes, as house-roofing material, or as a base for betel-nut gum. On bazaar day, the trail is filled with mat-covered "viking ship" wagons loaded with melons and vegetables. Straw hats and shoes usually dangle from the prow of the "boats." All the neighboring villagers then assemble at the great bazaar for a day of merrymaking, feasting, bargaining, and bartering of goods.

As the bazaar was the only place where food could be

purchased, I usually ate in native homes. Scrambling up the bamboo ladder, I would take my seat in the family circle around the stove. Resting in the center of the split bamboo floor was a mass of mud hollowed out at the top and emitting smoke and flames like an active volcanic crater—this crudely fashioned structure is the typical Shan "stove." True, the smoke is annoying to the natives, but neither do mosquitoes like the atmosphere. Of the two evils, the natives prefer the smoke. The simple meal of these hill folk usually consists of smoked rice, red and green hot peppers, and a cube of brown sugar or jungle figs from the trunks of the native fig tree. In one corner of the room of every house is the little figure of Buddha with right hand touching the earth. The Buddha altar is covered with gifts of flowers, food, and feathers from the peacock, whose image is the national emblem of Burma. In another side of the room, human infants sleep cosily in small bamboo hammocks tied between the corner walls. With one hand, the mother swings the hammock by means of an attached jungle rope, while with the other, she works deftly at the loom. In quiet contentment, these folk live their simple life, ignorant and unmindful of the great world of affairs outside of their jungle home.

CHAPTER XLII

Into the Jungle Mountains of the Federated Shan States

At Wapong I started on an oxtrail over fertile, high, rolling plains, emerald green with tall grass and jungle vegetation. Scattered sporadically throughout the plain were great balls of foliage-covered cliffs, while along the southern and northern horizons were outlying ranges of camel-humped mountains.

Except for a small band of red-bloused, black-shirted travelers with their bed mats rolled upon their backs and wicker basket "pockets" hanging from their hips, the beautiful plain seemed to be devoid of human life. A huge white Buddha, carved from the solid rock cliff halfway up a nearby mountain side, lent a touch of weird unreality to the whole scene.

In the vicinity of the Buddha were circular and rectangular caves cut into the rock, unmistakably by human hands, as were those in the cliffs of Bamian in far-away Afghanistan. However, as I could locate no trail through the cobra-infested jungle grass to the site of these strange carvings several miles off the road, I had to be satisfied with a distant perspective. While cycling along in solitude, I wondered if my late discovery was known to the outside civilized world. Surely these mountain-side carvings were far enough off the beaten track to have escaped notice of the few European travelers through the region.

My thoughts were suddenly interrupted when I left the high plateau, and plunged abruptly down a gorge into the densest jungle growth I had yet seen. A heavy rainfall bent feathery bamboo shoots across the road; long rope vines and roots dangled in my face. Though the incline was quite precipitous, the mud and slime were so deep in the trail that I had to pedal vigorously downhill. When I stopped to rest, the cycle was self-supporting, so deeply entrenched was it in the muck and mire.

Thus far, I had been fortunate at river crossings where I had always located dugout canoes, or large rafts consisting of two hollow banyan logs tied together with bamboo, and "manned" by women with long bamboo poles and oars. However, at the 800-foot-wide Nampang River, eighty-five miles from Loilem, I found neither rafts nor natives. They were either on the east bank of the river, or else had already been washed away by the swollen stream. (Life is cheap here—if a whole village is washed away and all its inhabitants drowned—well, they're just drowned—that's all!) Through the heavy din of rain, it was a waste of time

[326]

and energy to try to make myself heard by whatever natives there might be on the east shore of the mighty river. My only alternative was to crawl into the little zayat on the river bank and wait for the rain to cease. Twenty-four hours later, it was raining harder than ever. With energy and food supply exhausted, no help in sight, and a whole day wasted in the sticky heat beside the mosquito-infested, miasmal jungle river, my morale had almost reached the breaking point. I could stand it no longer. Anything was better than this horrible waiting.

Few people know the extreme joy and horror of intense solitude. It is one thing to stand alone in the bracing atmosphere up in the land of the sky and watch the setting sun send a rainbow of colors across the snowy mountain peaks far below; but it is an entirely different matter to sit in the foggy jungle swamps reeking with poisonous vapors and deadly insects.

With my dah I cut a dozen huge bamboo poles and tied the ends together with rattan to form a crude raft. By means of a split bamboo paddle, I launched vigorously out into the swirling stream with Bucephalus on board, and headed diagonally against the current toward the dark green eastern bank. The rain had ceased, and dense masses of white clouds began rising above the surrounding mountain vales.

As the opposite bank loomed nearer and nearer, I was about to give vent to my feelings with a loud shout of joy when closer observation revealed that it was merely one of the many large islands in the middle of the river. For nearly two more hours, I weaved through the islands before reaching the opposite shore, thankful to be alive and able to continue my journey.

On the twenty-five-mile trip, down to the next great river (Salween), I crossed hundreds of large colonies of ants which had built mud passageway tubes, not only across the road, but also up the towering cement-like

[327]

trunks of jungle trees, finally culminating in big mud nests around the forks of branches. Upon locating one of these ant houses in a small tree near the ground, I threw a rock into the very center of the nest. Immediately, thousands of big red ants came tearing out like a swarm of disturbed hornets.

I spent three precious hours at Takaw on the banks of the Salween before I could persuade native boatmen to carry me over. Though no wider than the Nampang, so deep and swift is the Salween that it is reputed to be the most dangerous crossing of any river in southeastern Asia. Too, it was now at highest flood stage, and huge logs and other debris, covering the entire surface of the water, swirled dangerously fast down the stream.

Three women and one man finally volunteered to take me across in a narrow dugout. In spite of their foresight in rowing almost a mile upstream in comparatively calm backwater near the bank before launching out into the stream, so powerful was the current that we came to the opposite bank several miles below the landing and again had to toil vigorously with the bamboo paddles up the eastern bank. But for uncanny balancing ability of the squatting rowers, our boat would have surely capsized in midstream when a fifty-foot log dashed full into the side of the boat, whirling it round like a top.

At Nawngarn, on the eastern bank of the Salween, I found none other than Captain Robert, High Commissioner and Ruler of the Shan States. He had just arrived at the P.W.D. (Public Works Department) bungalow from Rangoon after a quick trip by air, auto, and finally, pack train of donkeys. He was now on his way by elephant to Kentung to investigate the recent opium-smuggling situation between Kentung and the Siamese border country, a question which had been seriously discussed sometime previously by the League of Nations. Since Captain Robert was traveling only eleven miles per day, he did not expect to reach Kentung for several weeks. As I expected to reach Kentung in two days, I refused his invitation to tarry and travel leisurely through the jungles with him.

When I left after tea, Captain Robert presented me with a handsome head-hunter sword taken from a native of Myitkyenia on the Tibetan border. For thirty-five miles I wound steeply up a rocky, muddy, slippery trail over which many sparkling waterfalls poured. The wayside trees were regular botanical gardens with shrubs and flowering bushes of many varieties growing in the forks of the branches far above the ground or along the tree trunks themselves. Also different varieties of large fern completely covered the trunks of many trees from top to bottom. Beautiful mosses clung gracefully to the rocky cliffs. Many large mossy-entranced caves dotted both sides of the deep gorge. It was interesting to speculate whether leopard, tiger, or bear occupied them.

My speed was less than two miles per hour, as I not only had to plough through mud three feet deep at the "buffalo wallows" every few yards along the narrow trail, but it was also necessary to drag my heavy cycle over huge trees which lay across the road. It was impossible to circumvent these fallen monarchs of the forest as a rocky cliff soared up on one side of the trail and a precipice dropped down the other.

Snakes stretched across the trail also occasioned much delay. Barefoot and barelegged as I was, it would have been suicide to attempt to run across them. Nor could I afford to coax the slimy creatures too vigorously to move, as they might move in the wrong direction. The going was easier after I surmounted the high pass and started down to Mongping. Snakes were more numerous and always presented themselves unexpectedly around bends in the road; but I managed to cycle down part of the trail, and hold my feet over the handlebars when Bucephalus ran

[329]

over one.

Thousands of long-tailed, black-faced grey monkeys swing through the tangle of jungle rope vines in the trees alongside the road. I would have enjoyed diving into the dense foliage and capturing one but the risk of snake-bite was too great. However, I did venture a short distance into one of the luxuriant banana coves to satisfy my hunger.

Beside a mountain stream at Hsengmong, I watched a Lahu tribesman make water-ground meal by means of a peg axle water wheel. At each revolution of the wheel, the pegs on the axle pressed down the handles of long wooden hammers, which, upon being released, pounded heavily upon wooden drums of wheat.

Down the last sixteen miles of steep mountain trail to Mongping, my ,progress was impeded by cave-ins, covering the path with tons of mud and debris, and by washouts, leaving yawning chasms in their wake. The natives must have heard that drain ditches keep trails from eroding, for I found foot-deep trenches across the road, every few hundred feet, with high bamboo embankments above each trench, literally barricading the trail so that I was compelled to stop and climb over each such obstruction.

Near Mongping, I experienced one of the most ludicrous accidents of my wandering career. The road had been washed out for several feet beneath a thin crust surface of mud. As we passed slowly and unsuspectingly over the danger zone, Bucephalus had a five-foot "sinking spell," so that only the top of my head was visible above the road surface. The strange feature of the accident was that, after the fall into the soft mud and sand, my relationship toward Bucephalus remained in status quo. The cycle was still in an upright position and I was still sitting in the seat and wondering for a brief moment if the world suddenly had come to an end.

The rest of the muddy trail was so chopped and churned into a deep quagmire by buffalo, that I was surprised at

Bucephalus' ability to plow through it all. After smashing through particularly difficult stretches of deep mud, I always looked back and wondered how we did it!

In general, cycling was possible only on the six-inch-wide "shoulder" of the trail, hanging precipitously over the yawning river chasm below. It was dangerous business, as the slightest slip in the wrong direction might mean sudden death. However, two even greater shadows hovered over my peace of mind. Aside from the probability of Bucephalus breaking down, there was likelihood of my having a sudden attack of malaria or snake bite far up on the untraveled jungle trail. Already at Takaw, while waiting for my dugout to cross the Salween, several dreaded Anopheles malaria-bearing mosquitoes had bitten me before I could kill them. Nor were pythons on the path the least of my worries. More than once, what seemed to be a coil of ordinary jungle rope vine dangling over my trail, dropped suddenly—but a fraction of a second too late—behind my bicycle, in the writhing form of one of these powerful serpents.

When I finally reached the edge of Mongping, I broke through one last barricade on which was attached a sign with the words: "Road to Kataw absolutely impassable"— and I had just traversed this same "impassable" road!

After the past few nights of lonely solitude in zayats in the depths of the jungle, with only howling beasts and buzzing mosquitoes to keep me company, I was glad to spend a night at the Roman Catholic Mission Station at Mongping. As guests passed through the village only once every two or three years, Father Monghisi's extra bed was occupied in the interim by a nest of hornets. Since there was not room for both of us in the same room, I managed to evacuate the hornets without casualties resulting on either side. I then enjoyed the rest of the weary before setting out the following morning on the long, long trail, a-winding into the land of my nightmares.

CHAPTER XLIII

Cutting Through to Kentung

Father Monghisi was up at daybreak, singing hymns with his flock of Shans in the little church. For ten long years he had loved and labored with the savages in Mongping, a typical Shan village of 142 houses with an average of five inhabitants per house.

Except for a few Catholic converts, the people belong to the strange Shan animist sects worshipping the evil spirited "nats." The commonsense basis of their belief is that the "Good Spirits" being inherently good, will never injure them. The Good Spirits are neglected. But the Evil Spirits, being inherently wicked and ready to harm the people without provocation, must be continuously worshipped and favored with sacrifices. Chinese influence is also evident in their universal worship of Adam and Eve.

It is among these queer people that Father Monghisi expects to spend the remainder of his life without ever once returning to his native land. While I enjoyed a simple breakfast, Father Monghisi played, first upon his little home-made guitar, and then upon a "wind bellows" baby organ.

As I cycled down the trail between long rows of tall, slender betel-nut palms, Father Monghisi, standing in the doorway of his study, giving two little sick native children some medicine (he was village preacher, postmaster and physician), his tame white pigeons sitting on either shoulder, his long grizzly beard flowing down to the chest of his black priestly robes, his eyes peering anxiously over the top of his spectacles as he put a big spoon into the mouth of one of the children, was a never-to-be-forgotten picture.

Near Ping Pong the jungle crowded in so closely upon the narrow trail that a thick, young bamboo shoot caught in my rear wheel and broke a spoke, the first such casualty Bucephalus had ever experienced. Shortly afterward, a rock in the trail gashed completely through the front tire and both sides of the inner tube. Handicapped by an exhausted supply of patching glue, I was compelled to spend two anxious, but successful, hours vulcanizing on the leaking tubes part of the rubber heels of my old shoes which I had tied onto my knapsack.

Father Monghisi had said that the road was flat all the way to Tongta, thirty miles away, before climbing again. Immediately after leaving Mongping, however, I ascended several thousand feet in altitude in a steady twenty-mile climb up the beautiful winding gorge of the Nam Haum River. Women in the deep forests were gathering betel nuts, wild figs, and other fruits, and were stripping bark from saplings for use in weaving baskets and mats. Most of the women of the Shan hills wear no clothing from the waist up, though some of the unmarried girls do wear small jackets unbuttoned down the front to ventilate their otherwise bare and exposed bodies.

Near Tongta, I ran into a tribe of animists in which the women wore short, black-pleated dresses (the first women I had seen in dresses since I had left Europe six months previously), networks of silver metal embroidered in their hair, and forehead headdresses of colored beads, similar to those worn by American Indian princesses of two centuries ago. Beautiful beaded bags were slung around their waists. Long mats, spread across their backs, furnished partial protection against the rain; the men wore great umbrella coolie caps over their heads. Both sexes smoked long, slender bamboo pipes.

Ofttimes as I cycled noiselessly behind one of these wild mountaineer tribesmen, he would draw his long, gleaming dah from its wooden sheath, and fall into a frightened, yet defiant, position of defense. But more often, upon being surprised by my onrushing bicycle, they would forget their dignity, dash madly for the nearby bushes, and peer out like monkeys as I passed by. Domestic animals were more stubborn and troublesome. These stupid beasts would neither step out of my trail nor stand firmly until I passed. Instead, they would run for ten or fifteen miles, stirring up the muddy trail directly in front of me, before finally granting Bucephalus the right of way.

Though tough going at first, it was a great experience to climb six thousand feet up from the sticky, depressing heat of the river gorge to the bracing atmosphere of the mountain peaks where it was so cold that the breath came like great puffs of smoke from my mouth. In spite of stops at cold mountain springs around each bend in the road, I averaged seven miles per hour, and reached the zayat at Kuilong, on top of the pass, in time to crawl into my sleeping bag and watch the sun set in a rainbow of colors across the raining thunderheads far below.

Next morning, after a hurried breakfast of popped rice, I plunged down the twenty-five miles of red, muddy trail, through icy rain and dense layers of cloud to Kentung, lying three thousand feet below, in the midst of a beautiful valley cupped in by concentric circles of cloud-enshrouded blue mountain ranges. Kentung was once a large lake, until a narrow gorge outlet drained the lake for the beautiful plain as it stands today.

To some people, the novelty of splashing barefoot through three-foot-deep mud, stagnant and reeking with miasmal odors, would be a thrilling experience; but to me, the novelty had worn off several hundred miles earlier.. By the time I reached Kentung, the bottoms of my feet had been ground into bloody masses of jelly by sharp rock and gravel in the mud. Because of dozens of falls, both Bucephalus and I looked as if we were made of mud; we were by no means presentable when we plowed up to the door of the famous Buker brothers, American missionaries of Kentung.

[334]

Bucephalus stops
to look over a rice field
of upper Burma

Fire by friction

Paradise at Pangwai
(Bucephalus and me with
Dr. and Mrs. Telford)

Kaw home in
Kengtung hills

This is why Bangkok is called "the Venice of the East"

Golden pagoda

Wat Benjamale, acme of Siamese architectural perfection

Most beautiful tombstones in the world are these pagodas covering the bodies of the first four kings of the present dynasty

My University of Georgia stickers boastfully and brazenly state: "A man from Georgia needs no introduction." Always my very decided Southern drawl had been the talisman, winning my way into the family circles of all the missionary homes in which I had visited in the Far East. Nor did it fail in the present instance where I was again welcomed like the Prodigal Son returned. Dr. Buker spent nearly two of the early evening hours in cutting small pieces of rock from my feet while Mrs. Buker held a flashlight over the bloody scene.

They insisted that it was impossible to reach Kentung by any vehicle other than airplane during the monsoon. They assured me that I did not cross the Salween River as it was considered to be extremely hazardous even in dry season and by iron-cable ferry at that. As for crossing the flooded, log-laden torrent in the middle of the monsoon in a slender little dugout—why it was absurdly impossible! And how did I manage to escape the dreaded king cobra as I crossed the rolling plains of jungle grass, literally alive with teeming thousands of these deadly reptiles? As they told me of their own narrow escapes, even during dry season, in this poisonous snake-infested region, native police entered with information and inquiries, which proved to the amazed doctor that I had really bicycled across this purgatory and not merely dropped in like a bolt from the blue. The police had received wireless messages from worried officials at Taunggyi, Loilem and other stations along the route of my progress. Even the High Commissioner, who was still marooned at Takaw, had sent a number of wireless messages ordering a band of local tribesmen to find the body, should I fail to turn up at Kentung on schedule time. Now that I had done the impossible by cycling down to Kentung, I was confronted with the far more difficult problem of getting out again!

CHAPTER XLIV

Paradise at Pangwai

During my week's stay in Kentung, I occupied the home of Raymond Buker, preacher and twin brother of Dr. William Buker, the physician. At the time of my visit, brother Raymond Buker, a former record-breaking track man of the American Olympic team, was away from home on a visit to Tibet and China. His home was full of huge tiger and leopard-hide rugs. As these animals are so numerous in Kentung State and inflict serious losses of life, both of human beings and of livestock, the natives are constantly warring with them, not only with bows and arrows, guns and traps, but also with strychnine-permeated carcasses of domestic animals, which tigers and leopards frequently kill and nibble upon one night, returning the following night to finish their hearty meal.

During my brief stop-over in Kentung, three tigers were killed near the village. The natives throw the beautiful hides aside as worthless; but the bones, claws, and teeth are ground and sold to the Chinese at a high price because of their remarkable medicinal value. Two days after my arrival, the most highly cherished and valuable of all medicines was found in the stomach of a giant python killed on the edge of the village. The python had crushed every bone in the body of a young deer and swallowed it whole, like a big chunk of sausage. When the python was cut open, the deer was found bathed in a thick coating of saliva. This saliva was scraped off and sold for a small fortune to the Shanese folk, who must take this medicine at least twice annually to build up enough reserve energy to last throughout the year. Our own cook, who made such delicious buffalo-buttered waffles (buffalo butter resembles pure white lard but tastes even better than American creamery butter), pilau, and other delicacies,

[338]

was feeling depressed and listless until he took his dose of python saliva and felt "like a million dollars," as he proudly stated, using an American slang expression, which he had learned from the Bukers.

Almost half the Shans of the wilder regions are lepers. The fragile-nerved young American had best not enter the wilds of the Shan States if he cannot endure looking at the backs of human beings, alive with wriggling masses of maggots eating into the flesh of their "living-dead" victims, walking the streets unmindful of their horrible condition.

The tung oil tree, so much in demand in American and British markets, is indigenous to Kentung, and Dr. Buker lets the able-bodied members of his leper colony cultivate these trees in order that the colony be self-supporting. Otherwise, he would be unable to procure medicine for the natives who would rather die than pay for it. As the few Civil Service hospitals, scattered throughout the British Empire, furnish medical and surgical treatment free of charge, it is but natural that the natives look to financially depleted American hospitals for the same service.

Dr. Buker took for granted that I should come down with malaria within a few days. For one to traverse this terrible region, even in dry seasons, without contracting malaria, cholera, dysentery, dengue fever, bubonic plague or some other added attractions thrown in by Mother Nature for good measure, was contrary to unbroken tradition. Even then the dreaded Bubonic plague had broken out in Kentung, and the doctor and his family were suffering from the effects of anti-toxin shots in their arms.

None of the older natives suffer from severe attacks of malaria. As children, they contract the disease and have so many recurrent attacks that by the time they reach maturity (if they are fortunate in surviving till then), they have become immune. However, they pay for this immunity, in the enlarged spleen which must constantly battle the infection. It is noteworthy that most Shan natives have huge protruding abdomens, caused, not primarily by overeating as is generally and erroneously supposed, but by an overworked, enlarged spleen.

Kentung was truly a breeding place for leprosy, malaria, and other diseases, and in spite of the wonderful New England hospitality of the Bukers, I was glad to accept the invitation of a Scottish missionary and his Canadian wife to spend a few weeks resting in their home, at the end of the trail at Pangwai, six thousand feet up in the picturesque, animistic-tribe country, overlooking the beautiful Kentung basin. With a telescope, I could look through my bedroom window and see the Buker home four thousand feet below.

While at Pangwai, we suffered a shortage in our milk supply when a big leopard killed our water buffalo. However, we "got our man" on the following night by employing the usual stratagem of baiting the half-eaten buffalo with strychnine.

Every few days leopard, panther, tiger, python, and king cobra hides were brought to Dr. Telford by natives; also they brought many "baby" lizards five and six feet long, like the big water monitors I had seen scooting across my trail between Rangoon and Meiktila, on the road to Mandalay. (I refer to these lizards as "babies" because the authoritative Bombay Natural History Magazine, edited under the auspices of the British government, in a recent issue insists that these creatures, especially those of Burma and the Archipelago, are not full grown until they have attained a length of eight or ten feet.) After looking at these lizards, one can understand that the natives need resort very little to their imaginative powers to build the monster blue and red-eyed dragons which invariably adorn the pagoda entrances throughout southeastern Asia.

In addition to these sinister denizens of the immediately surrounding jungle, the most dreaded of all jungle

[340]

enemies—the Anopheles malaria-bearing mosquito—confines his habitat to the lowlands, whereas at Pangwai the cold, bracing atmosphere is healthful.

Even though midsummer, I slept comfortably under a half-dozen heavy wool blankets. At night, the stars twinkling merrily through the crisp, still air with the occasional tinkle of pagoda bells (like sleigh bells) was just like Christmas time. During the daylight hours, I lay reading or looking out at the indescribably beautiful sunrises and sunsets across the big thunderheads, far below the panelled walls, gigantic windows, and open fireplaces of my room.

I felt as if I were again in the Neuschwanstein dream castle of the Bavarian Alps. I had been snatched from purgatory and transplanted in a dreamy paradise. The forest primeval rolled out in emerald waves far below, with a sea of big clouds resting on the crest of each green wave till their rain-filled bags exploded on the valley beneath. Having thus performed their earthly mission of raining potential jungle flowers over the countryside, they plunged joyously skyward, swimming into my room on their heavenward journey, pervading the atmosphere with damp, grey nothingness till they soared higher into the ethereal blue, and finally hovered in white splotches only a few feet above the housetop, waiting like obedient guardian angels for Mother Earth to call them down again to water the green garden of earth.

As there were no native bazaars in the vicinity of Pangwai, we had our own little garden of delicious wild fruit and berries (pineapple, papaya, banana, mango, and strawberry), sweet American Indian corn, sweet potatoes, green beans, cabbage, and other vegetables which thrived in the fertile jungle soil.

On rainy evenings, when the wind howled outside, tigers roared in the jungle, and billowy grey clouds zoomed past our windows, Dr. and Mrs. Telford and I sat beside the

[341]

cheery logs, blazing in the open fireplace, and enjoyed our game of "lexicon." More enjoyable still was it to look down in the daytime at the heavy rainstorms in Kentung valley while at the same time all was clear and cold in these high hills.

One cannot truly appreciate one's native country until after an absence from it of several years in strange lands. Surely one can love his own country without becoming hopelessly lost in an all-consuming flame of narrow-minded nationalism. But, alas! in nearly all of the forty-three countries, both civilized and uncivilized, through which I cycled, the one great prevailing evil was (and still is) a spirit of hyper-nationalism. How pathetic that people of one country should be so wrapped up in themselves as never to realize that there are peoples of other countries who eat food, wear clothes (some of them), and behave like human beings just as they.

Dr. and Mrs. Telford are only conscientious missionaries like the hundreds of others who have lost themselves in service on the outermost fringes of civilization; but if our world civilization survives, it will be due largely to the work of these missionaries who, since the days of the Apostle Paul, have sown more seeds of international understanding and cooperation than all the trade and peace treaties of all time.

END OF PART SEVEN

[342]

"Though riders be thrown in black disgrace,
　　Yet I mount for the race of my life with pride.
May I keep to the track, may I fall not back;
　　And judge me, O Christ, as I ride my ride."
Douglas Hyde

PART EIGHT

SUNSET SHADOWS ON THE SUNRISE TRAIL

CHAPTER XLV

Big Game Hunting on a Bicycle

Crash! Another giant banyan tree fell across my path as I guided Bucephalus down the stormy trail from Pangwai and headed into the vast, dangerous jungles near the northern borders of Siam.

At this season of the year no one had even attempted this trip even by water buffalo, or by elephant, and I was already too aware of the truth of my Rangoon friends' statements that an airplane was the only feasible mode of travel. But I had come too far to turn back at this stage of my journey. The road ahead couldn't be any worse than that poorest possible excuse for a trail which lay stretched out behind me, a ribbon of blood-red mud alive with creeping and crawling creatures.

My chief concern now lay in the danger of malarial infection. But surely I was immune to this fearful fever as hundreds of mosquitoes had already bitten me with apparently no ill effects. In fact, I felt so physically fit as I sauntered up the stormy trail from Pangwai, singing in the rain as loudly as my lungs would let me, that I could but wonder if it were not almost sacrilegious to be thus in such high spirits in the face of the full fury of the forces of nature.

I had survived the snowstorm and avalanche in my lonely climb to the summit of the Matterhorn; had not drowned when swimming at high tide in the Blue Grotto on the Isle of Capri; had not roasted alive when spending the night in the crater of old Vesuvius; had not gone mad at the

[344]

tom-tom rhythm of the Nubian dancers deep in the African desert, nor lost my heart (at least, not completely) at the singing of the little Norwegian lassie far up in the frozen north.

I had not even lost a single one of my nine lives in crossing the wilderness of Sinai, where half-starved desert wolves moved in all too close circles about my camp, nor through Palestine, where the Arabs were bent on killing me at every turn; nor through Persia, where I had my only actual hand-to-hand fight with an armed bandit. I had even gone alone and unharmed through the wild tribe country of Afghan cave dwellers, a region which a few foreigners may have seen; but if they did, they never lived to tell the tale!

Perhaps the memory of these escapades had made me over-confident as I poised for my final plunge through the jungle to the peaceful Pacific.

In my previous travels, I had found it difficult enough to avoid suspicion, even without carrying weapons. Being unarmed, the government officials had let me pass, and the most savage of all natives had hailed me for this foolhardy courage, whereas had I been armed, they would have slain me at the slightest suspicious gesture on my part. Even wild animals had seemed to respect me more because of my unprotected state. Whenever beasts had made murderous advances toward me, a few well directed stones had been enough to discourage and send them away. In short, I had actually been safer without weapons than if I had carried a nest of machine guns with me.

The very idea of buying a gun now at this late stage seemed to invite disaster. Though I was now nearing the end of my long zigzag trail around the world, I did not dream that it was just the beginning of trouble, and that the supreme thrill of my life lay hidden in the depths of the jungle just ahead. Thus unaware of the unwelcome, but fitting, climax to my great adventure, I set out through

[345]

lightning, thunder, and rain into this almost trackless portion of the Shan jungles.

Having rested at Pangwai and recuperated from the ill effects of my stoned, bruised, and cut feet, I was in a perfect frame of mind and body even though it was a steaming hot day in August with the worst road still between me and Siam.

It took nearly the whole of the first day to reach the main trail at the foot of the mountain. As my little Lahu escorts did not know the path any better than I, we went off on a dozen side trails to as many Kaw villages and back again before striking the right path. The gate entrances to all of these Kaw villages were covered with wooden birds, animals, human figures, spirals, and other charms to keep out evil spirits. My entree into the peace and quiet of these villages was always the occasion of holy terror among the inhabitants, who grabbed their huge umbrella hats made of palm leaves, and fled for their lives.

My progress was further impeded by numerous pony caravans coming up the steep mountain side, each procession headed by a man beating upon a huge iron gong with such determined force as to dwarf even the sound of the incessant rain, thereby frightening away all evil spirits. Every horse in these trails seemed to consider it his duty to fall down in the one-foot path as I approached.

Finally, after wading through several waist-deep streams, I struck the main trail and sent the Lahu escorts back to Dr. Telford where they were to spend the remainder of the day setting out tung trees. As there were no bridges between Loimwe and Siam, it was necessary to wade through the smaller streams, and waste several hours building bamboo rafts to cross the larger ones, just as I had done in crossing the Nampong and other rivers on the road from Mandalay to Kentung. At other times, I was

[346]

ploughing knee—and sometimes almost neck—deep, in watery mud with Bucephalus balanced across my shoulder. Landslides constantly blocked the road. The incessant, heavy downpour of rain, which had been beating upon the earth for more than two months. was gradually making it impossible for man or beast to travel the trail.

Near Mungpeah I carried Bucephalus over a landslide dump of about thirty feet in height, blocking half the trail and caving the other half of the trail into the river gorge hundreds of feet below. Looking down from the dizzy height, I noticed the shattered remains of a double-teamed oxcart on the river bank immediately below my perilous position. Later that same day, I learned, at Mungpeah, that two oxen, a man and his family of five had met death at that point.

Toward evening of my second day out from Pangwai, a most heart-breaking incident occurred. I did not lose my life, but the next worst thing happened. In crossing a shallow stream about forty feet wide, I mired up over my head in the slimy water, and ruined a roll of fifty splendid pictures of wild, animist tribesmen of this region.

The strain was beginning to tell upon me and I nearly collapsed in the middle of several swift streams, where my legs trembled so much as to send out little waves against the onrushing flood. At such times, it was necessary to marshal every ounce of reserve energy into action in order to get through without being swept off my feet. To lose one's footing in these mountain torrents meant more than a mere ducking; it meant death. Instead of ignoring the beauties of nature around me while I fought against rain-storm, fatigue, disease, and death, my mind's eye grasped eagerly at every wayside thing of beauty, from the large rainbow-colored butterflies in my trail to the giant, red, florescent flowers, resting against their verdant jungle background.

Three days out in the jungle I was delighted to run into a

small colony of Kaws, with their customary cone-shaped headdresses, lavishly embellished with coins, rings, square lumps and round balls and beads of silver, beaded sashes and dahs around their waists, and the usual long pipes in their mouths. Shortly before reaching the village, I had put the "finishing touch" to my already injured feet by stepping on a sharp rock, which slashed a three-inch gash all the way across the ball of my right foot. For two days my trail had been one of bloody footprints, left behind at each step through the green, stagnant mud. Looking down at the blood oozing from my helpless foot, I suddenly realized, that even though I had learned to ignore excruciating pain, it was now a race against time to reach civilization before gangrene, blood poison, or other infections set in. If only I had the physical strength to pull through!

It was only noontime, but my aching body could go no farther. I decided to stop for a day of rest with the Kaws. Unsteadily I climbed up the bamboo ladder of the nearest hut and collapsed at once into deep slumber upon the bamboo floor before my amazed host had time either to remonstrate or greet me.

Several hours later, I was brought to life by the smell of barbecued dog. My native family had smoked the meat in a big straw coolie hat, suspended about one yard above the fire, on the mud foundation in the middle of the floor. They had then split open the chunks of meat and were roasting the pieces between split bamboo forks held over the fiery coals. One woman then removed another coolie hat filled with smoked rice. After the rice was crushed as if it were dough, the feast began, and I joined the family around the fire. Only hunger gnawing at my empty stomach could have induced me to partake of the dog meat.

The one redeeming feature of our dessert, of stewed snakes, was that the meat was not difficult to swallow; it slipped easily down the throat like okra or oysters.

[348]

After this typical Kaw meal, I lay down for a night's repose. All children of this region go naked both day and night except for a coin necklace which jingles like an alarm clock each time the wearer moves. Too, the slightest movement of anything upon the springy bamboo floor produces the same startling effect as an earthquake. With the children, dogs, and cats around me squalling, barking, and meowing; a whole flock of bantam roosters and jungle fowls crowing on the bamboo poles overhead; the pigs, bullocks and buffaloes grunting and snorting under the house floor directly beneath my bed; and the mosquitoes playing hide and seek in and out of the ragged holes of my old mosquito net, it was not the most enjoyable night of my life.

Before leaving next morning, I presented some of my prized souvenirs to the family, not only as tokens of gratitude for their hospitality, but also as necessary measures to lighten my load. Unable to wear anything except a loin cloth through the steaming, reeking jungle, I presented the old tribesman with my heavy water-soaked Bavarian buckskin shorts. To his wife, I gave my can of tooth powder, which was still half full even though I had used it consistently for the past fourteen months. To the children I consigned half of my precious supply of iodine and mercurochrome for their own cut and bruised feet. It was almost like a last will and testament!

In turn, my family showed their appreciation by giving me a hot lunch of dog curry wrapped in jungle leaves and tied with strips of bark.

At the end of the "road" back at Pangwai, Dr. Telford had given me a last word of warning: "August is the wettest, hottest month of the monsoon season; the jungle undergrowth is now at its thickest, and tigers are bolder in their daytime ramblings. It is also the mating season for the deadly king cobra. At this season of the year, the king cobra scouts around his nest with head high in the air, looking for trouble. When he sees you, it's no use trying to escape; he is too fast. Stand by and throw your sweater over his head as he strikes. When he has untangled himself from this, shield yourself with a shirt. By the time you have utilized all your clothes in this manner, the snake has exhausted all of his venom in the clothing, and his bite is no longer deadly."

I was fortunate in meeting my first cobra while still in the high mountains near Mungpeah, where occasional dry stretches permitted cycling; in the flatter part of the jungles farther down, even walking was nearly impossible.

As I stopped to rest on the top of a pass, a beautiful arch of rope-like ribbon glided along the gully beside me, its sinewy form swaying slowly from side to side, like the long neck of a fleeing giraffe. In spite of the dangerous situation confronting me, I could not keep from admiring the graceful movements of the cobra. But when I looked at the cold, steel eyes sparkling just above the little forked tongue which was expressing annoyance and hatred in lightning-like flashes from the mouth, I read murder in them, and all my sense of beauty and admiration was frozen.

As the pilot, by the "feel" of his wheel, can tell several seconds in advance that his ship is about to change its course, so, too, could I look in that snake's eye and see that he was about to attack.

I forgot all about Dr. Telford's warning to stand my ground and throw my sweater, et cetera, over the snake's head. Anyway, I had nothing to throw except my bicycle! In spite of the constant, heavy downpour of rain, the temperature was about 120 degrees. Sickening, smoky vapors rose from the ground. I was drowned in my own sweat even more than in the hot, sticky rain.

I jumped on Bucephalus who immediately went into high gear. The reflex action in my legs acted a fraction of a second before the cobra's spring, but I had not moved quickly enough to steer entirely clear of my adversary. However, the snake had missed his mark, and landed, head foremost, into the spokes of my rapidly rotating rear wheel.

For fully ten seconds there was a sickening, spluttering sound as the snake's head and body were ground into sausage on the chain and rear axle of my cycle, the bloody mass of flesh splashing against my legs as it fell to the ground.

Just as I began to breathe with a moderate degree of ease, I looked back at the writhing fragments. To my horror, I saw another towering snake in close pursuit!

Surely this was an hallucination. It just wasn't right for another snake to take up where his companion left off. Nevertheless, when that ribbon of death started advancing, poor old Bucephalus really showed speed.

The trail was steep, but smooth and not very muddy. It was perfect for fast, yet dangerous, cycling. Rather than face the cobra, I much preferred taking a chance upon slipping off the trail into the deep ravine below. As I started around a big horseshoe curve, I was delighted to see the snake already more than twenty yards behind, and fast losing ground.

Two minutes later, at the bottom of the bend in the road, I was about to congratulate myself upon winning the race when that same shadow of death loomed up over the high embankment above my head. My God! Twice I had been double-crossed!

Dr. Telford did not tell me that these snakes had sense as well as poison. The cobra had made a bee-line shortcut across the hill instead of following the winding road! So far as I know the king cobra and the bush master are the only snakes that will actually look for trouble and pursue a human being. These cobras attain a length of ten to twelve feet and travel with about one-third of their body in the air. This old fellow was about four feet tall when in action.

[351]

How long he followed me, I do not know. That horrible picture, hovering over my head, was enough. After that, I did not look back again for fear of staring into those terrible eyes.

Racing madly down the remaining two miles of good trail, Bucephalus splashed on through the steaming jungle, without slackening his pace until late in the afternoon, when we reached the bank of a large river. Instead of lying down on the bank to die like a rat, I cut bamboo poles, bound them together with rattan to form a serviceable raft, and poled Bucephalus and myself across—to new dangers.

Mosquitoes were so annoying in this region that, in spite of the sultry heat, I donned my remaining clothes; shoes and boots were too heavy for use in the deep mud. However, before the expiration of another week, nearly every strip of cloth was torn from me by rain, mud, and jungle growth. My bare feet, struggling under the weight of a heavy cycle and 150-pound knapsack, looked as if they had been run through a meat grinder. Each footprint was dyed in blood worse than ever.

The only food I could get from the scattered wild tribesmen of this region was the usual parched rice, smoked dog, and snake meat. Yet, as in other wilder countries of the world, I found these savages to be genuinely concerned with my welfare.

At night, I sat on my little bamboo platform in the depths of the jungle and enjoyed the beautiful "headlights" of the "tiger, tiger, burning bright, in the forest of the night"—why did the tigers always creep stealthily within fifty feet of my split bamboo bed, stand and gaze in silent meditation for hours, and then, as silently steal away?

True, all tigers are cowards unless they have once tasted human blood and thus become man-eaters. But alas! This region is all too famous for its man-eating tigers. First, they nab helpless old women and infants; then, they fearlessly attack the strongest man.

[352]

Only once did I meet with a tiger who stood his ground against my bicycle bell. For two days and nights, the old cat played with me as if I were a mouse, constantly dogging my footsteps but never actually attacking. Only occasionally, I caught glimpses of the huge yellow form as it flashed through the thick jungle growth; but the excited chatterings of the monkeys overhead, and the frequent snap of a twig, were grim reminders of the tiger's presence. When I stopped at night, his green eyes blazed with restless anticipation. He was waiting—waiting until I should fall asleep. Then, it would be much easier. But it was easier for me to stay awake the first night than my "close friend" imagined!

Not daring to venture from the muddy trail in search of food in the thickly foliaged jungle, I had eaten nothing all day. Having carried Bucephalus on my shoulder, through endless miles of slime covering the lonely trail, I was actually too fatigued to sleep; yet strange as it seems, I had really been more alive that horrible day than ever before in my life.

With death threatening at every moment, I drank in the beauties of life while I could. Never had the tangled masses of richly hued flowers blazed so beautifully against the emerald walls of the jungle growth, as on this day when I expected them to be my funeral wreaths. So brilliant were these blossoms that my eyes seemed to burn every time I looked at them. Then fearful doubt crept into my mind, when I discovered that my eyes began to burn, whether I was looking at flowers or not!

A sickening, chilling aching sensation possessed me. It was an unnatural sort of cold feeling that I knew could not have been caused by the hot monsoon rain, nor were the terrible feverish pains, piercing through my body, caused by cuts and bruises. I sat in mental and physical anguish, half afraid to guess what was happening.

Upon stretching my stiff limbs at dawn, I groaned loud

enough to startle even my watchful wayside companion. The tiger seemed bent upon attack, else his glassy eyes would not have stared at me all through the night, and he would not have remained in the edge of the jungle to haunt me by day.

If I could only reach the Catholic Hospital at Monglin before my strength or the tiger's patience failed!

However, I had now reached the lowlands again where the mud was waist deep in many places and cycling was not at all possible. To plough through this region was a tough job for one in perfect health; in my feverish condition, it was only a matter of time before I should collapse.

I did not heed the occasional fearful noise, or gleaming golden form only a few yards away in the jungle; nor did I notice the endless stretches of mud which lay before me. I clung only to the vision in my mind's eye of Father Lawrence's hospital in Monglin.

Several times when I felt myself sinking slowly up to my neck in slimy sand, I tremblingly mustered all my strength to pull out of the sloughs, holding for dear life to the bicycle which had enough surface tension to keep it from sinking. I then literally lay down and dragged across these would-be watery graves, dragging myself and Bucephalus out of danger.

It would really have been a pleasant death to have allowed myself to sink listlessly beneath these mud pits. There was something soothing about the cool soft mass which helped to alleviate my burning fever. It suddenly appeared absurd that I should keep struggling from the mires only finally to die a more horrible death in the tiger's jaws.

So long as there is life there is hope, but all this second day I had again gone without food and was wondering if the tiger had such a gnawing hunger as I. It was also my second night without sleep, as I sat shivering from unnatural chills in the steaming hot mud in the middle of the

[354]

trail, so near and yet so far from civilization.

On the third day,. I arose again from my living death, in the depths of the jungle, and staggered forward in a final desperate push to Monglin.

Still the tiger had not attacked, but I had lain all night on the open trail in a heavy downpour of rain and had barely been able to rise again at dawn. We both knew that the next time I should fall, I would never rise again.

The suspense was so great that I had to divert myself with singing or else go crazy. There was a pathetic touch of irony in the fact that I could think of only one song, "Tiger Rag." All day long I sang, prayed and pleaded "Hold that Tiger! Hold that Tiger!" Several times the tiger roared at the proper time like his poor imitator, the blowing trombone.

All day I trudged wearily, leaning heavily on old Bucephalus. Late in the day I came upon a small clearing, and saw in an enclosure the remains of a young goat, near a rickety bamboo platform. Exhausted, I leaned Bucephalus against a tree and pulled myself up this platform and sprawled out, tired in body and spirit. "All things come to them that wait."

I knew that the tiger would not approach until nightfall. Yet this made the rest of the afternoon seem all the more miserable. The suspense was unbearable.

When the tiger finally emerged from the twilight shadows, my brain and body were so fatigued that they refused to react. I sat stupidly staring at the shadowy form as it crept closer and closer—I looked upon the scene as a mere spectator.

I wondered why some one didn't shoot the brute; then the ghastly truth suddenly dawned upon me that if there was any shooting to be done, I was the one to do it. The tiger had paused near the goat, only a few feet away, and was crouching as if ready for the final spring at me. I wanted to reach for my knife but was unable to move.

[355]

Even my eyes were fixed in a frozen glare at the tiger. Thunderous rumbles rolled around the jungle.

The end came quickly. A terrible pain shot through my body as if the blood in my veins was liquid fire. I tried to close my eyes, but the lids were sheets of flame which threatened to burn the eyeballs from their sockets. A series of freezing chills shot down my spinal column. I could no longer see the tiger. Suddenly, everything was black, and I remembered nothing else.

*　　*　　*　　*　　*　　*

At Father Lawrence's hospital at Monglin, a gaunt rooster, perched upon the head of a bed, crowed loudly enough to wake the dead. The Mother Superior was busily shooing a hen and her brood of chicks out one door of the sick room while an old sow and litter of pigs entered another. Father Lawrence was examining a thermometer, which he had just removed from the mouth of a patient. A grinning Lahu Tribesman, bearing a large tiger skin in his arms, rushed into the room and exclaimed in perfectly good Italian, "Padre, here is the tiger you wanted me to skin yesterday."

The Padre turned toward his patient and remarked: "Temperature 107 degrees, but you'll live. Lucky for you, one of my faithful Lahus found you in the jungles three days ago when he was out looking for stray water buffalo. Another day, and it would have been too late. Jungle malaria is no respecter of persons, you know. One tiny mosquito bite may prove as fatal as that of a snake or tiger."

"But—but, what about that thing?" I stuttered, pointing in amazement at the huge tiger hide which Father Lawrence had spread across the foot of my bed.

"You mean the tiger?" exclaimed the Padre, a gleam of satisfaction plainly visible in his eyes. "Oh, yes. It was found dead—poisoned—near the half-eaten body of the young goat in front of your last resting place. I thought you might like to keep the hide as a souvenir."

[356]

CHAPTER XLVI

Out of the Valley of the Shadow

To me, it was the Providence of God that there should be another hospital in Kentung State besides Dr. Buker's. That hospital is the Catholic Mission Hospital of Monglin, a little village high up in the Shan jungles near the Siamese border! Had the hospital been in any other part of the world, I would have died in the jungles, and set out upon my last Great Adventure into the land from whence no traveler returneth.

Mosquitoes had infected me with the worst attack of malaria Padre and Mother Superior had ever seen. For two days I had been in a comatose state, and they were uncertain as to whether I should ever awaken. However, in the interim, my temperature soared so high that bodily heat actually burned out some of the malarial germs in my blood stream, and I awoke to see Mother Superior peering anxiously down at me. The blankets of my wooden bed were drenched in perspiration, and my bronzed hide had been transformed to lily white.

While the Padre administered quinine injections in both of my arms, I looked around to see that I was not the only inmate of the hospital ward. In addition to a score of pitiful boys and old men with gigantic tumors, goiters, cancers, and other obvious diseases, there was a steady stream of fowl, pigs, and other denizens of the barnyard prowling through the room. In spite of Mother Superior's remonstrances and exhortations to the contrary, several pigs liked the atmosphere of the room so well that they stayed for the night.

Mother Superior evidently thought my constitution to be made of iron as she loaded me with enough rich, greasy pastries and sweetmeats to kill a hard-working ditchdigger. In order not to hurt her feelings by openly refusing the carefully prepared food, I "passed the buck" by slipping the dishes to my fellow brothers in misery. Thus, as the huge quantities of food placed before me always disappeared, she was highly pleased. In the late afternoon, I could look out the door and watch Mother Superior in her glory, as this dignified (?) old nun played hop, skip, and buck dance with a hundred or more little native children.

At night, my head whirled and pains shot throughout my body as if the blood in my veins were liquid fire. I lay sleepless in my bed of miserable torture, as in a suffocating vault, and I did not improve during my first six days in the hospital. But for the comforting presence of Sister Maria, a beautiful, dark-eyed Italian girl, who kept constant watch beside my wooden bed throughout these long, horrible nights, I, no doubt, would have given up the ghost.

Sister Maria had been only nineteen years old when she had left her home in Naples the previous year, to spend the remainder of her life in nursing the wildest of Kentung State tribesmen. Feverish and delirious as I was, whenever she spoke, her voice recalled a vision of my beautiful cave on the Isle of Capri, where I had lived in such wondrous contentment exactly one year earlier—why, Capri was nestled like an exquisite jewel only ten miles out in the bay from Naples! Inquiry soon led to discovery that my nurse had also visited the Isle of Capri, and explored its natural wonders as I had done, though of course not in the same fashion.

If only my physical condition could have improved, I would have been satisfied to spend the remaining three months of the rainy season with Father Lawrence, Mother Superior, and Sister Maria; but in spite of their splendid efforts, I grew weaker each day. It was plainly evident that I could never recover as long as I remained in the low, unhealthy climate of Monglin. After much persuasion, I induced my friends to let me attempt to make a dash, in a bullock cart, across the border to Chiengrai, Siam, where I would have better chance of recovery in a more healthful climate.

After paying my driver six rupees, I set out across the flat lowlands for Siam. I nearly collapsed from sheer weakness and giddiness, before the straw-filled cart had rambled two miles to the first big river ferry. Here my driver refused to go farther and I sat in the cart all day, looking at the raindrops on the river and waiting in vain for my driver to finish his piping and drinking with the ferryman. That night, spent on the floor of the river-bank hut, was the most horrible mentally and physically that I have ever experienced. Millions of mosquitoes seemed to soar up from the stagnant pools beneath the house and pounce upon me, together with fleas from dogs, and lice and mites from broods of chickens around my bed.

Next day, my driver was still inclined to remain in status quo. He had sent a message to Padre saying he was afraid to go farther because of stories which the ferryman had just told him of several carts being completely engulfed, and their passengers suffocated by a horrible death, in quicksand beds along the road.

Padre had already gone back into the hills on his mission work when the letter reached the hospital, but one of his assistants immediately sent a letter to my driver informing him that as one cart had recently succeeded in making the trip from Siam, he could do the same in reverse style. He also pointed out that my life was in his hands and further delay would mean death to me.

Nevertheless, my driver was not to be moved. At last, I had found a Shan who did not adhere to the teaching "Te leh tegeh te, suh leh tegeh suh" (if we live, we live together; if we die, we die together).

In disgust and desperation, I told my driver to go to hell. I grabbed Bucephalus, crossed the river in a dugout, and started staggering through the mud on the seemingly

[359]

impossible task of reaching Chiengrai, Siam, nearly a hundred miles away. How I managed to accomplish this feat in my weakened condition will always remain a mystery to me. From the very start, I felt as if I were going to drop senseless in the mud at any minute.

"The spirit was willing, the flesh was weak"; yet the spirit proved to be mightier than the flesh, and I ploughed the first thirty miles to the border solely on will power and sheer determination.

The rain ferreted down into the jungle growth with the mighty roar of breakers on a stormy beach. The mud seemed a horrible live thing clinging to my legs and wrapping around Bucephalus' wheels, with the sickening suction of octopus tentacles.

The physical agony of cutting myself to pieces through this awful morass was bad enough, without the mental torture of knowing that I was stubbornly, yet certainly, fighting a losing battle.

Like Hercules cutting off the gorgon heads, I ripped successfully through the tenacious tentacles of stinking bogs, only to fall in the clutches of even more murderous mudholes. Bucephalus and I kept fighting, but with a horrible feeling of impotence, like flies struggling in a jar of honey.

I had not really and truly slept a single night since leaving my little dreamy mountain-top paradise at Pangwai, and I had not retained a mouthful of food for the past six days. Malaria had burned out every ounce of fat and reserve energy; my skin was stretched so tightly over the hardened muscles and bones of my body that I looked like a skinned cat (and, felt like one!). The bottoms of my feet, and the palms of my hands were reduced to raw flesh and blood, bones and tendons showing all too visibly through great gashes in the gory masses of ground meat. Though my feet were more completely pulverized by the constant grind through the muck and mire, some of the worst gashes were inflicted in my hands by falls every few feet along the way. So frequent were my falls that there's no doubt but that, on this terrible journey, I traveled at least forty miles in vertical falls, whereas I lunged horizontally forward only thirty. As for time and energy expended, twice as much of both were required to bring me to my feet after falling, than to carry me forward on my journey.

It was more than enough to test the fibre of our physiques to plough through these low plains of plain hell and high water, but worse still were the occasional little rises over which my "trail" painfully crawled—hills of the same fiery red as those of my native Georgia, and much slicker even than icy alpine passes in mid-winter. Every time Bucephalus started up and over the top of one of these rises, we immediately became backsliders and sat in the soft, slimy scum of earth, like Fallen Angels in Paradise Lost.

Just as hot water gives one a cold sensation, so too did my sad situation provoke laughter. All too frequently, I stepped forward a dozen times not only without moving an inch nearer the hilltop, but even sliding all the way back to the bottom to lose the fruitful labors of the past ten minutes. It was so sad it was actually funny, like the fat lady I once saw trying to go up the down escalator in a New York department store. Every time she took a step upward the escalator brought her a step downward. But she was a plucky old sister, and in one amazing burst of speed and endurance she advanced almost to the top step before disaster stepped in; she lost her footing and slipped back to the bottom step, only to rise, gird her loins, adjust the war feathers in her hat, grit her teeth, and renew her charge up the flighty stairs.

Perhaps this was just one way God had of giving me a dose of my own medicine. I had faint recollections of the boyish pleasure I used to get out of putting poor little black ants just inside doodlebug holes, and watching them climb in vain against the fine sand walls till their weak little legs could wobble upward no more, and the big-hearted old doodlebugs came and put them out of their misery. If only my own inevitable end could come as quickly as extinction did to those innocent little ants, sacrificed upon the altar of my childish whims!

To strain vainly up slick hills, with not quite enough gravel imbedded in the mud to secure a footing, but still enough to slash my body to a bloody mass, as I catapulted downhill with Bucephalus on top of me—well, it began to be too funny!

Hot water may give one a cold sensation—misfortune may have a funny feature to it, but it can be overdone! Make the water hot enough and one doesn't experience an occasional chill—he gets a permanent cold sensation. Make an experience harrowing enough and one may go permanently and happily "haywire."

Whether justified or not, the fact remains that I was gradually becoming hysterical, and hilariously happy because I was no longer helplessly lost in the Shan jungles—I was enjoying with my folks back home those highly entertaining, kaleidoscopic pictures of a young American fighting for his life through an endless trail of bogs and buffalo wallows. Whenever he sank up to his waist, I thrilled to see, and hear, his heartbeat in the jerky flow of blood through the almost bursting blood vessels in his arms and neck, like the straining throbs of an old model-T running on two cylinders up a steep grade.

It didn't occur to me that this pitiful American was myself. But I marvelled that he kept plugging along, when all his physical energy had obviously been expended before he even started out on this desperate dash.

I knew a Georgia sharecropper who could keep a model-T going long after it was supposed to be headed for the junkyard. When gas gave out, he fed the engine with some of his "corn likker"; when the tire sprung leaks, he stopped up the holes by pouring sorghum cane syrup inside the tubes. But I couldn't understand how a human machine kept moving, after it had already given out of gas, its tires cut to pieces, and the whole chassis apparently ready and willing to "give up the ghost!"

I began to sicken at sight of these scenes of slow but certain death. Siam and safety lay in the grey mists just beyond the distant horizon, but I could easily see the shadows of Death hovering closer and closer to the youthful cyclist.

Several times I breathed sighs of relief when I thought those enveloping black shadows had blurred this picture from me forever. But each time, the boy tore loose from Death's grip, tottering forward with body bent almost double from the weight of the bicycle on his shoulder, but with his head held high so that I saw the strangely familiar light in his eyes. He was dreaming of home across the sea—the home he should never see again. My God! Dim reality returned just long enough to convince my feverish mind that this young American and I were one and the same person; his dream was my own!

Then the most wonderful of miracles occurred. Despite my high fever and delirious state of mind (or perhaps because of it) I saw the steeple of the Methodist Church steeple right straight ahead only 12,500 miles away in the distance and only a couple of hundred yards from my home. Back home every morning I would roll over and look at that steeple from the big window at the head of my bed to know whether or not it would be a sunny day. And, despite the heavy monsoon rain and mud that engulfed me here in the jungles of Southeast Asia, I could clearly see that steeple glowing radiantly in the early morning sunlight, and I knew that if I could take a step in that direction, and then another, and that even if I fell, if I could pull myself up again and stagger on and on, further and further towards that steeple until I was within its shadow, then I

[363]

would be home.

It is surprising how difficult it is to kill a fellow who has a purpose in life—and did I have a purpose! No one ever wanted anything as much as I wanted to get home. There were plenty of reasons for wanting to live, but for the present, all were lost in one all-consuming desire to get out of this green hell. Nothing else mattered.

And so I pulled myself up, put my bicycle on my shoulder, took a step forward, and fell. Then I rose again and staggered on. And on.

But for one portion of hope, one portion of faith, and a double portion of the grace of God, I would be rotting today in the ooze and slime of those jungles.

About two o'clock in the morning I stretched out on the bamboo floor of a little house, built against the very side of a new bridge over the river, connecting Siam with the Shan States. It had taken all of the first half of the night to "navigate" through the last couple of miles of three-foot grey mud through Mesai, the last town in the Shan States before crossing into Siam. More than once on this last little stretch, I had fallen and felt it impossible to continue the journey; but as my hopes dimmed, the vision of home brightened, and I again mustered my imaginary strength together and pushed onward.

For fear of waking up dead, I was half afraid to go to sleep. I finally succumbed to the rest of the weary, waking at high noon, surprised to find myself not unreasonably sore, stiff, and weak. After purchasing a quantity of Siamese "lady finger" bananas and several tins of condensed milk, I climbed a ladder up to the uncompleted bridge, crossed to the good paved road of Siam, and breezed down the fine jungle highway to Chiengrai, fifty miles from the border. I arrived at Dr. William Beach's Presbyterian Hospital late in the afternoon, apparently none the worse for my trip, except that the muscles in my legs had been so strained as to make them almost useless for a few days.

I had heard of certain aboriginal tribesmen who were so healthy that they not only survived axe or sword cuts which would kill the average white man, but their wounds healed in only a few days' time. I didn't realize that my skin had reached this same highest state of health enjoyed by my aborigine brother. Fortunately a strong constitution and common sense do not necessarily go hand in hand. Otherwise, my constitution would be hopelessly weakened since I certainly had exercised very little common sense in plunging through the impenetrable Shan jungles in the middle of the wet season.

As the rice-transplanting season was in full swing, all the natives were at work in the fields and could not afford to be sick. Consequently, as the beautiful hospital at Chiengrai was now practically empty, Dr. Beach pounced upon me at once as a fit and first-class patient to keep his restless staff of expert assistants busy.

Thus, for the second time in a week, and for the second time in my whole life, I was a patient in a hospital. Both Dr. Beach and I expected that I would collapse. I hurried to bed, waiting for and expecting the worst, but the worst never came. It was almost embarrassing to lie down to die, and persistently get better instead of worse. Though my room was on the second floor of the hospital, at my request trusty old Bucephalus was brought up to keep me company.

In a few days, I was hobbling around the room on crutches to save pressure upon my battle-scarred legs. Later, I was allowed to ride around the city in one of the thousands of bicycle taxis one sees throughout Siam. Within a week, I had passed the Valley of the Shadow, and was on Bucephalus again riding down the royal road to Bangkok.

END OF PART EIGHT

[365]

"A line of palms in the distance
        And feathery green bamboo,
A hut of thatch and a brown man,
        And a lazy old caribou
And all over jungle and rice plain
        The blue of heaven's dome;
Some of us call it Siam
        And some of us call it home."
                    Hazel E. Hanna

PART NINE

CHAPTER XLVII

Biking to Bangkok

From Chiengrai to Lampang my way wound around
rolling mountains, between precipitous limestone cliffs
with palms and other tropical foliage on top and huge
caves dotting the sides, through tangled masses of dark
jungle with occasional little open patches of emerald green
rice fields, up dashing mountain streams to their sources
near mountain tops, and down beside another on the other
side of the range. Quite frequently, elephant trains crashed
into my trail, each elephant carrying in his trunk a huge
log from the nearby, heavily timbered, teakwood forests.

Unlike any other country in the world, Siam has a
beautiful network of paved highways extending from the
far reaches of the wild border jungles to the rail terminals
leading into Bangkok. Here all roads—even buffalo and
bullock trails—end, and farther progress must be made via
train. Thus Bangkok, a city of a million inhabitants, has no
motor road outside its city limits, whereas the little village
of Lampang boasts a fine paved highway penetrating
through Chiengrai to the jungle borders of the Shan States.

In crossing the Mekong River I marvelled not only at its
size, but also at the fact that it is the only river in the
world which flows in reverse order for six months in
every year. The reason for this unnatural phenomenon is
that the great lake, into which the river empties below
Angkor in Cochin China, is normally far below the level
of the river between the lake and the ocean. During the
rainy season the lake level rises many feet and the water

flows to the sea; but during the dry season, the lake level is so low that the river turns around and flows backward until the lake has been refilled. The houses in this lake region are all perched on unusually high poles to surmount the difficulties of the changing waters. Several weeks later when I again crossed the Mekong in Cochin China, the lake had not yet been refilled by the monsoon rains and the river was still flowing "upstream."

Fifty miles above Bangkok, I stopped at Ayudhya long enough to inspect Asia's largest bronze Buddhas, the old elephant kraal where wild elephants were captured, the ruins of the old Royal Palace, and other remnants of this once great Siamese capital which suddenly perished at the hands of Burmese invaders in 1767.

In Bangkok I gave Bucephalus a well-deserved rest in a bicycle repair shop, and adopted one of the thousands of Siamese bicycle taxis as my sightseeing conveyance. This most popular, and universally used, vehicle consisted simply of ricksha attached to front wheel and frame of a bicycle. My taxi driver assured me that he would drive me throughout the city, all day long, for ten setangs (ten setangs equal four and one-half cents; 100 setangs equal one tikal, pronounced "tickle"). After so many months of self-conducted tour, it struck me as an interesting change to sit back and let my "taxi driver" carry me where he wished.

As Bangkok is the religious capital of the five hundred million Buddhists scattered throughout the Far East, my "conducted tour" naturally led to some of the hundreds of beautiful old and new pagodas and temples dotting the city.

We climbed the Buddha-studded staircase, winding up the man-made mountain of brick and mortar (formerly completely covered with gold) to the white pagoda of Golden Mountain temple; visited the exquisite marble temple, Benjama Bo Pili, a paragon of symmetric Siamese architecture with tiny flame motifs, of tapering golden points, protruding from the tops of each of the little sections of orange and green tiled roofs, superimposed one on top of the other in well-balanced order, from either side of the temple, to a single little roof topping the whole.

Near the Royal Palace we passed the historic old swinging gate, where, as among Kaw tribesmen of the Shan States, all the inhabitants who wish good health and a fertile harvest, must take part in the annual swinging ceremony.

In the beautiful garden behind the Marble Hall of Parliament, I paid my respects to the world's only sacred white monkey and two white elephants. The snowy-white monkey came up to all expectations; but the elephants, each in a little palatial home and with several royal servants of his own, were not the most beautiful sights in the world. Toe nails and eye pupils of these weird freaks of nature were strangely white while their bodies were motley masses of flesh-colored patches dotted with sporadic specks of grey. Long, red-tinged white hairs completed the comical coloring of their bodies. When one of the royal keepers let me feed sugar cane to the elephants, these long-tusked creatures surprised me with little "curtsies," bending low on the left front and two rear knees, bowing heads and raising trunks.

Admission into the Grand Palace of the King was not so easily obtained. The little King was vacationing in St. Moritz, Switzerland, and had given his mother to understand that he had just as soon remain there and play in the snow, as pretend to be King of Siam. (Since the recent rebellion, the King had been only a figure-head of the new parliamentary government.) Not being able to appeal directly to the King for an invitation to visit his palace and the adjacent world-famous Temple of the Emerald Buddha, I lost several hours in vainly seeking admittance, before learning that the Royal State Railway had authority to grant the permit. Even then, I was not presentable until

Shorts are "indecent" and therefore not allowed within the palace grounds

They keep out evil spirits

'Mid pleasures and palaces of King of Siam (The world's most beautiful skyline)

Note Tamarind trees

Bat boy

*Leading across to the temple
is a great causeway*

I had obtained a new suit of clothes, as the office of the Royal Household strictly outlawed, from the palace grounds, any ladies without hose or men dressed in knickerbockers, shorts, blazers, sweaters, or other "indecent" European clothes.

It was almost noon before, correctly attired, I presented my coveted permit to the right royal reception committee, at the gateway to the royal grounds, which contain the world's most beautiful skyline. Its wealth of towering temples and colonnaded pagodas are covered in thick layers of pure gold leaf, and dotted with semi-precious stones and glazed glass.

Draped around the outside of the serrated walls, enclosing these edifices of glistening splendor, is an unbroken hempen rope which helps keep out evil spirits. Instead of flying over the wall and into the holy temples, even into the Grand Palace itself, evil spirits are content to stop and rest on the rope outside.

As added protection against the entrance of evil spirits, huge glazed monsters are stationed, with clubs in their hands, just inside the inner entrances into the Temple of the Emerald Buddha.

Almost a mile of gold leaf and oil painted murals, on the arcade walls, surrounding the magnificent Temple of the Emerald Buddha, portray the life of Buddha, battles of good and bad demons, and the whole of Siam's classical history.

The temple staircases culminate in the figures of five golden-headed dragons, the five heads spreading out at the foot of the staircase like a fan and rearing menacingly upward like a nest of hooded cobras.

In the central temple are thrones of jewel-studded gold and of pure marble as in Gulistan Palace in Persia. Towering high above the seven-tiered, golden embroidered, umbrellas of royalty, behind the marble altar, the Emerald Buddha is perched in dazzling splendor on the apex of the golden pyramid throne. A single emerald jewel, the size of a golf ball, graces the center of the Buddha's bronze forehead. Beside the alabaster vases on either side of the marble altar are two orange candles, six feet in height and one in diameter. These candles, presented to Buddha by the late king, had burned continuously for nine months, yet they had decreased only a few inches in stature. Perhaps they will still be burning at my next visit to Bangkok.

Spread out in real splendor, on the vari-colored marble floors around the base of the pyramid throne, was a strange assortment of gifts which imparted a pawn shop, or old-curiosity-shop, atmosphere to this sacred shrine. In addition to tiny gold and silver trees with golden birds and animals, fighting or playing beneath the branches, there were other slightly more exotic gifts, which Siamese pilgrims felt sure would appeal to Buddha's broadminded tastes. Among these latter gifts was a big American-made grandfather clock, sitting conspicuously at one corner of the throne!

In addition to the halls of Coronation, and of New Year's celebration, and the marble baths, where his Royal Highness performed hebdomadal ablutions with great ceremony, I visited the hundreds of other great palace halls and temples of inestimable material wealth and inde-scribable artistic beauty.

Even topiary art in the twisted tamarind trees, in the main courtyard of the Grand Palace, reflected unique Oriental beauty in their branches of cut and tied balls of green leaves.

At the many little shrines dotting the courtyards and temples were little Buddha figures in prayerful attitude, with palms of hands together before their chins—the iden-tical attitude of the Siamese as they greet friend or stranger. One Siamese politely salutes another by placing hands together at the chin, and at the same time curtsying, by bowing the head and bending the knee. I also noticed that, regardless of his station in life, every Siamese stoops embarrassingly low every time he passes near a white person.

Such humility was carried to an extreme state as I was snapping pictures near the exit from Grand Palace: A young passerby evidently laboring under the false impression that only very wealthy tourists took pictures, immediately paid me the usual humble respect of bowing almost to the ground and, in addition, grabbed both my ankles and sprawled flatly across the dirty ground to show that his humility was worthy of a few setangs. As the youth refused to arise, or turn loose my ankles, unless I either gave him a few setangs or a sock on the jaw, I gave him the setangs. After all, was it not a ticklish compliment to my vanity to be mistaken as a millionaire after my previous six months of savage existence?

The afternoon was brought to a browsing close in the city's covered bazaar and pawn shop district, where every article imaginable was on display—silver cups to hold ancestors' ashes, gold and silver laced baskets to hold betel nuts, bronze cowbells, gongs, python drums, silk robes, razor blades, sandalwood figures to be placed on graves of deceased relatives, paper monsters used in popular Siamese silhouette shows, teakwood elephants, lizard-handled spoons, and even five and ten-barrelled cannons, like those I had seen in the National Museum a few days earlier.

Even more interesting than cutters of genuine jewels were the native manufacturers of synthetic emeralds, which they made by melting scraps of pure emeralds, and then injecting jets of air, to form tiny bubbles in the solidifying mass, which imparts to it a striking semblance of the streaks naturally occurring in genuine jewels.

It is not in every city in the world that one can walk through town in his pajamas without creating a riot. Bangkok is the exception. Just as night shirts are the usual

[374]

street wear of the Near East, so are pajamas (particularly black satin) customary for the Far East. On my last day in Bangkok, I took advantage of the opportunity of a lifetime to don my pajamas and promenade unnoticed up New Street! "New Street" is the oldest street in the city. Forty years ago when it was first built there was no other street in this great Venice of the East, whose network of canals are still the main arteries of commerce and transportation just as is true in many other Eastern cities today.

I was enjoying immensely the novelty of walking native fashion up this "main drag" of Bangkok, and enjoying too the uncanny skill with which street urchins played the popular game of Taakraw—keeping a half-dozen bamboo balls in the air at the same time by merely bouncing them up with feet, head, or shoulders—when suddenly, a cold chill of embarrassment shot down my spinal column, as I heard my name called by the decidedly American voice of a young lady in a passing bicycle taxi. Had I been suddenly transplanted to Times Square, clad in these same satin pajamas, I could not have felt more awkward than at that moment. I dashed for the comforting concealment of the covered bazaars, with my ears tingling from the peals of laughter the demure little nineteen-year-old daughter of my Presbyterian Missionary friend had showered upon me.

At the invitation of a Protestant minister I attended services in the native church. The sermon was a warning that the seventeen signs of the second coming of the Messiah had already been fulfilled and the end of the world was nigh at hand—those not already in the fold were hopelessly lost.

As the minister was a converted Chinaman, who spoke broken English to a French woman, who in turn interpreted and translated it to the audience in Siamese, it was almost midnight before the sermon could be completed. Several times when both preacher and interpreter lost patience with each other, the nerves of all concerned were soothed by singing psalms to the tune of "How Dry I Am," "Good Night, Ladies," "Show Me the Way to Go Home," and other popular American tunes which the natives like so well, and which consequently are adopted by missionaries and sung, with religious verses adapted to them.

On through the night the preacher wrestled with the devils in his audience; by the time the services came to a close, I decided the millennium really was so near at hand that it would be of no avail for me to start out at this late hour on my straight and narrow path.

At dawn I continued my zigzag trail around the world. Though not at all superstitious, still I was glad that instead of going west in the beautiful but slightly depressing wake of the setting sun, my trail should lead me ever toward the Land of the Rising Sun (which of course is Georgia and not Japan).

John Ruskin truly said that "all travel becomes dull in exact proportion to its rapidity." I had certainly traveled slowly enough and with never a dull moment either. However, by the time I completed my final bicycle jaunt through the wilds of Indo-China to the peaceful shores of the Pacific, I would be "fed up" with exciting experiences and ready, willing, but not financially able, to pay for a quick, "dull" passage home on the China Clipper.

CHAPTER XLVIII

Angkor, Castle of the Sleeping Beauty

There are four "possible" ways of reaching Angkor from Bangkok: via ocean steamer to Saigon and thence up the Cochin China highway; via inland waterways; via train across the flooded rice fields and swamps to Aranya Pradesa and thence down the French trail through Cochin China; or, finally, via airplane.

[376]

As it was the usual procedure for Bucephalus to bike through the impossible, we did not hesitate to start up the railroad tracks stretching out toward Saigon, 1400 kilometers away. Unfortunately, all railroad tracks look alike, and I wasted six hours cycling up and down the railroads leading to Chiengrai in the north, Petchaburi in the south, or various spur tracks leading to no place in particular, before I finally struck the one and only track leading toward Indo-China.

For the first thirty kilometers my progress was so impeded by deep drain ditches, sliced at six-foot intervals across the narrow shoulder of the elevated railway, that I attempted to ride the rails, with the result that my bicycle tires slipped and tripped me headlong into the miry rice fields. By the time I had repaired my own bruised physiognomy and Bucephalus' flat front tire, it was already late twilight.

A short distance up the track ahead of me two old rams were bidding each other goodnight by backing up fifty feet in opposite directions and then dashing their heads together in real battering-ram style. The impact seemed not only to leave the combatants uninjured but even inspired to back off and try it all over again. As I looked back at the railroad extending toward the dying day, like two thin ribbons of gold between fields of rice, waterlilies, and lotus blossoms, then looked at the gathering gloom of night which in a seemingly similar endless expanse lay ahead, I felt like doing battle with the rams, to see if it would knock any sense into my own head.

Already Ruskin's theory of slow travel was growing a little stale. Still, it had been an interesting day watching all sorts of irrigation wheels in action and wondering what sort of contraption I would next see. Dotting the landscape by the hundreds and thousands, were huge cloth-sail windmills connected with paddle wheels, which forced the canal waters the necessary few inches up to the level of

[377]

the rice fields. In many of the great paddle wheels, pegs were inserted in each end of the axle on which native men and women walked, thus furnishing motive power in place of the windmills. Still another popular irrigation contrivance was the oblong water shovel, suspended by a rope from an arched bamboo framework till it barely touched the water; thus, the operator need only push it, pendulum-like, from the canal stream into the trench adjoining the rice fields.

Shortly after sunrise, I reached a welcome change of scenery in the padeng forests (wood oil trees) at Krabenburi.

The last hundred kilometers to Aranya, after leaving the misty mountains of Prachinburi, carried me through beautiful jungles richly colored by nature, not only in the form of myriads of luxuriant blossoms and green masses of plant life, but also with every color and size of animal and bird life from lizards, leopards, and tiny brown sparrows to wild elephants, huge white storks, and black and white striped pelicans with orange heads, yellow beaks, and flamingo-pink tails.

Having already enjoyed an overdose of jungle experiences in other countries, I was glad to reach the end of the little foot-wide railroad trail and start down the broad highway across the wild marshes of Cambodia on the road to Angkor.

I found an ideal resting place on the shores of a mirrored lake, which reflected to perfection the delicate colors of the sunset sky. The only sounds breaking the peace and calm of twilight were those of the occasional splash of the oar of a lone native fisherman far out across the waters, the note of a songbird bidding his neighbor goodnight as he flew homeward, or else the mellow croaking of awakening frogs.

However, I had long since discovered that man cannot live by beauty alone. With no sign of food in sight, there

[378]

was nothing to do but continue my journey to Sisaphon, the western-most jungle village of Cambodia.

Here I spent the night with the French Prefecture of Cambodian Police. His home, a gigantic teakwood structure with columned veranda all the way around the house, reminded me of old Southern Colonial style except that it rested "jungle fashion" on stilts of ten-foot-thick logs.

The old gentleman had lived in this wild region for so many years that he had gone almost completely native in his epicurean taste. For supper, we had birdnest soup flavored with snails, and green herbs. He even used chop-sticks so that he could dip his unseasoned, baked chicken in platters of ginger sauce.

The redeeming feature of the meal was a large bottle of vin rouge, the only sparkling sign of civilization in this little lost world. The wine loosened the tongue of my queer old host and, in breathless volubility of mixed French and Italian, he began the romantic story of his wanderings from his native Corsica. The excitement of meeting a white person, the stimulating effect of the wine, and the vivid memories of his boyhood home, were too tiring to the aging mind of the speaker. He had scarcely reached the point of departure from his island home before drowsy slumber overcame him and he drifted off to dreamland. As I was up and away next morning before my feeble host arose, the story remained unfinished, leaving me wondering what winds of fate had blown this old soldier of fortune over the seven seas and finally landed him in such a God-forsaken spot as Sisaphon.

The heat was so terrific and the cool luxuriant jungle growth crowding in on both sides of the road so inviting, that I stopped at every wayside village to see what I could see and eat. In addition to oranges, limes, and grapefruit, the milk of green coconuts proved a refreshing life-saver in this country of malarial water.

At one nameless village I found not only one giant

[379]

coconut palm growing from the top of a big banyan tree, but just across the trail was another identical phenomenon of nature! Huge ant hills, like ancient pagodas, dotted the countryside.

In the multitude of jungle rivers and irrigation canals, Cambodian children swam about on their waterwings, which consisted of the dried trunk of a banana tree under each arm.

The women of the tropics wore tiny hip cloths and nothing above their waists—not even a head of hair, that is so characteristic of Chinese city women. Instead, their heads were cleanly shaven, leaving them looking like peeled onions. On the other hand, the men wore long jet-black locks of hair, but no clothes of any description except an occasional loin cloth.

While cycling at breakneck speed down the flat stretches of green-wreathed road, I was just congratulating Bucephalus and myself on the success of our globular circumnavigation, when the entire left pedal arm worked loose from the crankshaft and fell to the ground. Only the tiny screw which held the two pedal arms bolted in place was lost, but how much such little things count! Like the lost horseshoe nail which eventually caused the loss of a battle, that tiny little screw killed the locomotion of Bucephalus. Without my trusty steed, it was almost impossible to complete the journey on my bruised and battered feet. It looked as if the venture would end in inglorious defeat.

Nearly a thousand kilometers of jungle trail still lay between me and Saigon and it was nearly five thousand miles to the nearest screw like the one I had lost!

Like a drowning man grabbing at a last straw, I took the tin top from my water canteen, and, with a sharp-edged flint rock as my only tool, cut a rectangular piece of metal from the center of the cap and wedged it into the armpit of the pedal. Though I expected the pedal arms to fall off at any moment, they were destined to "stay put," not only to Saigon, but even now they remain on Bucephalus as he rests in peace in the Smithsonian Institute.

It was nearly dark before I cycled into the Chinese hotel at Siem Reap where I sat on the dinner table and sipped tea with the proprietor and other guests.

In the morning, August 24, as I started up the six-kilometer jungle trail from Siem Reap to Angkor, the gold and blue sunrise sky became overcast and heavy with dark clouds. Hundreds of wayside doves moaning their love notes helped to put me in the correct frame of mind to conjure up the past and walk with the ghosts of Angkor's dead.

It was a perfect setting for my visit to Angkor. If tourists wish to see the jungle-buried city at its best, when the dancing figures trip lightly from their niches in the mosaic walls, the long columns of bas-relief soldiers march along the arcaded corridors, and the old priests who once dwelt in these temples walk about mumbling their prayers to the thousands of Buddhas perched in every corner and on every pedestal of Angkor's palatial buildings, they must pick a dark, gloomy day in the middle of the monsoon season in late August; then they may be sure of walking back through these echoing corridors of time, without having the spell of the living past broken by the presence of noisy tourists.

All my life I had listened longingly to stories of the surprisingly varied and unique styles of architectural beauty manifest in the man-moated mansions of this matchless dead city.

One of the most fascinating features of the Lost City had always been the veil of mystery surrounding the history of its birth, life, and death. The French are gradually solving this mystery and thereby removing one of the many attractions to the place—or are these discoveries increasing interest in Angkor? Just as Rome is of greater interest to

[381]

us because of our knowledge of old Roman history, so too, may mysterious Angkor prove all the more marvelous when its enshrouding veil of secrecy has been thrown aside.

I had walked with the ghosts of the glorious past: at Pompeii, overlooking the beautiful blue Mediterranean with Vesuvius hovering menacingly overhead; at Babylon, in the flats of the "Garden of Eden"; at Petra, in the red-hot desert hills of Trans-Jordan; at Ray, in the wild wind-swept plains of northern Persia; and now, it was almost unbelievable that I should walk up the miles and miles of magnificent galleries and precipitous temple stairways of the world's most beautiful dead city, half-hidden beneath masses of moss and banyan trees in the jungles of Indo-China.

My first glimpse of Angkor Vat was through a maze of banyan trees. The symmetrical towers of this great temple reflected perfectly in the lotus-dotted lake, even though the grey stone steeples did seem to melt away into the grey clouds of almost the same hue. Leading across to the temple is a great causeway of rectangular, irregular-sized stone slabs twelve feet above the water. A few finely carved pillars still remain, to show that formerly pillars ornamented both sides of the promenade from water edge to the top.

Banisters of dragon serpents, supported on lion-like feet, culminate in huge five or ten-headed dragon fans, reared up cobra-fashion almost exactly like those lining the stair-ways of the temple of the Emerald Buddha in Bangkok.

Halfway up the "grand slab" avenue to the temple is a kilometer-long structure with double galleries extending about a quarter of a mile on each side along the moat. The candlelabra sticks, of spiral-chased stone in the windows of this and the other Angkor buildings, are as delicately and beautifully carved from solid granite as our modern skilled craftsmen can carve in wood!

[382]

The grand avenue ends in a series of dragon and lion-lined stairways, leading to the temple's outer square of double galleries with their two miles of unbroken battle scenes in bas relief on the outer walls. One could spend many months looking at these miles of soldiers marching in clock-like precision, this gory chaos of elephants tearing enemy victims to shreds, the hook swords depicted in the act of pulling out the insides of other victims, and the ghastly expressions placed on the faces of the fighters by the unknown artist who sculptured this great masterpiece in stone.

The double columns of the inner gallery are carved in semblance of praying priests and dancing devils, the latter on lotus leaves and with snakes entwined about their necks.

Today the only inhabitants of Angkor are great armies of giant red ants, bats, snakes, lizards, monkeys, and in some of the ruins in the more impenetrable parts of the jungle along the Siem Reap River, there are even tigers, leopards and other animals. Great ant hills now block the corridors and palisades where once human industry prevailed. Dragon lizards, from a few inches to several feet in length, scamper along the narrow passageways.

Having received my share of exciting experiences with snakes in the Shan jungles, I was glad that the only grim reminders of those dangerous days were the shedded hides of cobras strewn along the halls of Angkor. Like the former human inhabitants these snakes seemed to have left their shells of splendor and vanished from the face of the earth.

Millions of bats fly in the eternal twilight of the corridors and domes of this dead city. Except for the occasional chatter of monkeys or phrenetic movement of a giant lizard, the only audible sounds are the squeaks of these myriads of bats, echoing and re-echoing like real ghosts of the past, and the patter, like green peas on a tin roof, of the heavy and incessant rain of the bat dung on the granite

[383]

floor. I advise all visitors to Angkor to take with them flashlight, umbrella, raincoat, hightop boots and south-wester hat (topee o.k., if you are not particular about getting it soiled). So voluminous is the shower of bat dung that the black-clad, black-haired, brown-skinned Bat Boy moves silently all day every day from corridor to corridor and temple to temple, sweeping up the huge piles of dung into his round wicker basket and dumping it into the moat.

It was this interesting little employee of the French Colonial government who nearly frightened me out of my wits when I bumped into him while groping through a pitch black dome of Angkor Vat. It was he, the only other human being at Angkor, who followed me all morning and took pictures as I posed in the palisades of the palaces. It was he who also favored me with timely warnings about steering clear of the center of Angkor Vat dome, and all others topping various buildings of the city, where yawning chasms lay in the inky darkness before my unsuspecting footsteps.

As I zigzagged through the thirty-square-mile area comprising the old city limits of Angkor, stone carved lions and snakes peeped out of the jungle undergrowth in almost too realistic fashion in such a natural setting. Scores of Buddhas rested peacefully in the depths of the jungle with vines and roots of banyan trees framed around their gilded bodies. Near the more accessible of the thousands of red-and-gold -painted wood, stone, and bronze temple Buddhas were offerings of food, paper flags, bits of colored rags, sticks of incense, and piles of human hair, so great as to put the floor of any Saturday night barber shop to shame.

Near the vaults of the Dead Buddhas, at the base of gracefully columned Pnom Bakheng pagoda, I found the most unusual single feature of Angkor's remains: the supposedly actual footprint of the Living Buddha. Evidently Buddha is a big man as this gilded impression of his footprint is three feet deep, three feet wide and seven feet long!

Cycling over the damp moss-covered trail into the vast moated square called Angkor Thom, I passed between terraced walls of life-size stone elephants whose trunks extended to the ground to form a columned arcade alongside the wall.

While paying my respects to the human-faced towers of Bayon and gazing at the Angkorites military exploits, so boldly emblazoned in bas relief figures along its lower galleries, I was startled by the machine-gun-like rat-tat-tat of a woodpecker on a nearby tree, as if the battle on the wall had suddenly come to life.

Penetrating into the inner recesses of the jungle city, past the multiple-headed monsters lining the entrances to the Prah Khan palace, I came to a colossal gateway through the center of which extended natural columns of banyan roots from a giant tree growing in impressive splendor on the very top of the granite gate. Within the portals of this gate were several large buildings partially concealed beneath forests of banyan trees and other jungle foliage growing over the towered house-tops—nature's own tombs of this dead city.

The going was so difficult and dangerous through these bewitching old edifices that I did not tarry too long for fear of running into animals which had adopted these dark recesses as their lairs. Too, the great roots hanging down through the roofs and sides looked so snaky that had I seen a real python hanging down a vine-clad wall, or entwined about an old Buddha statue or colonnade, I would have undoubtedly mistaken it for a root.

As the shadows of night were already creeping through the cracks and crevices of these old edifices, I hurried on to the picturesque shrines of Neak Pean, the brick-towered temple of Pre Rup in Baray district of Angkor, and the great crystal lake covering several square miles in its

[385]

rectangular area and adorned at the ends with Venetian-like bath steps.

Two hours later I was seated on the veranda of my Chinese Hotel Barak at Siem Reap and dreaming of the delights of the day, while khaki-clad native boys dashed about with their lantern-lighted bicycle taxis, like myriads of will-o-the-wisps sailing to and fro through the dark street.

CHAPTER XLIX

Siem Reap to Saigon

It is surprising how even little things one learns as a child prove to be valuable later in life. Thus at the hotel in Siem Reap where meals were brought up to my veranda according to orders, I had to ransack my brain for ways and means of making the waiter understand the order, as food was not present so that I could point out my choices—and of course the waiter spoke no word of any language except Chinese. To convey the idea that I desired chicken I made shadow pictures of a hen on the wall and even let her lay an egg and begin to scratch and cackle. I evidently succeeded for the waiter brought up scrambled eggs as well as chicken.

I had a terrible time convincing the waiter that I wanted some French fried potatoes (not that I liked them cooked in such fashion, but that's the only way they know how to cook them; it seems that they bake sweet but not Irish potatoes here). He followed me through the process of digging up, peeling and slicing pomme de terre, but when it came to my dropping them in a frying pan and letting them "sizzle," a cloud of confusion and doubt came over his homely face, and repeated pantomime on my part, through the whole process, was of no avail. Suddenly a faint glimmer of light burst through the foggy sea of doubt

[386]

in his mind and grabbing the imaginary frying pan, the waiter chipped my imaginary potatoes in it, flipped the pan up and down letting the potatoes "sizzle" (sound from his lips) as I had done, and looked at me with an eager, questioning countenance asking if "that" were the right food. It was now my turn to look dubious and uncertain as I had never heard of potatoes in process of cooking being flipped in the air, like pancakes tossed by skillful New York side-street cafe cooks. In fact, I wasn't sure but what he meant pancakes; but as his illustrated language had all the marks of potatoes with this one exception, I answered in the affirmative. However, I was really not at all sure what was coming until the potatoes were set before me. This was just one of a thousand such incidents that made my days all the more interesting.

Bucephalus was beginning to develop serious aging pains more annoying than interesting. At Bangkok, after his terrible grind through the jungles of the Shan States, I had given him a new set of "insides" in the crank shaft and rear axle and had had no further trouble except the loss of a screw. Now the sprocket was again shot to pieces. "This stocky old steed which had climbed up the highest of the Swiss alpine and Himalayan peaks could scarcely hold its own on a level road. When the grade was slightly uphill, the chain held no grip in the worn-out axle, and I had to get off and push.

Fortunately, four days after leaving Siem Reap, we were able to cycle into Saigon, on our own power as the road was flat as a pancake, through emerald green rice and golden corn fields; rubber, coffee, tea, and cinnamon plantations; banana, betel nut, date, and coconut palm groves; watermelon, peanut, and potato patches.

The road was lined with thinly clad women clogging along to market with huge baskets of vegetables suspended from one end of the long pole balanced across their shoulders, one or two children riding snugly in a basket on the other end, and frequently a baby at its mother's breast even as she jogged down the road at the typical Chinese trot.

All of these peasants wear gigantic umbrella straw hats (many covered with colored, embroidered silks and satins), which serve not only as headgear, but also as plates for food, basins for pouring water on self and water buffalo, and even as a shade over baby's hammock as it lies stretched between two poles in the rice fields, while mother is plowing or planting the paddy seed.

The main farm implement of all Cambodian peasants is the scythe-shaped, two-pronged knife with a metal blade at one end to use in cutting crops, and the wooden blade at the opposite end to use in prodding the shanks of lazy buffaloes.

Here, as in the rest of southeastern Asia, the chief pastime of children is "aquaplaning" on the backs of buffalo swimming in deep water of the rice field irrigation canals. If the Hawaiian surfboard enthusiast thinks his sport is thrilling, he should try it "Chinese style." As long as the buffalo swims smoothly with head out of water or sinks his whole body simultaneously a few feet beneath the surface, the going is pleasant enough; but when he does a nose or tail dive so that both ends don't go down at the same time, the rider, standing on his back and holding for dear life to the tope tied through the buffalo's nose, is sure to get a ducking.

My last stop in the interior of Indo-China was at Hotel Kompong Thom, which as the name signifies (Kompong means "bank of river" and Thom means "big") is on the banks of a big river north of Great Lake. A river steamer filled with French marines was in dock and all hotel rooms were booked, but the manager, Paul de F. Goubert, insisted that I stay as special guest in his own suite of rooms.

In signing his memoir book I was astonished to see

notations by Osmyn Stout and Charlie Chaplin, the last two Americans who had visited this spot.

Monsieur Goubert, a bachelor, kept for company a house full of pets, varying from blue-eyed Chinese cats to a pair of beautiful baby panthers he had found only the week before in a rocky crevice in the jungles, a few hundred yards across the road. He insisted upon giving me the panthers, but I assured him that balking Bucephalus was giving me enough trouble without inviting more.

At Kompong Thom I crossed the red river Mekong, last great obstacle separating me from the Pacific. This flooded river was almost at a standstill, as Great Lake was not quite filled to capacity and the river was still undecided whether to flow toward the China Sea or "upstream" into the lake.

On the eastern bank of the Mekong I stopped to "refuel" with a few pounds of barbecued venison which a native hunter had just prepared in a great charcoal mud-furnace by the water's edge.

Late at night as I cycled into the still streets of Saigon, I was impressed by the sights of so many ricksha coolies sleeping between the shafts of their parked vehicles. All their lives they were with their two-wheeled contraptions, twenty-four hours a day, just as Bucephalus and I had been for the past eighteen months. To them "home" meant nothing more than a straw mat beside their ricksha on the tropical tree-lined streets of Saigon. To me, it has been a sleeping bag beside a bicycle wherever in God's great out-of-doors night had overtaken us. To the Afghan nomad ever wandering, not in search of Maeterlinck's elusive bluebird of happiness, but in search of a livelihood in the form of greener pastures for his sheep, camel, and goats, it meant practically the same thing.

While cycling or riding in rickshas around the city, I took hundreds of "natural life" pictures at the botanical gardens, temples, markets, and street corners.

[389]

*Crossing Mekong,
the only river in the world
that flows upstream*

*Saigon
street scenes*

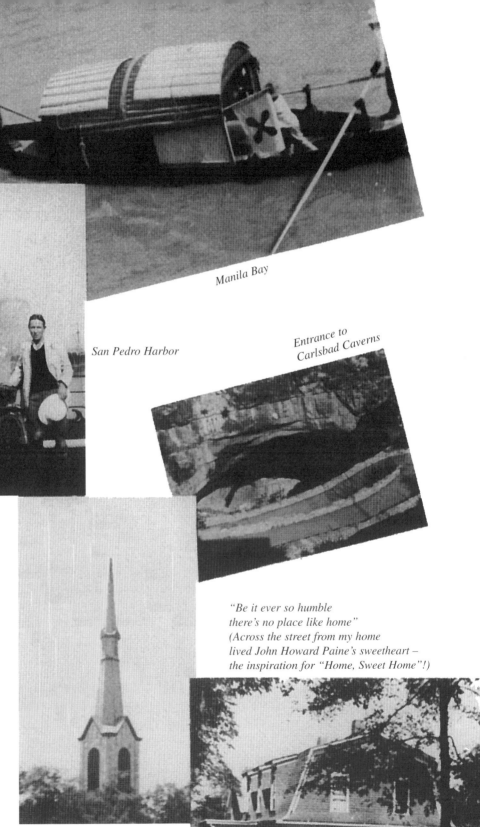

Manila Bay

San Pedro Harbor

Entrance to
Carlsbad Caverns

*"Be it ever so humble
there's no place like home"
(Across the street from my home
lived John Howard Paine's sweetheart –
the inspiration for "Home, Sweet Home"!)*

*First Methodist Church
steeple, Athens Georgia*

I warn all visitors against letting Chinese take pictures for them. In the first place, the odds are a hundred to one that he will be unable to secure a native who is willing to take the photo. When, however, one such is found and given proper instructions, just as it seems that he is about to take the picture, he will either put his hand completely over the front of the lens and pull the trigger or else he will turn the camera skyward and click the shutter a half-dozen times to see if it really does "click" as he has been told. Ninety-nine times out of a hundred that I had natives take snapshots, they ruined the picture by clicking the shutter again just as they were about to hand me the kodak. The hundredth time, my accommodating coolie merely sighted through the camera without ever pulling the trigger.

While wandering through the one hundred per cent native city of Cholon (I was the only foreigner among the two hundred thousand Chinese in this large suburb of Saigon), I stopped at a local theater to see what a typical Chinese play was like. The performance surpassed my wildest imagination and left me stunned.

Upon entering the theater at six-thirty p.m., a half hour before scheduled performance, I noticed that it was filled with a motley crowd of querulous, stentorian-voiced old Chinese washer-women and coolies. All suddenly vanished at eight o'clock when the ticket office opened and blue-pajamaed girl ushers took their places along the now empty aisles.

For five cents I obtained one of the finest and most expensive seats in the house, excepting the box seats of the front row where, I soon learned, a rich man paid the huge sum of twenty-five cents to do as he pleased—keep his hat on his head, throw cigar butts or rotten tomatoes at actors, and make any sort of disturbance with impunity. He even had his own private waiters and food vendors. The scene reminded me of English history's Elizabethan

"Dandy," who paid for the privilege of sitting on the stage to display his fine clothes and abuse the actors in general.

The Cholon theater orchestra consisted of a brass horn, two snake-charmer flutes, two two-string Chinese violins with their little python drum covers, a pair of castanets, and cymbals.

The raising of the green dragon curtain was preceded by a fifteen-minute cymbal solo, accompanied by a mad rush of spectators from the gallery above to standing room in the pit in front of the footlights.

Someone's dog in the middle aisle set up a mournful howl, and a few seconds later one of the big tom cats running rampant through the building chased a wharf rat beneath my bench. The crowd began chattering and moving about noisily, while fruit peddlers screamed out their wares as if trying to drown out the "music" and voices of the actors. The play was on!

Throughout the entire performance the vendors bellowed from the corners of the theater, and the peripatetic and loquacious audience continued its frolicking.

Occasionally, during a very dramatic moment in the play,. a fat Chinese spectator on one side of the theater would recognize a friend on the far side of the building and immediately conversation would start, as unself-consciously as if they were alone out in the paddy fields instead of in a crowded theater.

What was even more astonishing, all the so-called "backstage" hands made it a point never to leave the stage. Thus, while the exalted High Priest character in the play sat upon his throne, one of the shabbily dressed stagehands leaned against the priest's chair; another occupied a conspicuous position in front of the priest, where he could see and enjoy the acting as well as the audience. All stage windows and doorways were crowded with ragamuffins and stagehands, who were continually walking across the stage mingling with the actors, making the audience realize that they were very important, too, by picking up chairs and setting them back again just to test their stability. They also put cushions on the floor for the actors' use every time the latter had to get down on their knees.

These cocky stagehands removed all interior decorations as soon as they became unnecessary, even though the actors, while in the middle of a speech, occasionally had to be asked to "please step off the rug," or "step aside so that we can move this table."

In one scene while a "dead" heroine was being removed on her sleeping couch, consisting simply of a plank across two chairs with a wooden block as a pillow, one of the stagehands carelessly knocked the block off the plank so that the poor heroine nearly broke her head, much to the amusement of the audience.

To an American, it is surprising how little the Chinese spectator is annoyed by the antics of these stagehands. The stagehand, dressed in his ordinary street pajamas or plain hip towel, is easily overlooked when contrasted with the extravaganza worn by the actors.

The simple-minded audience is attracted by showy display and mimicry. Craving action and splendor of dress, it is distracted by too much dialogue. Thus the crowd threatened to stampede when the hero spoke too long, but was immediately entranced when he went through pantomime of the fire-building ceremony and the heroine washed clothes—common everyday duties, familiar drudgery of every member of the audience, yet the source of much enjoyment to watch the actors do it.

The hero was quite popular with the spectators since he could turn his eyeballs so far wrong side out that only the glassy whites of his eyes were visible as he stood before the floodlights and sang in the traditional chanting manner, while the cymbals clashed between each phrase of his speech.

Evidently cymbals furnish the favorite "music" to the discordant ear of the Chinese. Even between scenes the cymbals had no rest, but kept up a thunderous din by periodic clashing, which kept reverberating through the building like the droning motors of an air fleet.

I could never have endured the show as long as I did had the heroine not been a demure little paragon of loveliness in her beautiful "blue-grotto blue" pajamas, a huge red poppy and a cluster of cherry blossoms adorning her silky black hair.

I left the theater at three a.m., just after the hero had swallowed a banana whole and been permitted to marry the heroine. Unlike our American plays which end with "they married and of course lived happily ever after," the Chinese play frequently conforms to real life by letting the story begin with the marriage ceremony. As the Chinese honeymoon was just beginning at three a.m., I began to fear that the show would never end.

Tired but unperturbed, Bucephalus carried me down the shadowy streets for my last ride on Asiatic soil.

END OF PART NINE

"The road is wide and the stars are out and the breath of
   the night is sweet
And this is the time when wanderlust should seize upon
   my feet
But I'm glad to turn from the open road and the starlight
   on my face,
And to leave the splendor of out-of-doors for a human
   dwelling place.

"I have never seen a vagabond who really liked to roam
All up and down the streets of the world and not to have a home;
The tramp who slept in your barn last night and left at
   break of day
Will wander only until he finds another place to stay.

"A gypsy-man will sleep in his cart with canvas overhead;
Or else he'll go into his tent when it is time for bed.
He'll sit on the grass and take his ease so long as the sun
   is high,
But when it is dark he wants a roof to keep away the sky.

"If you call a gypsy a vagabond, I think you do him wrong,
For he never goes atraveling but he takes his home along.
And the only reason a road is good, as every wanderer knows,
Is just because of the homes, the homes, the homes to
   which it goes.

"They say that life is a highway and its milestones are the years,
And now and then there's a toll gate where you buy your
   way with tears,
It's a rough road and a steep road and it stretches broad
   and far
But at last it leads to a golden Town where golden Houses are."

Joyce Kilmer

[396]

PART TEN

CHAPTER L

Piloting Across the Pacific

As a rice boat carried Bucephalus and me across the glassy surface of the China Sea on a sultry thirty-first day of August, I sat on the front hatch and read from a Philippine Island newspaper: "Mr. B—, in commenting upon his 80,000 miles of travel on the United States Air Lines last year, states that 'flying gives one a feeling of freedom and power which does not result from the use of any other form of transportation.'" I could not restrain a smile of pride as I read this article and looked across the hatch at my battle-scarred bicycle, which had rolled 25,000 miles around the globe under the powers of my own visceral dynamics. When a plane refuses to function further, the pilot is out of luck; but when Bucephalus found it impossible to plough through jungles or surmount rugged peaks, I had merely turned carrier instead of rider—that, to me, was a feeling of real power, freedom, and a mastery of one's fate.

At Manila we touched earth for the last time in the Eastern hemisphere. After a week of pleasant cycling through the picturesque plantations of the Philippines, Bucephalus and I boarded the S. S. Hanover, bound for San Pedro, California, with a heavy shipment of copra and a couple of hatches of brown sugar and rattan.

As we sailed out of the bay on our twenty-seven-day trip across the sea, the China Clipper roared overhead with a letter which would reach my family in four days to tell them that I was homeward bound.

[397]

I was signed up as an A.B. (able-bodied) seaman instead of ordinary work-a-way or utility man. A half-dozen of the crew had deserted at Shanghai, and, as several more refused to come aboard at Manila, the Captain had no other alternative than to list me as a regular seaman on the ship's articles—not bad, getting paid sixty-seven dollars and fifty cents per month for having the time of my life! It was much better than paying five or six hundred dollars for a boring passage.

Day in and day out, from four to eight o'clock in the morning, I stood behind the wheel high up on the bridge and piloted the boat through the inky darkness to the silver streaks of dawn and finally down a golden pathway of liquid light toward America. From four to eight in the evening I steered up the luminous trail blazed by the rising harvest moon. It was one endless succession of memorable dawns and twilights almost too beautiful for me to share alone; all the rest of the crew, except the lookout in the prow of the boat and the fireman in the engine room, were sleeping.

When there were too many clouds to tell where the sun should be, I first set my direction by compass, and then steered by the guiding form of a horizon cloud directly in line with the prow of my boat. At night, when the moon forgot to rise in time to guide my turn at the wheel, I kept my eyes constantly upon an eastern star, alert to correct the slightest deviation from the course instead of carelessly letting her run wild and then having "quite a time" guiding her back into the right direction.

"A ship is like a human being," warned the Captain, "if you let her stray from the straight and narrow path, she's a goner. It's less trouble to keep the old boat in a straight line than to bring her around once she's started slipping.

"Yet there's one funny thing that's different about a ship. She'll dip her head into the briny deep and plough straight through any storm, whereas she'll skid all over the ocean when the water is calm."

At dawn we passed Formosa while the Big Dipper blazed brightly in the middle of the sky overhead, and the beautiful Southern Cross hung over the last of the Philippines' thousand-and-one-islands still wrapped in their blankets of clouds which, in the early hours of the morning, looked like silvery lakes twined about the bases of the island mountains.

The Captain strictly forbade any animals on board but his two cats, but he permitted every sailor to keep canaries which were usually named after the port of call where they had been purchased. When news spread through the ship that "Saigon"—the pride of the first mate's little aviary—had laid an egg, it created more excitement than the radiogram from Hawaii telling of the storm brewing several hundred miles dead ahead of us.

But the sailors had other forms of entertainment than playing with canaries. As the Hanover had visited Kobe, Yokohama, Shanghai, Saigon, Singapore, and nearly a dozen ports of the South Sea Islands before picking me up at Manila, they all had enough edifying (?) experiences to discuss for the first half of the return trip; the last half of the crossing could be spent in anticipation of adventures in the next port of call.

During the heat of the day, little blue-steel-looking copra bugs oozed by the millions from the hatches, and swarmed over the ship's deck. I could endure these new playmates and take them as a matter of course, but one night I discovered new cousins to the copra bugs that could not be so easily endured. During the first few calm nights at sea, I had slept out on the hatch in the stiff sea breeze where I could taste the salt air and count the liquid lightning streaks of stars shooting across the sky, like flying fish rocketing for a few brief moments through the sunlight before sinking again into the briny depths of darkness.

[399]

But when gradually swelling seas drove me inside, to my horror and discomfort, I became aware of scores of bedbugs emerging from cozy spots in my mattress, I began to do battle at once, but these plucky little creatures refused to be exterminated and seemed to be endowed with supernatural powers of reproducing themselves manifold like the mythological Gorgon's head which was always replaced by several more heads every time one of them was cut off. Finally, after a sleepless night spent in fighting a losing battle, I pitched mattress and bedding into the ocean and dived into the good old sleeping bag which carried me around the world without ever once becoming infested with such terrible insects. After a thousand nights parked out on Mother Nature's clean snowy-bosomed peaks or soft desert sands, my "Schlafsac" was as fresh and clean as the day I had bought it in Cologne.

Even more annoying to some of the sailors than bugs, were "ghosts" which haunted the ship. On her previous trip to the Orient, the Hanover's first mate had died at sea. Yet, several of the crew swore to me that, two months after he had been sacked in limestone and iron-ballasted canvas and buried in the briny deep, he had one day appeared as usual in his white uniform at the doorway of the fo'castle where they were painting.

"He stood there quietly watching us for fully five minutes before turning and slipping away as silently and suddenly as he had come," exclaimed the wild-eyed boatswain as we sat at supper, steadily swallowing potatoes as if they were mere pills.

Shortly after sunrise on Sunday, September 13—our sixth day at sea—a static series of whistle blasts called all hands to fire-drill, with the sole exception of the Captain and me. Even the Captain wore a life preserver, though I, as pilot, could not.

All day long the Pacific showed no signs of being

anything but peaceful. Like the China Sea, it was as quiet as an old mill pond. As the Hanover cut through the mirror-like surface of the deep blue water, reflecting in unblurred perfection fleecy white clouds dotting the sky in lacy patterns, I felt as if I were crashing through polished mirror paintings, like those I had seen in the native shops of French Indo-China.

Toward evening, the Pacific became decidedly unpacific. A steadily blowing southwestern gale began to whip the ocean into creamy caps which assumed alarming proportions of height, until forty-foot walls of water were crashing across the ship, as high as the bridge where my pilot house stood. For five days the storm raged unabated. The Hanover continued to advance steadily in spite of the blasting bombardment of the waves, which struck broad-sides with the force and thunder-like booming of great cannon, crumpling and carrying away the iron-barred railing on the starboard side as if it were made of paper.

Unceasingly, mountainous masses of white foam loomed up like ghosts out of the darkness, down upon the little ship's deck far below. Yet, each time the towering walls of water seemed to completely engulf and "swamp" our boat, the Hanover proudly rose up so that half the froth would go under instead of over her. Looking through the spray-drenched air to the ocean waves towering on either side above the ship gives the spectator the impression that he is on a submerged submarine.

Luckily all ventilators had been plugged with wooden stoppers and canvas coverings and all loose deckgear stowed away before the storm struck, since it gradually grew worse even though the skies were crystal clear. Phosphorescent sea creatures floundered over the ship's deck and permeated the thick air like myriads of fireflies in a South Georgia swamp. The raging wind howled with the same sound as desert sand storms, stiff blasts through pine forests, or around corners of old houses on cold winter nights.

[401]

Sleep was impossible in my fo'castle quarters with the waves pounding against its sheetiron walls and roof. One gigantic wave broke through the two-inch porthole glass of my cabin and nearly drowned me before I could clamp an iron cap over the gushing hole.

On the fourth day of the storm, our ship was still bobbing up and down, in a sea churned to foam, when the crest of a giant wave swept away one of the middle deck ventilators.

"Water pouring into the engine room," yelled the excited fireman.

The same wave which put the ship's boilers in danger of explosion had swept through the windows of the Captain's cabin on the second deck. Thinking it high time to shift courses, the Captain rushed breathlessly up to the pilot house and gave orders to abandon our due-east course, against the battering broadsides of the ocean waves, and ride out the storm in a northeasterly direction toward the Aleutian islands.

It was almost impossible to get from sailors quarters in the fo'castle to the pilot house steps, or to the bridge deck, until we stretched a long cable to which we might cling along the middle deck.

All things, both good and bad, must come to an end. Saturday, September 19, the stormy gale calmed down to a gentle breeze and the water gradually resumed its usual pacific form with scarcely a ripple disturbing the glass-like surface. The magic spell of the big round rising moon quickly changed the molten gold waters in the wake of the ship into soft, silvery sheen and sent a dazzling silver-white shaft of light down our long, long pathway to California.

Scores of sea gulls, skimming a half inch above the smooth surface of the water, occasionally put on the "brakes" and playfully surfboarded on their breasts against the crest of a little swell or traced graceful lines in the inviting liquid, as the tips of their wings touched the surface in "banking" around a curve.

Several big hippopotami-looking sperm whales came to the surface to spout off steam which they seemed to have held throughout the storm.

As Captain Massey already had made a good offing toward the Land of Nod, and was blissfully snoring below, I ventured to give chase to the whales. However, I soon learned that playing "follow the leader" with a whale and a whale of a ship was an entirely different matter from big game hunting on a bicycle!

That night, through the ventilator up from the Captain's cabin to the pilot wheel, I heard "California Here I Come," among other radio selections coming four thousand miles across the waves from sunny San Pedro.

After my turn at the wheel, when I had retired to the restful watch in the prow of the boat, a din of noises arose through one of the ventilators above the fo'castle dungeons: the crew was celebrating the "calm after the storm" with a little radio party of its own. There were so many good programs on the air that the men kept tuning in from one to another without stopping. As no two persons were able to agree on any one program, their evening's entertainment threatened to end in discordant dissatisfaction, until I came to the rescue by sticking my head down the ventilator and announcing myself in solemn voice as "Saint Peter of San Pedro, the Golden Beach Gateway to Heaven."

My program, though leaving the audience speechless for a few minutes, was finally drowned out with Bronx cheers when I began interrupting my own speech (just an old American custom which Germans and people of other countries can't understand) with a few refreshing advertisements of Alka-Seltzer "fizzes" and a couple of "Socks, socks; we're the Interwoven pair, now we're going off the air," et cetera.

[403]

Sunday, September 20, was a quiet day of rest for all except the pilot and the firemen. After all, a ship cannot run of its own accord any more than can a bicycle. All morning I stood behind the wheel and listened over the radio to the Christian services in a Philippine Island church. All afternoon I rode Bucephalus around the ship's deck "just to keep in practice."

As the next day, September 21, was still Sunday, we again tuned in on church services—this time from a station in Salt Lake City—during the night we had crossed the international date line and had moved the clock back twenty-four hours so that we got the full benefit of an extra Sunday. But had my globe circling jaunt been westward instead of eastward, I would have lost instead of having gained a day.

For the next two weeks our boat sailed across a beautiful smooth sea. The moonlit nights were so bright and the air so transparently clear that clouds actually reflected in the polished mahogany, ocean ballroom floor.

While I was at the wheel at 4:58 p.m., Friday, October 2, we passed Conception Lighthouse. Two hours later the golden moon rose over Santa Barbara. At dawn of October 3, the sun rose across San Pedro as we wove through the long lanes of battleships to the docks.

I was ready to continue next day with the Hanover as far south as the Panama Canal, where Bucephalus and I had wild plans of disembarking, bucking across the mountains of Colombia to the headwaters of the Amazon, and then floating via raft and river boat all the way down that mighty river through the heart of South America.

But after we landed at San Pedro, Bucephalus and I never again saw the Hanover. My family, evidently suspecting that their wandering boy might go off on a tangent, had hitched up the old family chariot and rattled all the way across the continent to nip just such plans in the bud.

[404]

For a week we rambled up and down the West Coast, zigzagging back and forth through the national parks and painted deserts and petrified forests, before striking out in a bee-line across the southern route toward the old red hills of Georgia!

In Carlsbad Caverns several days later, while sitting in inky darkness beside the Rock of Ages, the sixty-million-year-old stalagmite deep beneath the surface of the ground, a clear voice began singing that great old hymn:

> "Rock of Ages, cleft for me,
> Let me hide myself in Thee."

Then I realized I was really in the heart of America.

Ten days after leaving Carlsbad Caverns the old family chariot pulled into Athens, Georgia, at three o'clock in the morning.

When I awoke in my own bed, it all seemed like a dream. As my eyes wandered about the room from one familiar object to another—the landscape sketches my mother had painted in her youth, my grandfather's old clock in one corner of the room, the deer antlers and muzzle-loading shotgun over the mantlepiece, and my shelves of books just as I had left them "millions" of years ago when I had started around the world—I was still unconvinced. The only thing which seemed real to me was old Bucephalus, a battered and bruised wreck of his former glory, but still standing staunchly beside the door as if waiting for the command to continue our march.

Perhaps it was only the softness of my snow-bank bed high up in the wild Afghan mountains or the soothing sound of shifting sands far out on the Arabian desert which made me sleep so peacefully and dream thus of home.

Surely my whole trip across the peaceful Pacific to the homeland was a lovely dream. That vision of the Rock of Ages had been too ethereally beautiful to be real, and the feeling of security and stability too wonderful as I lay

[405]

safely anchored as in Abraham's bosom, after so many ages of wandering on Life's wild and restless sea. As for that desperate dash through the monsoon jungles of the Malay States, it had certainly been only a horrible nightmare—I must have had that terrible dream while sleeping on the sticky burrs beneath the spreading chestnut tree down in sunny Italy.

Yes, it was all too good to be true. It was just another of my vivid dreams of home as I lay somewhere in a foreign field waiting for the dawn of a new day. In the morning my dream would fade away when I awoke, and I would pack my sleeping bag on Bucephalus and bike across emerald meadows, down glacial peaks, or beside azure waters, in my eternal wanderings toward the Land of the Rising Sun.

However, one look out of the window of my bedroom dispelled all doubt as to the reality of the dream. In my wanderings I had missed the familiar sight which had always confronted me when I looked out of my window. Now as I looked upward at the majestic Methodist church steeple glistening in the golden sunlight of the early morning, I knew I was home.

Memories of the last sermon I had heard in the old church still lingered in my mind and heart. After portraying Paul's journey through life the preacher had closed with a quotation of that great apostle's last words as he reached the end of the trail: "I have fought a good fight; I have finished my course; I have kept the faith; henceforth there is laid up for me a crown of righteousness which the Lord a righteous judge shall give me at that day."

Just how far this beautiful text could be applied to my own journey, I was too sleepy to consider. It was enough that at last I was safe at home. With one last look at that supreme symbol of security and stability for which my restless soul had been searching, I turned over and slept the peaceful, dreamless sleep of the weary.

THE END